DISTRIBUTED TEAMS

The Art and Practice of Working Together
While Physically Apart

John O'Duinn

Cover design and illustrations: Catherine LaPointe Vollmer
Editor: Linda George

v1.0: 08-Aug-2018
v1.1: 16-Sep-2018
v2.0: 20-Jan-2021

ISBN: 978-1-7322549-2-3

Contents

Introduction From The Author

When I first published this book in 2018, I wanted to provide practical help to existing distributed teams[1], as well as encourage others to create or join distributed teams. Now, in January 2021, I'm writing this revised edition during an ongoing COVID-19 global pandemic.

The economic, business and human cost of this pandemic is still unfolding, but some things seem clear.

Organizations with office-centric cultures were forced to change to a distributed teams model very quickly—at the same time as they struggled to keep their businesses afloat in a sudden global economic downturn. Government agencies found themselves struggling to keep up with the sudden record-level increase in demand for services—at the same time as disruptive government office closures forced staff to work from home. All with little warning.

Humans familiar with office-centric work were forced to start working in distributed teams immediately, with little (if any) training. Those with children had further complications due to childcare, school, and university campus closures. And of course there are the direct health concerns of this global pandemic, especially for those with elderly parents, pre-existing medical conditions or working high-exposure, location-dependent essential jobs.

Even for those already comfortable with distributed work, these are not "normal" times.

---

[1] The terms "distributed teams," "virtual teams," "remote work," "work from home," and "telework" are confusingly overlapping terms. In this book, I use the term "distributed team" to describe people who work together even though they are not within physical arm's reach of each other. For more on this, see "Terminology." The terms "co-work" and "cowork" are also evolving, so for consistency I've chosen to use the term "cowork."

This global "work from home experiment" has been ongoing for several months now, and it's unclear when—or if—people will be able to safely return to their empty offices. The ability to work well in distributed teams is now more important than ever.

Early in my career, decades before COVID-19, I stumbled into my first distributed team. I assumed this was a normal way to work. It took a few job transitions for me to discover that not every company is distributed, and some handle this better than others! Even within the same company, I found some teams handle being distributed better than other teams.

As a computer engineer, manager, director, founder, consultant and mentor, I've now worked in several distributed companies for over 28 years, led distributed teams for more than 14 years, and coached/mentored startups on effective distributed teams for more than seven years. Throughout it all, I had to learn how to lead, manage, and work in a distributed team. All at the same time. All on the job. Without prior training, I was literally making it up as I went along, recovering from my own mistakes and learning from others about what did/didn't work for them. To this day, I still make mistakes and keep learning. Whenever possible, I try to only make *new* mistakes.

Throughout those experiences, I've continuously honed a set of common techniques and practices into the book you are now reading. Although most of my career has been in the software industry, there is nothing specific to the software industry in this book. In my work, my consulting, my workshops, and while researching this book, I've worked with people in distributed teams across many different industries[2] and countries. I've looked for common threads of what worked—and didn't work—for company founders, hedge fund managers, software developers, data scientists, accountants and CPAs, book publishers, economists, political organizers, recruiters, military personnel, career government employees, executive assistants, therapists, and various medical roles.

When we improve how teams work, we improve the lives of humans on those teams. This is true whether everyone works in

---

[2] These interviews were all informative, helpful, and brutally honest—so whenever requested, I've changed their names throughout this book.

one physical office or on a fully distributed team. However, distributed teams have additional significant benefits in terms of workplace diversity, disaster resilience, environmental impact, economic development, city planning, housing—and yes, cost savings for employers. After years working in various distributed teams, and especially since the start of this pandemic, I've seen these wider benefits first-hand. From these experiences, I believe now more than ever that enabling more humans to work in distributed teams will benefit society and literally change the world.

John O'Duinn
20-Jan-2021
San Francisco, California, USA.
email: feedback@oduinn.com

How to Use This Book

It's hard to find time to read a book these days. Over the years, I've bought many weighty management books—most of which ended up half-read, gathering dust with a bookmark somewhere in the middle. Because of this, I wanted this book to be down-to-earth, practical, and immediately useful.

I wrote this book using short, easy-to-read English words instead of formal management English[1]. Each chapter is intentionally short enough to read in one sitting: over lunch, during a long commute (if you have one), or late at night after a busy day. Each chapter has simple practical takeaways you can use to make life better today. Each chapter is self-contained, so if you have a specific area of interest you can jump straight to that chapter.

The chapters in this book are organized into three sections:

◆ The first section ("Why") details why distributed teams are good for business, good for the environment, and good for diversity. I intentionally provide lots of supporting data throughout, to help reframe some recurring remote vs. office debates, as well as the "should we return to the office after COVID-19" debates.

◆ The second section ("How") covers tactical essentials like dealing with lots of emails, running efficient video calls, handling meetings, and tracking status of work across time zones. Helpful in any work environment, and live-or-die essential in a distributed team.

◆ The last section ("Humans and Culture") focuses on more advanced topics such as hiring, firing, reviews, promotions, handling personal isolation, and group culture.

If you find yourself in your first distributed team because of COVID-19, just start at the beginning. The carefully chosen

---

[1] No "Dilbert Bingo" here, dilbert.com/strip/1994-02-22.

sequence of chapters is a good default path. I wish I'd had a book like this when I joined my first distributed team, and I hope you find it helpful.

If you are already familiar with working in a distributed team and you picked up this book after some frustrating "remote" problem, jump straight to the relevant chapter. Be aware that sometimes the problem you want to fix is a symptom of a deeper root cause elsewhere. In those cases, I've cross-linked between chapters, to help you quickly address the symptom and then also address the root cause.

If you already work in, work with, or lead high functioning distributed teams, I hope you find ideas in this book that help improve how you already work. If you have any battle-tested ideas that are *not* covered in this book, please let me know. I'd love to hear any suggestions that you think might help improve this book—and help humans work together while physically apart.

Why

The Real Cost of an Office

Takeaways

◆ Offices are expensive and distracting to set up and to operate. This is true whether you are considering getting your first office—or whether to return to an empty office after a prolonged closure.

◆ An office that is too big is a recurring financial drain. An office that is too small or in the wrong location impacts hiring. Moving your office later, as you grow, impacts the employees you already hired.

◆ Having no office lets you hire better candidates, hire faster, and improve diversity in your organization.

◆ Being distributed requires you to crisply organize all communications. This is important for all organizations as they grow, whether you start as three people in a garage or three people in three garages.

The COVID-19 global pandemic impacted workplaces with varying severity depending on location.

In some locations, the impact of COVID-19 has been low enough that offices remained open. In these locations, deciding to set up an office is still an expensive decision that complicates, not liberates, the ongoing day-to-day life of your company. Technologies change. Market needs and financial budgets change. Product scope changes. Business plans change. Companies pivot. Physical buildings stay where they are[1]. Before you rush into the mechanics of creating a physical office, pause to ask yourself: What problem

---

[1] ...unless the office buildings are in an area prone to earthquakes, typhoons or hurricanes!

do you think an office will help you solve, and what recurring costs are you getting yourself into?

Meanwhile, in other locations, COVID-19 has forced office-based organizations to evacuate their offices at short notice and start working from home. For many organizations, this was their first long-term office closure and the sudden transition was often disruptive. Over time, changes to internal processes, leadership style and organizational culture helped the humans adjust to working together while physically apart—but the rapid transition is fraught with peril.

For organizations that survive this transition, it's natural and healthy for humans to view this sudden change as temporary, until everyone goes back to "life before COVID-19".

I am often asked to comment on when and how organizations should return to their offices. Usually the question is framed as "When COVID-19 is over…" and with unspoken concerns about the recurring financial cost of these empty offices, broken internal processes, growing human burnout and fading team culture. Humans are a social species and we crave social contact with other humans[2]. It is a natural and real human desire to want to go back to the office, because we miss the impromptu social contact with coworkers. Humans we spent most of our working days with before COVID-19. However, what most people actually want is to go back to *life* before COVID-19, without the ever present concerns of a global pandemic, social distancing and economic disruption.

We do not have a time machine.

Whenever offices can reopen safely, they are likely to be significantly changed from office life we remember before COVID-19. As I write this, in January 2021, official health guidelines are still in flux, but so far include mask requirements, temperature checks on entry, changes to HVAC systems, significantly reduced occupancy in open plan offices and meeting rooms, removing coffee machines, water coolers and closing communal kitchens. And that's just once you arrive at your desk. Reduced elevator occupancy will increase wait times when you arrive at the building, or want to leave at the end of the day. And

[2] For more on this, see "Feed Your Soul."

the idea of being on pre-COVID-19 crowded rush hour public transit and sidewalks is concerning for many. For parents, the situation is further complicated by school closures.

The business costs of an office described in the rest of this chapter are true for those considering getting their first office as well as for those considering whether to return to their existing empty office. If you already have an office, and it has been closed for months because of COVID-19, I recommend immediately focusing on operational efficiencies, human communications and leadership as described in this book.

Encourage others across the organization to help improve communications, fix process problems and improve operations efficiencies with phrases like "It looks like offices will remain closed for a few more months, so for today, lets work together to improve how we…" These improvements are good to have, even if you later move back to your newly reopened office. Focusing on these improvements now can buy you time while you research your decision, but at some point, there needs to be an explicit go/ no-go decision about whether your organization will *ever* return to an office.

When making this decision, beware of the sunk cost fallacy[3]. Also beware of the optics of spending money on an empty physical building, and then spending additional money to make the office "COVID-19 safe" while at the same time deciding to reduce costs by removing humans from your payroll. Decisions like this are a clear signal of leadership priorities—visible to everyone, inside and outside of the organization—with predictable impact to morale and retention.

"Don't tell me what you value. Show me your budget, and I'll tell you what you value."

President Joe Biden

---

[3] Just because you already spent a lot of money on a fancy office does not mean you should continue spending even more money on it. In August 2020, Pinterest paid $89 million to cancel their lease of a new unused office building in San Francisco and REI sold their new unused HQ building outside Seattle for $368 million.

Business Cost

By encouraging employees to work from home, Dell has saved $39.5 million in real estate costs over the last two years, with ambitions to have 50% of the global company work from home by 2020[4]. Aetna has been encouraging employees to work from home since 2005 because it improves their hiring, their retention, and they save $78 million a year in real estate costs[5]. Each year. Similarly, by encouraging staff to work from home, the US Patent & Trademark Office was able to grow from 6,000 to 10,000 employees without increasing office space, a recurring savings of $19.8 million each year[6]. FEMA, GSA, IRS, NASA have also made large investments in "telework"[7]. Unilever saved 40% on office leasing and maintenance costs simply by having more people work from home. No wonder JetBlue, British Telecom, McKesson, United Way, and others were already doing the same, before COVID-19.

If you reduced how much money you spent on physical offices, what else could you do with that money and organizational focus? Conversely, if you decide to set up an office, you are committing money and leadership attention to the long-term consequences of this brick-and-mortar cost.

Deciding which city, and which neighborhood in the city, is the best location for your office is not as easy as you might hope. Sometimes the answer is "near the CEO's home," or "near the offices of our lead investors." However, it is important to also answer questions like "Where will we find most of the talent we hope to hire?" and "Where will most of our customers be?"

Calculating the size of your new office requires thinking through your hiring plans—not just for today, but for the duration of the

---

[4] "Dell 2020 Legacy of Good Plan."

[5] From reuters.com, "In telecommuting debate, Aetna sticks by big at-home workforce."

[6] US Merit Systems Protection Board, "Telework: Weighing the Information, Determining an Appropriate Approach."

[7] "Understanding Government Telework" by Weinbaum, C. et al, RAND, 2018.

multiyear building lease. Accurately predicting hiring for multiple years into the future is tricky, especially when starting a company. Without historical trend data for workload or hiring cycles, you can try aspirational estimates, ask others who have created similar companies, or use plain old-fashioned guesswork. Too small of an office can cause an unwanted hiring freeze (if you stay), or cause you to lose existing valuable office employees (if you later move to a bigger office at a different location). Too big of an office commits the company to a recurring financial cost for the unused office space—a financial drain you can sometimes reduce by spending even more money and human attention negotiating commercial subleases and dealing with tenants.

Renting coworking spaces is one popular solution for avoiding long-term leases, offering the flexibility to quickly increase or decrease office size. Originally used by solo entrepreneurs, now approximately 25% of coworking spaces are used by employees of traditional companies, extending their existing office space to support location or travel flexibility.

This "Office as a Service" flexibility comes at a price. Coworking spaces usually cost more per square foot than traditional office leases, although they include prearranged maintenance staff, utilities, and the month-to-month lease flexibility to quickly expand or shrink as needed. There are also risks: After your initial team starts, later hires could be blocked because all available space might be rented out to others. In addition, the coworking center might change hands or go out of business, disrupting your organization in ways that a traditional lease would not.

An even more flexible approach is to rent meeting rooms by the hour from "Meeting Room as a Service" companies, with slightly higher, fully loaded operating costs.

All of the other office costs outlined in this chapter apply equally to coworking spaces and leased offices.

If you believe that you need an office, be aware that you are committing your company to a series of ongoing expensive logistics and operational mechanics to set up and run your new physical office. Here are some examples:

- Negotiating, signing, and paying leases that impact your company's financial burn rate. Every month.

- Hiring staff who are focused on running the physical office, not focused on your product.

- Hiring architects and builders; obtaining construction permits; and building the physical office space, bathrooms, and kitchens.

- Choosing, buying, and installing desks, chairs, ping pong tables, coffee machines, and fridges.

- Setting up security door badge systems, alarm systems, printers, internet providers, secure Wi-Fi, and phones.

- Debating floor plans: do you want offices with doors, or cube farms, or open plan? For offices with doors, decide who will have one and explain to everyone else why they cannot. If you choose open plan, do you design a bright, airy space with high ceilings that feels spacious and lively because of the echoes of human cross-chatter across crowded bull pens of desks? Or do you design a library-quiet, cave-like environment with accent lighting to avoid reflections on screens and encourage focused work with minimal interrupts?

- Negotiating seating arrangements, including who gets a window and which teams can reserve nearby empty tables for future hires.

- Rethinking your vacation and sick day policies so humans who are sick don't feel the need to come into the office, causing other healthy humans at the office to become sick[8]. This is annoying when dealing with cold or flu season; it is scary when dealing with COVID-19 (Corona virus), H1N1

---

[8] Moving office workers from private individual offices to an open-plan space increased sick leave absence by 62%. "Sickness absence associated with shared and open-plan offices—a national cross-sectional questionnaire survey," by Pejtersen J.H., et al.

(Swine/Avian flu), MERS or Ebola[9]. For more on this, see "Disaster Planning."

All of these examples have serious ongoing consequences for the company. They all take time, money, and—most importantly—leadership focus away from the purpose of the company: hiring humans to create and ship product to earn money. Maintaining and running a physical office takes ongoing time, money, and focus, so these daily distractions continue long after your new office opens its doors for the first time.

Having no physical office lets you sidestep all of these potentially serious distractions. Instead, you (and everyone else in the company) can dedicate time, money, and leadership focus to your people and your products. This is a competitive advantage over companies that pay for and operate physical offices.

One common justification for wanting an office is to help humans interact socially with their coworkers. Human contact is important. After all, humans are a social species and we use solitary confinement as a form of punishment. A physical office does not automatically solve this problem. Instead, I've found it more effective, more flexible, and less expensive to routinely bring humans together on a predictable cadence. For more on this, see "Bringing Humans Together" and "Feed Your Soul."

Hiring Cost

Having an office changes how you approach recruiting and hiring.

---

[9] For H1N1, MERS and Ebola, the companies I worked in required special authorization to allow employees to travel to these regions for work or vacation. They also mandated a work-from-home quarantine period for anyone returning from these regions before they were allowed to physically meet any coworkers or enter any office buildings. For COVID-19, most companies cancelled all travel and closed their expensive offices until accurate testing, vaccination or medical cures are available. At time of writing, this situation is ongoing.

When you decide to commit to a physical office, you bias towards hiring people who sit in expensive new desks and chairs that cost you money daily, even when they are empty. You are disappointed when good candidates turn down your job offers because of your office location. You pay to relocate people who would be great additions to your company, but do not live near your new office. You debate hiring the best person for the job versus hiring the best person for the job who is nearby or willing to relocate. You have a hiring freeze because you don't have a spare desk available. You need to sublease part of your new office space because growth plans changed when revenue didn't go as well as hoped, and that unused idle office space is still costing you money every month. Money you could use elsewhere.

I call this the "sunk cost of an office" fallacy.

Having no office gives you crucial advantages over your all-in-one-location competitors. You don't need to worry if the location of the office building helps or hinders future hiring plans. You don't need to worry about good people turning down your job offers simply because of the office location. You can hire from a significantly larger pool of candidates[10], so you can hire better and hire faster[11]. Companies that support at least some remote work also have better retention[12], so humans stay longer. This reduces the pressure to continuously hire and onboard new humans as others continuously leave. The super-hot hiring crises in some locations has encouraged more companies to try building distributed teams out of necessity. These are competitive advantages over your all-in-one-location competitors. For more on this, see "Recruiting and Interviewing."

---

[10] Job postings on stackoverflow.com get three to six times more applications when they say "remote": *Guide to Standing Out & Attracting Top Talent*, by Joel Spolsky, founder of Stack Overflow, Trello, and Fog Creek Software.

[11] On upwork.com, 25% of jobs are filled within 24 hours, and the average time to hire is only three days as detailed in: "4 Types of Companies That Can Benefit From Distributed Teams." Meanwhile, OwlLabs reported 33% faster hiring, although the exact amount of improvement probably varies depending on your industry and your specific organization.

[12] OwlLabs's "State of Remote Work 2017" survey found that employee turnover was 25% lower for companies with flexible remote work policies.

Diversity Cost

When you require people to come into an office to do their job, you reduce your ability to hire diversely.

There are qualified people with the right skills who would be happy to have the job, and who you would be happy to hire. Yet these candidates won't even apply.

Why?

Even if they applied, excelled at the interviews and were offered the job, they could not accept it—simply because they cannot reliably get to and from your physical office on a daily basis. For more on this, see "Diversity."

Housing Cost

People looking for work will relocate to regions where companies are hiring. Rapid growth industries can cause rapid population shifts. People can relocate faster than cities can react, so increased demand quickly overruns existing housing capacity, driving up housing prices and rents.

Companies that concentrate their employees into custom-built single-company "trophy towers"[13] dominate the financial revenue streams of larger cities. Each trophy tower generates lots of prestige and office jobs for that single employer in the short term, and the towers are profitable for construction companies. However, without also building housing for those new employees *at the same time*, these office-only buildings trigger rapid increases in nearby housing prices. This causes rapid gentrification, culture change, and social disruption as the humans who keep the city running can no longer afford to live there. For more on the environmental consequences of this increased commuter traffic, see "Commute Cost."

This increased cost of living for all employees matters to employers. Humans who commute to an office pay a larger

---

[13] Daniel H. Pink, *Free Agent Nation: How America's New Independent Workers Are Transforming the Way We Live.*

percentage of their salaries to live in smaller apartments, within commute range of the office. This impacts their ability to raise families, and it restricts the pool of potential employees to humans who are willing (and can afford) to live that way. Employers pay inflated salaries to make the expensive cost of living feel affordable to employees. In extreme cases, employers are building houses for their employees[14], or giving them recurring payments to offset increased housing costs near the office[15]. One fully distributed company, Zapier, is taking a different approach: they pay employees to "de-locate" away from Silicon Valley[16]. Meanwhile, in June 2018, the State of Vermont signed a law[17] encouraging remote work by giving tax breaks to humans who relocate to Vermont—specifically when their organization is not in Vermont[18].

Building more affordable housing after the fact will, of course, help reduce the cost of living. However, construction lead times for housing are long, and affordable housing builders are competing for the same land against more profitable luxury housing builders and even more profitable office building projects.

---

[14] In the 1870s, Guinness started building housing for Guinness employees in Dublin, Ireland. Some companies went further, building entire "company towns" to house their employees: Cadbury created the town of Bournville, England; US Steel created the town of Gary, Indiana; and DeBeers created the town of Oranjemund, Namibia. Communes and kibbutz continue this practice today. At time of writing, Google has approved plans to construct roughly 10,000 homes and apartments for employees in San Jose. Facebook announced that it is also planning large-scale housing construction "Willow Village," which will literally double the population of the town of Menlo Park. There are open questions about how long this new housing will take to become reality and whether residents will be required to move out if they change employers.

[15] Instead of building homes, some companies are choosing to pay recurring additional payments to their employees—above and beyond salary—simply to help offset the increased cost of housing near the office. Starbucks in Chendgu, China and Facebook in Palo Alto, California, are examples of companies experimenting with this.

[16] "De-Location Package: Keep Your Career and Live Beyond the Bay Area."

[17] New Remote Worker Grant Program, Vermont Senate Bill S.94.

[18] This legal policy is significant as people change jobs more frequently in society. For more on this, see "Distributed Teams Are Not New" and "The Final Chapter."

If you start building housing *after* people start migrating to a city for an industry in an up-cycle, you risk having the newly completed housing enter the property market just as the industry enters a down-cycle. Adding new housing to the market when offices are reducing hiring and people are relocating away to jobs in offices in other cities can cause a glut in the local housing market, causing a plunge in the housing market. As industries go through these up-and-down cycles they oscillate the real estate market in those cities. This boom-bust cycle disrupts the economy, social fabric, and quality of life for everyone in those cities—even those working in unrelated industries essential for the city's wellbeing. Examples include Manaus, Brazil, when the rubber industry collapsed; Rochester, New York, when Eastman Kodak went bankrupt; Jakarta, Indonesia, during the Asian currency crisis; Detroit, Michigan, when car companies downsized; and San Francisco, California, during the first dot-com crash in the early 2000s.

In San Francisco from 2013 to 2016, median prices increased 80% for single-family homes and 60% for apartments and condos[19]. In 2017, those single-family home prices increased an *additional* 16%. Since December 2014, literally *no* properties sold in San Francisco were affordable to a two-income family of teachers, police, firefighters, or EMTs. Since 2017, the same has been true for nearby San Jose[20]. This forces many people to live further away and commute longer distances, or relocate to find jobs elsewhere. Meanwhile, Detroit continues to auction off abandoned houses

[19] According to several Redfin articles (affordability for teachers, employees and companies relocating, and the housing affordability gap), and the Vanguard Properties quarterly newsletter for 2016 Q2 and 2018 Q2.

[20] As of May 2018, hsh.com noted that the median family income needed to buy property was $262,000 in San Jose and $182,000 in San Francisco. According to redfin.com, a 2017 San Francisco Board of Supervisors report, and San Francisco's job site, a teacher in San Francisco is paid an average of $59,700. San Francisco Deputy Sheriffs are paid $70,000 to $90,000, and Sheriff Cadets are paid $44,000 to $54,000. Buying is out of the question, and for most, even renting is hard because of "Rent Affordability Gaps."

starting at $1,000 each[21], while Gary, Indiana is selling houses for $1.00 (yes, one dollar)[22]. Each.

This disparity is not unique to the US. In Berlin, housing prices rose by over 20% in 2017[23]. In Ireland, the rapid influx of people moving to work in offices in central Dublin has caused housing prices to increase rapidly, becoming more expensive than housing in San Francisco and 10 times the cost of housing in rural Ireland—outside the commute range of offices in Dublin. No surprise that Dublin has quickly slid down to 47th on the Expat City Ranking[24]. Meanwhile in Japan, Yokosuka (on the outskirts of Tokyo) has started demolishing abandoned homes and creating a "vacant home bank" to attract buyers—while housing within commute range of corporate offices in downtown Tokyo remain expensive[25]. The same is happening with abandoned houses in Osaka and Kyoto—major towns in their own right. In Italy, the towns of Gangi, Sicily, and Ollolai, Sardinia, are selling homes for a token 1 euro (approximately $1.17 at time of writing)[26] while across Europe, entire castles with surrounding lands are for sale[27], many for less than the cost of an apartment in San Francisco.

Requiring humans to live within commute range of an office is a significant factor in this situation.

[21] Detroit Land Bank Authority, buildingdetroit.org.

[22] Mayor Karen Freeman-Wilson of Gary, Indiana, "SA chance to own a home for a dollar." modeled the city's new Dollar Home program on a similar US HUD program—which allowed Freeman-Wilson to get her first home decades ago, for $1.

[23] "Global Residential Cities Index 2017" by Knight Frank.

[24] Expat Insider, "The Best (and Worst) Cities for Expats in 2017."

[25] New York Times, "A Sprawl of Ghost Does in Aging Tokyo Suburbs"; japanpropertycentral.com, "Yokosuka City Forcibly Demolishes Abandoned Home."

[26] Ollolai, Sardinia is selling homes for $1.25.

[27] Related websites include dartagnans.fr, adopteunchateau.com, prestigeproperty.co.uk, and moulin.nl.

"The future is already here—it's just not evenly distributed."

William Gibson

Commute Cost

Rapid migrations of people can quickly overload roads and public transport systems that were already operating near capacity.

One part of the increased demand is caused by the rapid increase in the number of people using existing roads and public transit. Another part is caused by increased housing demand, forcing people to live further away from the office in more affordable housing, and then having to commute longer distances to their office. This combination of more humans commuting, with each human commuting further distances, causes a sudden increase in demand on public infrastructure.

It typically takes decades to build additional capacity for cars, buses, or trains. The practical consequence of rapid human migration is an increase in the average commute time, with everyday driving and overcrowded public transport systems fraught with unpredictable system-wide delays rippling outward if even one part goes off schedule. The average commute in the US has grown to around 30 minutes each way[28], each day. To put that in perspective, the average American now spends more time stuck in traffic each year than they do on vacation.

These numbers get even worse when you look at large metropolitan areas. For example, San Francisco's population grew by around 10% from 2000 to 2014[29]. In the same timeframe, traffic increased 70%[30]. In Silicon Valley, a *reasonable* commute has jumped to more than 60 minutes; the term "mega commuter"[31] is used for people who commute at least 90 minutes *and* 50 miles.

[28] "Silicon Valley Competitiveness and Innovation Project—2016 Update."

[29] "US Census American Community Survey (ACS)."

[30] "INRIX Global Traffic Scorecard, 2017," an annual evaluation of traffic in over 1,360 cities around the world.

[31] "US Census: Mega Commuting in the US."

Each way. Each day. Traffic delays increased 13% from 2010 to 2014, adding around 75 minutes to the average person's commute time every week—in addition to their regular commute time. Silicon Valley continues to set new records year over year[32]. In just a few years, their commute has jumped from eleventh- to third-worst commute in the entire US[33], and fifth worst in the world—ranked by Inrix as worse than driving in London or Paris!

Longer commutes directly impact life and health. More than 38,000 people were killed and 2.5 million injured in car accidents in the US in 2015[34], while one in three mega-commuters have recurring back or neck problems[35].

In Silicon Valley, commuting has had such a large impact on hiring that some companies pay to operate their own private bus networks. This allows them to hire people who would otherwise decline a job offer, simply because they live too far from the office to reasonably commute by driving or public transportation. These private bus networks grow larger each year. As of September 2016, nearly forty companies use more than 750 buses to transport their employees[36] around Silicon Valley. Demand is so strong for these busses that people are willing to pay more just to live near these private bus routes[37]. This raises rents on rental properties for all

---

[32] "Time Spent in Congestion," from the California Bay Area Metropolitan Transportation Commission, Sept 2017.

[33] The worst is Los Angeles, followed by New York City. For more details, see WNYC "Average Commute Times," and American Highway Users Alliance, "Unclogging America's Arteries: Prescriptions for Healthier Highways." The Metropolitan Transportation Commission report claimed it was second-worst.

[34] Chris Urmsom, "Google Self Driving Cars," SxSW 2016 and American Highway Users Alliance, "Unclogging America's Arteries: Prescriptions for Healthier Highways."

[35] Gallup-Healthways, "Well-Being Lower Among Workers With Long Commutes," 2010.

[36] Memo from the Metropolitan Transportation Commission regarding the Bay Area Shuttle Census, September, 2016.

[37] For the San Francisco Bay area, sf.curbed.com has links to data at craigslist.org, apartments.com, and others; "Tech shuttles are SF's biggest rental amenity, says apartment listing site."

residents of the city, even those who don't take those shuttle busses to work. These ever-present shuttle busses literally disappeared overnight when COVID-19 forced these software companies to close their offices and their employees started working from home.

For people working at offices that don't operate private bus networks, crowdsourced "casual car pools"[38] allow people to avoid crowded public transit by being a passenger in empty seat of cars of private individuals, while solo drivers get to drive to their office in faster carpool lanes by driving strangers to work.

In Jakarta, traffic is so bad that entrepreneurial humans stand near the start of carpool lanes so that they can be hired by drivers to sit as passengers in their car, allowing the driver to use slightly faster carpool lanes. At the end of the carpool lane they are paid, get out of the car, cross the street, and return with another driver eager to pay to use another carpool lane!

In Nairobi, the number of cars on the road doubles every six years[39], with associated traffic and pollution problems, because more roads simply cannot be built fast enough.

Last but not least is the environmental cost of this additional commuting, which can be the largest source of emissions. For more on this, see "Environmental Impact."

These quality of life, social, and environmental issues are direct consequences of deciding to have an office and then only hiring employees who will commute to that office. The various COVID-19 office closures globally have shown us just how much of an impact is possible[40]. Reducing the number of commuters, or even just reducing how often humans commute, has significant benefits all of us.

---

[38] Casual Car Pool News and SF Casual Carpool.

[39] The World Bank 2014, "A major African step to make sustainable transport a reality."

[40] NASA data on reductions of emissions "How to Find and Visualize Nitrogen Dioxide Satellite Data", 2020.

"Attracting and retaining employees who are more productive
and engaged through flexible workplace policies [like remote
telework] is not just good for business or for our economy—
it's good for our families and our future."

President Barack Obama

Disaster Planning Cost

Requiring people to work in a physical office makes your office an expensive single point of failure for your organization. If the office is unexpectedly closed for a few weeks, or if people are unable to commute to the office for an extended period, you now have a company-threatening business continuity problem to solve.

For more on this, see "Disaster Planning."

Communication Cost

Organizations thrive when they grow a culture of crisp, effective, and resilient internal communications. Having a physical office can mask the need to develop effective organizational and interpersonal communications.

Many all-in-one-location organizations only focus on internal communications after communication issues emerge. They view these issues as normal growing pains that can ignored—until forced to react as corporate productivity drops. Several organizations I've worked in had unintentionally grown a culture where employees ask (and re-ask) each other for updates—at the coffee machine, in email, or in status meetings—multiple times a day. This continuous retelling of a project's status is one way to keep everyone up to date, but it is inefficient, brittle, and doesn't scale. Miscommunications quickly arise when key employees are out sick, traveling for work, on vacation, or when the organization grows beyond the point where each coworker can realistically talk with every other coworker[41].

---

[41] The Dunbar number suggests a cognitive limit of around 150 people in a person's social network; Dunbar, *How Many Friends Does One Person Need?*

By contrast, humans who have only worked in successful distributed organizations can think their communication efficiencies just happen naturally. In reality, creating that efficiency takes intentional premeditated work: a distributed company *must* focus on crisp organization of all internal communications from the beginning, when the company is small, flexible, and its culture is still being formed.

Someone who has only worked in all-in-one-location organizations needs to be aware of the heightened importance of crisp communications when they join a distributed organization. Similarly, an organization morphing from all-in-one-location to distributed needs to be aware of the importance of crisp communications.

Crisply organized communication channels and a results-oriented workplace improve operational efficiencies of any organization—distributed or not.

> *"One day, offices will be a thing of the past."*
>
> *Sir Richard Branson*

Distributed Teams Are Not New

Takeaways

◆ Humans have been working in distributed teams for centuries.

◆ As new technologies become available, they change how we communicate and how we work.

◆ Each generation brings new perspectives to the workplace. The Millennial generation grew up as "digital natives" and are now the largest portion of the US workforce.

◆ Socioeconomic changes mean people change jobs more frequently, becoming less willing to relocate each time.

Humans have worked in distributed teams for centuries. When you look carefully, you can find examples of humans working in distributed teams throughout the Middle Ages, the Renaissance, the Industrial Age, and the Information Age.

Over time, as we improved how we communicate, we gained new abilities to work together while being physically separate from each other. These communication improvements literally changed how people work. Commercial organizations tend to adopt new advancements when they offer cost savings or a competitive advantage. By contrast, military organizations adopt new advancements much more quickly—because their lives literally depend on it.

Previous inflection points include the development of accurate long-distance navigation, railways, steam ships, and airplanes; and the invention of the printing press, telegraph, and radio.

Today's inflection point is a combination of affordable high-bandwidth internet, global video calls, and global travel—at the same time as significant socioeconomic changes.

Changes in Technology

During World War I, telephone wires were run through active battlefields so generals at headquarters could communicate quickly over long distances with soldiers on the front lines. Delays and miscommunications still happened if a wire was severed or front-line battles moved beyond existing phone wires—requiring humans to install new phone wires across active battlefields[1].

Field telephone on front lines in World War I

By the 1940s and World War II, communication technologies had evolved to the point that one specially trained soldier per team could be dedicated to carry a large fragile backpack radio—a labor cost well worth the improved communications and management coordination.

---

[1] Another new communication technology, "Braille," was invented by the French as a way for soldiers to read written commands at night, without a light, so they could avoid giving away their positions to enemy snipers.

US Marines in World War II

As technology continues to improve, these communication tools continue to shrink in size. Today, each soldier has night vision equipment and personal encrypted radios in their helmets. This allows them to coordinate securely with coworkers out of sight elsewhere in nearby combat theatre, as well as communicate with headquarters for advice, supplies, and reinforcements. Urban warfare and nighttime battles are now possible. These new communication technologies changed how soldiers communicate with each other, which changed how armies work.

A modern-day soldier with earpiece and microphone for secure communications, and helmet mount for night vision equipment.

The rate of change of technology continues to accelerate, in both military and civilian environments. Over the last few decades, "expensive new technologies" that allow you to talk with people far away (telephone), write on a portable device (portable typewriter), and create moving pictures (reel-to-reel movie cameras) are now routinely included for free in each new laptop computer and smartphone. These physical devices keep getting smaller, lighter, and less expensive every year. Again, changes to how we communicate let us change how we work.

> *"Adapting to new technologies brings with it many challenges. It's one thing to install new hardware and software. It's far more difficult to change people's brainware."*
>
> *Colin Powell*

Given the possibilities that these new communication technologies allow, and their widespread availability, we can now build companies that have customers all over the globe. So why do some companies still arrange their offices like this?

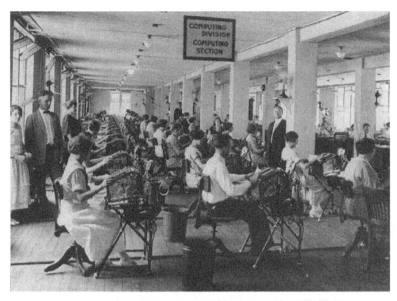

US Veteran's Bureau, early 1920s. Note the large, non-portable calculators used in the computing division.

This 1920s office photo was taken just a few years after the photo of the soldier in a World War I battlefield. As new technologies evolve, the military update how they communicate and how they work. So why do many companies still arrange offices and manage staff like this?

As it turns out, some companies asked this same question and decided to reduce the importance of an office or skip an office completely. In 1957, Elsie Shutt founded CompInc[2] in the US. About the same time, in 1962, Dame Stephanie "Steve" Shirley founded Freelance Programmers in England. Both companies are noteworthy because the founder was female, hired women engineers, and the companies were fully distributed—everyone worked from their homes. Hiring requirements included having a working telephone at your house! Employees drew flowcharts and wrote code at home, then physically mailed their work into headquarters so that others could type their code into mainframe computers. CompInc did projects for Harvard University and the

---

[2] Elsie Shutt was also the first female founder of a software company in the US. For more details, read *Recoding Gender: Women's Changing Participation in Computing* by Janet Abate, MIT Press.

US Air Force while Freelance Programmers grew to a $3 billion valuation (back when $3 billion was a lot of money!) working on notable projects like the black box for Concorde aircraft[3].

In the US, there has been an increasing trend of people working from home, growing from 2005 to 2014[4]. Then COVID-19 hit. As of September 2020, 42% now work outside of their employer's facilities[5]. Globally, in 2012, 17% of the workforce who could connect to their workplace online, worked remotely[6]. Since COVID-19, the sheer number of organizations declaring they're not coming back to offices is hard to keep track of—the best I've seen is a constantly updating article on Forbes[7]. Before COVID-19, some notable examples were:

- Aetna Insurance has around 35,000 employees. More than 43% of them work from home; the rest are scattered across more than 100 offices globally[8].

- Automattic (makers of WordPress) has around 1,100 "Automatticians" in 62 countries. They are 100% remote, with no office[9].

---

[3] For more details, watch Dame Shirley's TED talk or listen to her interviews with the British Library.

[4] This 103% increase excludes self-employed people, who would skew the number higher. For more details, see the Telecommuting Statistics at GlobalWorkplaceAnalytics.com.

[5] "How working from home is working out" Nicholas Bloom, Stanford Institute for Economic Policy Research, 2020.

[6] Full Ipsos / Thompson Reuters poll results: "The World of Work: Global Study of Online Employees Shows One in Five (17%) Work from Elsewhere."

[7] "Here's When Major Companies Plan To Go Back To The Office" by Rachel Sandler, 2020.

[8] Aetnacareers.com, "Reasons to Work at Aetna," and reuters.com, "In telecommuting debate, Aetna sticks by big at-home workforce."

[9] They did set up an office in San Francisco, and then sold it because few employees ever worked there! Related articles: "The company behind WordPress is closing its gorgeous San Francisco office because its employees never show up," and "Automattic Freedom: A Fully-Remote Team Talks About Remote Work."

- Dell has around 140,000 employees globally as of October 2017. Dell launched its flexible work program in 2009, with the goal of having at least 50% of its team members leverage work flexibility by 2020. While 18% are formally enrolled to work remotely[10], 54% already do so informally.

- GitHub (makers of github.com) has around 1,100 employees and four offices globally. Around 50% of their employees work from home.

- GitLab (makers of gitlab.com) has around 1,300 employees, globally, with no office.

- InVision (maker of InVisionApp) has around 700 employees globally, with no office.

- JetBlue Airlines has 17,000 employees scattered across 97 airport destinations plus their New York City headquarters. Some jobs require being on-site, but around 75% of JetBlue's approximately 8,000 reservation agents work from home.

- Mozilla (maker of Firefox) has around 800 employees globally. Of these, 60% work in one of twelve offices globally, while 40% work from home full-time.

- MySQL AB (maker of MySQL) has around 400 employees globally. Of these, 70% work from home full-time.

- Wikimedia (maker of Wikipedia) has around 300 employees globally. Of these, 60% work in or near Wikimedia's one office, while 40% work from home full-time.

"We are pushing for a culture where it simply doesn't matter where you work from."

Mohammed Chahdi, Global Director of HR, Dell

Changes in Internet Connectivity

Reliable, high speed, affordable, internet connectivity is essential for distributed teams. In the US, in 2009, there were around 34 million people working from home. This number was expected to

---

[10] "FY17 Connected Workplace," Dell internal report.

rise to around 63 million people by 2016[11], enabled in part by the availability of high speed internet. Since COVID-19, those numbers have obviously jumped with some estimates of 88 million people[12]. The success of Elsie Shutt and Dame Stephanie Shirley's distributed software companies in the early 1960s are even more impressive when you consider they had to use dialup phone connections and postal mail.

Internet connectivity was essential for me when I decided where to live—and sometimes when I decide where to vacation! Anecdotally, the same is true for many of my friends as well as current or former coworkers. Living and working in Bangkok, Barcelona, Berlin, or Boston is fine; living in a location without reliable high-speed internet connectivity is daunting. As high-speed internet rollout accelerates globally, the range of suitable locations increases. This allows high-tech workers to live wherever they find high-speed internet connectivity—choosing features that are important to them personally, like a stable government, good weather, and appealing local amenities[13].

Changes in Social Contract

Over the last 40 years or so, society has gone through seismic changes. The idea of a job for life is no more. Per-project jobs, freelance work, and gig work are prevalent in the free-agent economy. Whether this is good or bad is a separate discussion; the point is that the social contract has fundamentally changed.

---

[11] "US Telecommuting Forecast, 2009 To 2016" (source: Ted Schadler of Forrester) and US Bureau of Labor Statistics, "Job Flexibilities and Work Schedules News Release" 2019.

[12] US Federal Reserve, "Working Age Population, 2020" and "How working from home is working out" Nicholas Bloom, Stanford Institute for Economic Policy Research, 2020.

[13] If you are planning to relocate within the US with the intention of working remotely, you might find the live national map of broadband coverage useful (see broadbandmap.gov). For global analysis of major global cities, read the annual reports published by Mercer.

Across all industries in the US, across all generations, people change jobs every 4.1 years[14]. The baby boomers averaged a new job every 2.7 years[15]. In the computer industry, in hyper-competitive locations like Silicon Valley, the turnover is even faster, with average tenure at major tech companies ranging from 1.2 to 2.0 years[16]!

To see how quickly and significantly the social contract has changed, consider these quotes[17]:

> *"Maximizing employee [career] security is a prime company goal."*
>
> *Earl Willis, Head of Employee Benefits, General Electric, 1962*

> *"Loyalty to a company, it's nonsense."*
> *"Loyalty isn't dead, but rewarding loyalty without performance should be. It's shortsighted and wrongheaded."*
>
> *Jack Welch, CEO, General Electric, 2005 and 2009*

Most of the software engineers I know already work on a per-project basis, even though they are administratively called full-time employees. They are hired to work on a particular project—and after one or two release cycles, they'll leave to work on a new project at a new company before moving on yet again.

These 18- to 24-month transitions lined up with the *waterfall* delivery cadence that was used by a lot of software companies. Soon after each major release shipped, there would be a

---

[14] US Bureau of Labor Statistics, "Employee Tenure Summary" 2020.

[15] US Bureau of Labor Statistics, "Number of Jobs Held, Labor Market Activity, and Earnings Growth Among the Youngest Baby Boomers" 1978-2016.

[16] The "Business Insider summary of Paysa.com "Annual Disruptors 2017 Survey" noted average retention (in years) at Airbnb (1.64), Amazon (1.84), Apple (1.85), Facebook (2.02), Google (1.90), Microsoft (1.81), Oracle (1.89), Twitter (1.83), and Uber (1.23).

[17] This change is across society, and not specific to General Electric. I only used General Electric in this example because GE has been large enough, for long enough, that it was possible to find "before" and "after" quotes like this about the same company.

predictable flood of "goodbye" emails, internal promotions, and new-hire announcements as people celebrated their successful project release and left before the next project started. As more software companies change to an *agile* methodology, releasing smaller deliverables more frequently, I suspect that the average tenure will shrink further. This will be interesting to watch[18].

In many ways this feels similar to the movie industry's evolution from the all-in-our-studio model of the 1920s to today's model of hiring independent specialists for each part of a movie. How do you categorize a special-effects engineer or stunt driver working on a movie for a few months? Or a software engineer who switches jobs every 18 to 24 months? Or a tour of duty in the military? Or engineers hired for a few months because they specialize in complex skills that are only needed for a short project? Or an Uber driver? Or a sound technician at a concert venue? The line between per-project employee, contractor, freelancer, free agent, and gig worker feels very blurry[19].

Of course, there are also times when employees do not choose when to leave. A company is bought, merged, or acquired. Or it shuts down or goes bankrupt. Or it pivots into a new business direction where their skills are no longer needed. No wonder 65% of freelancers feel working with a few different clients is a *more* stable income stream than a job with one employer[20].

In this context, it is no surprise that people are less likely to relocate for each new job. For more on this, see "The Final Chapter."

Changes Across Generations

While I was writing the first edition of this book, my nephew arrived in San Francisco for the summer. I immediately brought

---

[18] Stock option vesting schedules help improve retention, but even these "golden handcuffs" only work until a nearby competitor offers even more valuable stock options.

[19] Reed Hoffman, founder and chairman of LinkedIn, offers interesting perspectives in his books *The Start-up of You* and *The Alliance*.

[20] Upwork's report, "Freelancing in America 2019."

him and his friends to a nearby cell phone store where they bought prepaid SIM cards and installed them into their Irish-bought Chinese-made quad-band smartphones. Within 24 hours of arriving in a new country they were standing on the sidewalk, streaming live video to their families in Ireland cheaply and reliably, using a small, portable, familiar device that fits in their pocket. They thought this was normal. They were stunned when I described the phone-attached-to-wall technology available to me when I first lived in the US, just like I was stunned when my parents described the technology available when they lived in South America during the 1960s[21].

In the context of this book, humans in my nephew's generation are important because they are "digital natives"[22], all born after MTV started broadcasting. These Millennials grew up using high-speed internet, group chat messaging, and free streaming video calls in their daily social lives. They expect the same in their professional working lives. In 2017, the Millennial generation became the largest percentage of people in the US workforce[23]. Sometime in 2020-2021, GenZ—the generation after Millennials—will become the second largest segment of the US workforce. As their numbers continue to increase and older generations retire, these digital native generations are changing workplace dynamics.

I was aware that, generally speaking, different generations had different comfort levels with current technology. But that moment, standing outside the cell phone store, showed me just how quickly and massively the mindset of these digital native generations will revolutionize the workforce. Their comfortable use of new communication tools is essential for effective distributed teams.

---

[21] My parents recorded audio onto reel-to-reel tapes, and physically mailed the reels back to Ireland. Many weeks later they eagerly sat down to play the tape reels that arrived back bringing news from family in Ireland.

It will be interesting to see what communication technology will be considered "normal" when the children of my nephew's generation enter the workforce.

[22] Term coined by Marc Prensky.

[23] "Millennials are the largest generation in the U.S. labor force" by Pew Research Center.

Millennials and GenZ do not expect a job for life. They are very aware how the Social Contract has changed in recent decades—and most have witnessed firsthand what happened to their parents who were laid off late in their career after decades working for one employer. To avoid the same fate, they diversify their career, switching employers when faced with a lack of promotion or learning opportunities. They expect to switch companies frequently throughout their careers—43% of Millennials and 61% of GenZ expect to change jobs within the next 24 months[24].

Anecdotally, there is evidence that Millennials want to travel and explore the world, living wherever they like, while working as Digital Nomads. By contrast, during the early stages of my career I had to relocate with each new job offer. So did many of my peers. My parents' generation was similar. As communication technologies improve over the generations, it becomes easier to find meaningful career-building work while pursuing the desire to explore the world.

Over time, as people start serious relationships with long-term partners who hold careers of their own, they start buying homes, raising families, and caring for aging parents. They become less willing to relocate for a new job, especially when they expect to change jobs again soon. At that point they tend to settle down in one location, which means they either limit themselves to working for a nearby company, or they work in remote-friendly distributed companies!

It is not surprising that surveys[25] of US college seniors and graduates found that 68% were interested in potential employers because of their remote work policy. This job benefit was more popular than traditional company perks like casual dress code (62%), free snacks and drinks (62%), or a pet-friendly office (31%). While some perks cost an organization money, the remote work policy is interesting because it was the most popular and it *saves* money. For more details, see "The Real Cost of an Office."

---

[24] "2018 Millennial Survey" by Deloitte.

[25] "RemoteCo: 10 Stats About Remote Work" and "US After College Report, 2015" and "AfterCollege Report, 2020."

Disaster Planning

Takeaways

◆ If the office suddenly closed tomorrow for a day, a week, or even longer, could your entire team continue to do their normal jobs?

◆ Rethink the traditional approach to Disaster Recovery. Use cheap, familiar tools daily instead of using expensive, unfamiliar tools rarely.

◆ We routinely build fault-tolerant systems. We need to build fault tolerant *organizations*.

When an organization requires people to be physically together in order to work, that location becomes an expensive single point of failure. Prolonged unexpected office closures[1] and public transportation closures[2] now become company-threatening problems.

Even something that sounds routine, like a snow day closure, can be very expensive. For example, in the New England region of the northeastern US, each snow day closure costs local employers $1.3 billion dollars[3].

[1] Spraying building for pests, a fire next door in another company's office, power outages, an earthquake, or worse!

[2] Hurricane Sandy (2012); Snowmageddon (2015); Snowzilla (2016); Hurricanes Harvey, Irma, and Maria (2017); Paris floods (2018).

[3] "Lost work hours from one snow day costs New England employers $1.3B" by globalworkplaceanalytics.com.

Some pre-planned events[4] give you advance notice to prepare. Civil unrest, man-made catastrophes[5], pandemics, natural catastrophes, and extreme weather events usually do not. The consequences are the same. While any one individual disruption might be a surprise, it is safe to assume that office closures and public transit disruptions will happen at some point—you just don't know when.

> *"If someone has the option to stay home, work from home, that's a great choice ..."*
>
> *de Blasio, New York City Mayor 2015 (in advance of Opening Session at UN, visit by President Obama and unrelated visit by Pope Francis all in Manhattan, NYC in the same week)*

Even organizations that do plan and train for office closures, usually only plan for short-term closures. It makes sense. Most office closures are brief and training for these is less disruptive to the organization. The COVID-19 pandemic in early 2020 caused long-term office closures globally. Organizations that had not trained for long-term office closures were disrupted—some more than others. Pandemics are not the only cause of long-term office closures. When Hurricane Sandy hit New York City in 2012, some people lost their homes. Some lost their lives. Many people were fine, though, and their homes and offices were fine. However, they could not get to the office because the subways were flooded and public transportation remained closed, long after the hurricane had moved on. Because their work was organized around being in the office, they found themselves attempting to learn how to work from home while already stuck at home.

---

[4] SuperBowl 50 in San Francisco 2016, Winter Olympics in Tokyo 2020.

[5] *What should I do with my life?* by Po Bronson includes a true story about a company that had an office in the World Trade Center NYC during the September 11th, 2001 attack.

New York City subway network closure, Hurricane Sandy, 2012

"Winter storms are always a wake-up call for companies that haven't adopted flexible workplace strategies. If people are already familiar with working remotely or telecommuting, when the weather stops traffic cold, they can keep right on working."

Kate Lister, President, Global Workplace Analytics

By coincidence, when the 1989 Loma Prieta earthquake hit, the State of California was running a study on the effectiveness of telecommuting. Because this study was already monitoring people's work before the earthquake, it was uniquely able to compare how quickly remote workers and office-bound coworkers recovered and resumed full work. Not surprisingly, the remote workers resumed work much more quickly—usually the same day or the next day—because they were *already used to working from home effectively*. By contrast, office workers were delayed by road and bridge closures. As the report dryly noted, "Repair of damaged telephone lines is generally much faster than repair of damaged roads," and "If many more organizations had adopted telecommuting prior to the earthquake, it is likely that the economic impact of the earthquake would have been materially diminished[6]." Similarly, during the 2010 "Snowmageddon" blizzards in the eastern US, the federal government was forced to close for four days at a cost of $70 to $100 million per day[7]—while federal employees who were already used to working from home were able to continue uninterrupted. The Congressional Budget Office noted that the five-year cost of implementing telework across those same agencies was $30 million—fully recouped in one half of one day of blizzard closures.

---

[6] "The State of California Telecommuting Pilot Project, Final Report," June 1990. A smaller scale study of New Zealand government was published in 2015 after a series of major earthquakes there. For more details, see "Disrupted work: home-based teleworking (HbTW) in the aftermath of a natural disaster" by Noelle Donnelly et al.

[7] "Federal Telework—Return on Taxpayer Investment" by Kate Lister (Global Workplace Analytics, 2013); "TELEWORK: Weighing the Information, Determining an Appropriate Approach" by US Merit Systems Protection Board, 2011; and the Society for Human Resource Management, "President Signs Federal Employee Telework Legislation."

Market Street, San Francisco after earthquake and fire, 1906

San Francisco and Silicon Valley, home to many global technology companies, are located in a major earthquake zone.

Most software companies have customers across the globe. Those customers expect their systems to keep working even when there is a local disruption to the vendor's local office.

When a software company has all of its servers running in resilient data centers (or in the cloud[8]), their unattended production servers might continue to run for a while. However, the company's day-to-day office operations—developing new software, deploying bug

---

[8] While "in the cloud" is a popular phrase these days, it should more accurately be written as "hosted on computer systems owned by an external service provider, located in multiple hardened data centers across multiple geographical locations."

fixes to production servers, holding meetings with clients, and collecting invoices—will all be disrupted if the employees usually work in an office, and that office no longer exists.

Could your company operate normally if your physical office didn't exist tomorrow?

You can choose to do nothing and be "surprised" the next time you have an unexpected office closure or public transit disruption. You can choose to spend time and money on a traditional disaster planning and disaster recovery ("DR") solution. You can choose to crisply organize how your company works so that the office is optional. Or you can choose to avoid setting up an office in the first place, allowing your company to sidestep future disruptions at the office. Crisp organization helps your company become office-optional, which creates a more fault-tolerant company and saves your company money!

The Traditional Approach

The traditional approach duplicates essential systems in a secure off-site location. If your normal office location becomes unusable, employees go to an alternate office location where essential systems are set up, ready, and waiting for humans to resume working.

This is trickier than it sounds.

Answering "What systems are essential?" depends on who you ask. Disaster Planning[9] is human-intensive, detailed, time-consuming, and expensive. If even one crucial but low-profile system is unavailable at the backup location, you will probably only find out when people start trying to use backup systems during or after an emergency. At that point it is too late to go back to the office to access the missing system or paper files. This analysis phase never ends—you need to keep updating your disaster plan as your business needs and procedures change.

---

[9] For simplicity in writing, I use Disaster Planning (DP) although terms like Disaster Recovery (DR), Business Continuity Planning, and Continuity of Operations (COOP) are also commonly used.

There is also recurring work to keep your backup systems up to date and refreshed with live production data. Here are two examples:

+ LDAP and VPN[10] servers need updating every time users join or leave the company, or change their passwords. If your company email server is in your office, transferring nightly or weekly backups of the live email server to the DR email server might suffice. For other companies, continuous up-to-the-second replication between mail servers is essential.

+ Paper files, such as financial records, patient medical records and customer invoices, must be physically duplicated and transported to the backup location in a timely manner.

The cadence and mechanics of these updates involves a tradeoff between business needs and cost tolerance. With more frequent updates the transition to the DR system will be smoother (should the need arise), but the cost of the system will increase.

Deciding where to put the backup location is also tricky. The backup location must be far enough away from the office that it is not impacted by the emergency that closed the regular office. At the same time, the backup location needs to be close enough that nearby employees can reasonably commute to the location. The backup location also depends on the type of emergency you are planning for. A good backup location while preparing for public protests is very different than a good backup location for terrorism, earthquakes, fires, or floods. For security reasons, some companies do not disclose the location of their DR systems until after the need arises, which can itself be a problem if people need to go to the no-longer-working office to learn the address of the DR location[11].

---

[10] Virtual Private Network

[11] One multinational company I worked for had a dedicated phone number that employees were expected to call during emergency office closures, to get timely updates on their offices. This number was intended for employees only, so to reduce the risk of external media calls, this number was unlisted. Despite repeated efforts to get the word out by organizing events in lobby and dining areas, posting on internal wiki sites, and sending regular company-wide emails, most people in the company had no idea this emergency phone number existed. When an accident cut electrical power to large portions of HQ, conflicting rumors and

In addition to backing up physical systems, there is a need to back up the human non-physical work procedures. In many organizations the how-humans-get-stuff-done reality of the workplace is poorly understood or documented. These undocumented human procedures are disrupted when key people quit, when they move physical offices, or when multiple people no-show at the same time—like during layoffs, pandemics, or a company emergency failover to the DR location. Understanding, documenting, and consistently following crisp organizational processes before any emergency arises helps humans take over the roles of any missing coworkers whenever an emergency does arise. This is essential for business continuity.

The Distributed Approach

To work effectively from home for an extended amount of time requires a combination of carefully chosen tools and crisply organized work habits for all involved.

A well-organized distributed team uses reliable, cheap, familiar tools constantly. This makes the group fault-tolerant and robust, and the tools are less expensive than traditional disaster recovery.

Most organizations are not crisply organized; they lack clearly understood protocols for coordinating work. In addition, humans often face too many conflicting sources of information. To compensate, humans form habits like daily standup meetings, status meetings, and corridor conversations, repeatedly discussing the latest status of their continuously evolving project. This recurring storytelling approach is so common that many people I've worked with view this as normal. In addition to being inefficient, this behavior is extremely vulnerable to physical disruption. Crisply organizing work around a written Single Source of Truth is crucial for resilient group communications. For more on this, see "Single Source of Truth."

---

misunderstandings caused people to drive to the office every morning just to discover that the office was still closed, turn around, and drive back home again. It took days for informal networks of humans using their cell phones to spread the word about current status of the closed buildings, as well as the existence of the still-unlisted emergency contact number.

Finding and fixing organizational weak spots is tricky. If you typically work in an office, try this experiment the next time you enter your office: Pretend it's your first day at a new company, seeing everything with fresh eyes as if for the first time. Note each process and action you do while in the office. Ask yourself how you would handle each one if you were to work from home tomorrow.

Here are some examples that are easy to miss:

- A giant physical sign in the office lobby announces "xxx number of days left before the release," or lists the remaining tasks for an upcoming project deadline. *Alternative approach*: Replace static signs and whiteboard notices with large monitors displaying live data from the system you use for your Single Source of Truth. This live data can also be viewed by remote people, as well as by people elsewhere in the office. This allows everyone to answer their own questions about current status, and encourages a culture where people routinely update the Single Source of Truth.

- A wall of sticky notes is used for tracking tasks on a software development team's agile or scrum board. *Alternative approach:* Move these to a bug system or ticketing system, flagged with the appropriate keywords and priority. Most ticketing systems have graphical interfaces that mimic the visual approach of a wall of sticky notes—without needing a physical wall, and without the single point of failure.

- Filing cabinets contain paperwork such as expense reports, HR personnel files, payroll records, medical records, and customer contracts. If these were lost in an office fire or soaked beyond repair by sprinkler systems, these original records would be hard to recreate. *Alternative approach:* Scan these records and store them in a data center with offsite electronic backups, or on a hosted Software as a Service ("SaaS") vendor. Keep the paper originals as backup copies.

- A status update happens during an informal corridor conversation, at the end of an unrelated meeting, at the coffee machine, or on the way to lunch. *Alternative approach:* Have the informal chat, then quickly update the Single Source of Truth so others can learn about it.

In general, ask yourself how you would handle every physical display, physical tool, physical document, and in-person human interaction you have in the office, if you suddenly needed to work from home tomorrow.

Of course, disasters do not just happen to offices; people working from home could have problems too. An earthquake damages someone's home. An ice storm in Canada traps humans in their homes with no electricity. Volcanic eruptions trap someone in a random stopover airport in eastern Europe. A work laptop is stolen from a rental car. A key employee is off the grid at Burning Man during a company emergency. Each of these examples have happened to me or to humans in one of my distributed teams. Each one impacted the individual who was involved, but did not take the *entire* distributed group offline at the same time. Because the group was distributed globally, it was less likely that the entire group would be disrupted at the same time.

> *"Sometimes the best transportation policy means not moving people, but moving their work... a trend known as telecommuting... Think of it as commuting to work at the speed of light."*
>
> US President George W. Bush

Experiment

Can you work your normal workday at home instead of at the office?

If you usually work in an office but occasionally work from home for a day, it might be easy to convince yourself that you already successfully work as part of a distributed team. This mistaken belief is usually held by people who intentionally only do focused solo work at home, deferring interactive work with coworkers until everyone is together in the office. If you only do solo work at home, your ability to work well with others still depends on you being in the office. This means your office is still an organizational single point of failure.

If you usually work from an office, try this one-day experiment. Do not go into the office tomorrow morning. Instead, work from home with no advance notice. For one day only. Don't reschedule your meetings or change the work you were planning to do. Attempt your normal workday: attend meetings, hold external customer conference calls, negotiate production calendars with other coworkers, do pair programming, plan budgets, give status reports to your boss(es), review contracts, handle personnel issues, lead team meetings, and so on. Do everything you would typically do during a full interactive day at the office, but from home— using only the items you have at home and the contents of your usual laptop bag.

If things go well, great.

If things do not go well, don't worry. This was only a short, one-day experiment. Worst case, you got some focused work done at home, and you can catch up on the rest of your work in the office the next day. And, you have identified several ways to improve how your team works. Once those improvements are in place, retry the one-day experiment and discover what else needs to be fixed.

Most people cannot do this well the first time because their organization does not have crisp organizational processes. Instead, their processes are shaped by humans they encounter while walking around the physical building[12]. By contrast, experienced distributed teams can handle this experiment just fine. Whether they are at home or in an office, they consistently use cheap, familiar tools and crisp human processes. Their location is simply not relevant.

If you are trying this work-from-home experiment in an organization that does not already have effective distributed teams, do this experiment on a Tuesday, Wednesday, or Thursday. Do not try this on a Monday or Friday. This is important to avoid any perception that "working from home" is a euphemism for taking a long weekend off work.

Continue this one-day experiment once a week for a few weeks. When you can routinely conduct your normal workday from

---

[12] Your organization has this problem if someone holds an emergency meeting inviting everyone nearby—simply because they are visible near the meeting organizer, regardless of whether they would be useful in the meeting. For more on this, see "Meetings."

home, ask another person in your group to start doing this one-day experiment. When that is successful, ask another person, and then another. When your entire team can do their normal work from home one day a week, slowly increase the cadence to two non-adjacent days a week. Then three days a week. Keep doing this until the trust and working relationships across the team work well consistently over several days a week, over several weeks. Only after all of this is normal should you consider working from home on a Monday or a Friday.

Congratulations! Your team has changed the office from an organizational single point of failure to being optional. Now, if there is an office closure, weather emergency, or public transit emergency, your team can continue working as normal. I've worked for several companies that had multi-day office closures or public transit disruptions. I've also worked in, and with, multiple organizations during the prolonged COVID-19 office closures in 2020. In each case there was no disruption to the distributed teams, because we were already effective as a distributed team; for us, the office was already optional.

Why choose to spend money to *add* an expensive single point of failure—an office—to your organization?

Some roles in an organization are clearly location-dependent. Lab technicians, brain surgeons, and people who operate some types of security-classified systems are examples of roles that need to be physically at their work location. For these roles, the physical office building is an operational single point of failure for your organization. In addition to short-term disaster planning, plans for long-term building closures need to be developed and tested for all these location-dependent roles. The COVID-19 pandemic uncovered which organizations had short-term and also long-term disaster plans.

Other roles appear to be location-dependent but could become location independent roles through process changes, tooling changes and/or training. Examples include roles that require wet-ink-on-paper signature approvals, use of desktop (not laptop) computers, and management pressures to work in the office.

Diversity

Takeaways

◆ Requiring people to commute to an office limits your ability to hire diversely.

◆ Companies with diverse teams produce better-quality solutions and are more profitable.

◆ Employee referrals remain an important tool for recruiting. If your social and professional networks are not diverse, it is unlikely that your referrals will be diverse.

Distributed teams tend to be more diverse than teams in a single location[1].

This diversity brings different perspectives when solving problems, which is essential for avoiding groupthink[2] and blind spots that can threaten the success of organizations[3]. This diversity of perspectives also improves the *quality* of the solutions

---

[1] Siebdrat, F., Hoegl, M., & Ernst, H. (2009). How to manage virtual teams. *MIT Sloan Research Management Review.*

[2] Cummings, J.N. (2004). Work groups, structural diversity, and knowledge sharing in a global organization. *Management Science.* Hambrick, D.C., Davison, S.C., Snell, S.A., & Snow, C.C. (1998). When groups consist of multiple nationalities: Toward a new understanding of the implications. *Organization Studies.* Hunt, V., Layton, D., & Prince, S. (2015). Why Diversity Matters. McKinsey.

[3] Janis, I. L. (1972). *Victims of groupthink: A psychological study of foreign-policy decisions and fiascoes.* Janis, I. L. (1982). *Groupthink: psychological studies of policy decisions and fiascoes.*

proposed[4], which helps diverse companies be more profitable[5] and outperform less-diverse companies[6].

When talking about diversity, it is easy to skip over practical realities. People with physical, mental, or emotional issues can find it very difficult to commute to and from an office on a daily basis. Caregivers might not apply for a job simply because of the distance between your office and the people they care for. Factors like these hamper office-based diversity efforts while also causing very high unemployment rates in certain sections of society—because of the commute, not their ability to do the work.

"Whether you're building a company or leading a country, a diverse mix of voices and backgrounds and experiences leads to better discussions, better decisions, and better outcomes for everyone."

Sundar Pichai, CEO Google/Alphabet

In this chapter I describe several different scenarios as if they were separate, without overlap. However, it is worth noting that some humans face more than one of these scenarios, and there are other scenarios that I did not include for the sake of clarity in writing.

---

[4] Mohammadi, A., Broström, A., & Franzoni, C. (2015). Work force composition and innovation: How diversity in employees' ethnical and disciplinary backgrounds facilitates knowledge re-combination. *Centre of Excellence for Science and Innovation Studies (CESIS), Sweden.* Rock, D., & Grant, H. (2016). Why diverse teams are smarter. *Harvard Business Review.* Feitler, D. (2014). The case for team diversity gets even better. *Harvard Business Review.* Page, S. (2008). The Difference: How the power of diversity creates better groups, firms, schools, and societies. *Princeton University Press.*

[5] Forbes Insights (2011). Fostering innovation through a diverse workforce. Barta, T., Kleiner, M., & Neumann, T. (2012). Is there a payoff from top-team diversity? *McKinsey Quarterly.* Delivering through diversity McKinsey (2018).

[6] Hunt, V., Prince, S. et al. (2018). Delivering Through Diversity *McKinsey.* Hunt, V., Layton, D., & Prince, S. (2015). Why diversity matters. *McKinsey. Hewlett, S, et al. How Diversity Can Drive Innovation (2013) Harvard Business Review.*

Physical Diversity

While recovering from some travel injuries, I spent almost two years on crutches, including six months of home nursing. During this time I discovered several fundamental logistical problems I had never even considered before.

I could no longer drive myself to my office; the office was too far to commute by taxi or public transport. Instead, I asked for favors from nearby coworkers, and organized my commute times and office meetings around the schedule of that day's volunteer driver. At the office I added time to my calendar for moving between meeting rooms (and buildings!) because I was so much slower on crutches, using a backpack to carry my laptop, notebooks, and medical equipment. Lastly, social lunches with coworkers were not practical, so I ate energy bars and napped under my desk to recuperate from my exertions—acutely aware of my sudden social isolation.

Thankfully, I was able to keep my job. I mainly worked from home while recuperating back to full health. I was lucky.

In the US, 41 million people have lifelong disabilities[7]. Of these, 28 million are working-age adults with no job—an unemployment rate of 62%[8]. Some of these disabilities prevent the person from doing work they are qualified to do. Others are still able to do the work they are qualified to do. The problem is not their ability or willingness to work. The problem is the twice-a-day obstacle course: the commute to an office, and the commute home. Every person I interviewed for this chapter all thought an occasional trip to the office, or to meet coworkers, was worth the logistical effort and stress[9]. They value the interactions and do not want to be isolated from society. However, reliably and consistently commuting to and from an office twice a day, every workday of every week, was a real problem.

---

[7] "Civilian Disability Status," US Census Bureau, 2019.

[8] "Cornell University Disability Statistics, 2018 Status Report."

[9] The State of California found that telecommuting caused a significant *reduction* in stress for mobility-impaired state employees. For more details, see the "State of California Telecommuting Pilot Project Final Report, June 1990."

Navigating within an office is also a challenge. To save money, open-plan offices are designed for a higher density of humans per square foot. In theory, people should be able to move around these high-density offices on crutches, in a wheelchair, or using a white cane. That theory rarely takes into account the reality of extra chairs, plants, rolling whiteboards, bags, coats, garbage cans, and other accessories that clutter the workplace, often completely blocking passage until someone unblocks the path.

One workaround is to acquire a desk near the office entrance, making it easier to get to the desk. However, this doesn't solve the problem of getting from the desk to meeting rooms elsewhere in the office, or navigating within a meeting room. In the narrow space between the walls and the meeting room table, chairs are often pushed back from the table by humans leaving the previous meeting.

Jane, an Air Force veteran with a master's degree and experience as a firefighter, was unemployed due to chronic and progressive medical issues. In 2011, Paralyzed Veterans of America introduced her to an employer looking to hire a full-time emergency services fire monitor. This role was sedentary in nature, and required in-depth knowledge of firefighter situations, including the ability to monitor specialized equipment, issue timely reports, and remain calm under pressure. When Jane started the job, she worked at her employer's office to learn her new job and build mutual trust. Then she transitioned to full-time work-from-home.

This work-from-home job lets Jane remain financially independent, productive, and gainfully employed. The job also reduced the commute logistics for Jane's caregivers. This improved the quality of life for all. And, the employer is happy with a dependable, well-educated, highly skilled, highly motivated employee.

Marcos, a coworker who is blind, described to me how much the weather impacts his hearing and his commute. Heavy rain or high winds make him effectively deaf[10] as well as blind. Heavy snowfall acts as a giant acoustic muffler, absorbing all of the familiar background noises he uses to navigate—and complicating his use of a white cane. It is not safe for him to leave home on those days, and he listens to weather forecast reports closely. This weather

---

[10] He called this "ear blind."

dependency means that he cannot accept job offers that require consistent daily commutes.

Fred, a software engineer who is wheelchair-bound, refuses to travel on public transport during rush hours because people getting on cannot see him in the crowd. They push others to "fill in that gap in the crowd over there," not realizing that he is sitting in that "gap," invisible because of the people standing around him. He has lost count of the times people were literally pushed into his lap. Fred was able to afford a handicap-accessible car, but the car introduced a different problem: the controls for his specially modified car are very hard on his hands and arms. (If you've never seen how these cars work, find someone to give you a test drive so you can appreciate the mechanics involved.) Fred's concerns about his hands and arms are well founded—he needs them to push his wheelchair and type at a computer. An injury would reduce his mobility even further, and could eliminate his only job prospects. To deal with this concern he limits how often he drives, and he only drives outside of rush hours. He avoids driving in poor weather or when special events might cause traffic jams. Sometimes he finds himself explaining the mechanics of his wheelchair life over the phone to a non-wheelchair recruiter who believes the commute objections are contrived.

Prolonged sitting is a health hazard[11] for everyone, including people in wheelchairs. During the day, Fred takes short breaks out of the wheelchair. He stretches and rolls around on the floor to help protect his spine from time spent sitting. This is easy to do at home but not in an open-plan office. Some companies have "privacy" or "nursing" rooms where he can do this, but it usually involves embarrassing discussions with nursing mothers who are surprised to find an adult male in "their" room.

"Don't hire people like you, hire your complements. You're white and male? Hire a woman of color. You're young? Hire someone older. Hire the things you don't have, like experience or a diverse perspective. Hire a wide range of ideas."

Guy Kawasaki

---

[11] Dunstan, D.W., Howard, B., Healy, G.N., & Owen, N (2012). Too much sitting—a health hazard. *Diabetes Research and Clinical Practice.*

Racial Diversity

Because of the lack of racial diversity in tech workplaces, and pressure from staff[12], some US-based companies started publishing racial and gender demographics of their employees with the mindset that they can improve what they can measure. These reports[13] show that African Americans[14] account for around 5% of employees at tech companies and around 2% at venture capital ("VC") firms. Latinos account for 1% of employees at VC firms. By comparison, the US population[15] is approximately 64% Caucasian, 16% Latinx, 12% African American, 5% Asian, and 3% "other."

Even after hiring, inclusion remains a problem, with 48% of African-American women and 47% of Latina scientists reporting being mistaken for administrative or custodial staff[16]. By comparison, this "only" happened to 32% of Caucasian women and 23% of Asian women scientists[17]. Lack of inclusion hurts retention, which makes it even harder to increase diversity.

[12] I believe Tracy Chou's viral post in 2013 was the tipping point for this trend. See "Where are the numbers?" on medium.com and "This Twenty-Something Forced Silicon Valley to 'Show Her the Numbers" on wired.com.

[13] Examples include "Strengthening Dropbox through diversity," "Driving Diversity at Facebook," "Diversity at Google," "Our workforce" at Microsoft, "Diversity at Slack," and "Tesla." A good general summary is "Diversity of Tech Companies by the Numbers: 2016 Edition," at pxlnv.com and "Five Years of Tech Diversity Reports—and Little Progress" at wired.com.

[14] In conversations about race and ethnicity, terminology can quickly become tricky. Throughout this book, I used the terminology provided in the cited references when identifying different races and ethnic cultures.

[15] US Census Briefs: "Overview of Race and Hispanic Origin: 2010."

[16] This problem is not unique to tech companies. The Wall Street Journal reported an invite-only formal event in 2003 where U.S. state senator Barack Obama was mistaken for a waiter and asked to get drinks by another guest.

[17] Williams, J.C. (2015). The 5 biases pushing women out of STEM. *Harvard Business Review.*

Diversity is being invited to the party; inclusion is being asked to dance.

Verna Myers

If your neighbors and your nearby office-based coworkers are predominantly the same race or ethnicity, you can improve diversity by hiring people who live outside your neighborhoods or nearby cities[18].

Some companies, like Automattic, will do trial hires, where a candidate is hired for a few weeks to work on a real project, with a go/no-go decision point at the end of the trial period. In general, though, many jobs are filled by referrals: people you've worked with before, whose skills you can personally vouch for. If a job requires complex skills that are hard to evaluate during interviews, it can be argued that the best way to know if a potential new hire will be a good fit for the role is if you, or someone you trust, has seen the candidate work well in similar situations. However, this raises the specter of bias if you only know others of your own race, ethnicity and socioeconomic background.

Lack of social diversity[19] makes it hard to improve organizational diversity. After all, if you are asked to refer candidates for a specific job vacancy, you can only recommend people you know.

Take a moment to ask yourself these questions: How diverse is your network of professional contacts? What about friends and social networks? If you don't have a diverse professional and personal life, how can you expect to make diverse referrals and foster a diverse, inclusive workplace?

Instead of creating a meritocracy (where you hire the best humans for the job), you can accidentally create a mirrortocracy[20] (where you hire humans who look and act like you).

[18] For example, see "Mozilla Diversity Data—EEO-1" (2015).

[19] Cox, D., Navarro-Rivera, J. & Jones, R.P. (2016). Race, Religion, and Political Affiliation of Americans' Core Social Networks, PRRI Research Report.

[20] Attributed to Mitch Kapor, founder of Lotus, Founding Chair of Mozilla Foundation and co-founder of other organizations. He attributes this phrase to his wife, Freada Kapor Klein, while the earliest written reference I could find was " Silicon Valley's Mirror Effect" by Joe Nocera, New York Times.

If you aren't happy with the diversity you discover in your social and professional networks, take intentional steps to diversify your networks. This helps you hear and understand different perspectives, which fosters inclusion.

If you are active on social media, seek out and follow others who are different from you. This also helps you avoid living in a social media echo chamber.

At professional conferences and local social events, make time to chat with humans who do not look, behave, or dress the same as you. If you find you have nothing in common with these other humans, then politely move on. If you find that your casual conversations are positive and friendly, then foster that contact—just like you would with anyone else you talked with at that event.

In the US, in 2015, 75% of whites only know other white people. Of the remaining pool of 25%, most (91%) only have one person of color in their immediate network.

Karla Monterroso, CEO, Code 2040

Invisible Diversity

There are many non-physical reasons for a commute to be a barrier.

Military veterans with PTSD can find sudden loud noises in crowded confined spaces stressful, which makes commuting a challenge on public transit or in rush hour. Some veterans won't even apply for a job because they know that if they get the job, they would be financially unable to relocate to a more expensive location near the office. This situation is complicated by difficulties translating military skills into civilian skills and acclimatizing into the non-military work culture. Unemployment rates for veterans are improving, but they are still significantly higher than unemployment rates for the non-veteran population[21].

---

[21] US Bureau of Labor Statistics, "Employment status of the civilian population 18 years and over by veteran status, period of service, and sex, not seasonally adjusted," 2016.

Four million adults in the US are on the autism spectrum, facing an 85% unemployment rate for life. Recognizing that the commute and the distractions of an office are a barrier for many, ultratesting.us was founded in 2012 to help people on the spectrum find meaningful work they can do from home. As a 100% distributed company, they currently employ people across 39 cities in 19 states.

One VP I interviewed at a Fortune 50 financial institution—I'll call her Amy—has an employee whose claustrophobia makes it impossible to take crowded public transport, drive in rush-hour traffic, or work in their windowless cube-farm office. Even though the company formally discourages working from home, Amy created an informal agreement with the employee. He permanently works from his home, and once a month he drives during midday non-rush-hour traffic to meet his boss for a one-on-one meeting outside in the fresh air. Then he drives home before rush-hour traffic starts. His boss is happy; she continues to have a great, loyal, employee who does good work. The employee is happy; he continues to have a good, productive job and is able to provide for himself without going on long-term disability.

Caregiver Diversity

In the US, 61% of families with two adults have both adults working full-time[22]. For each of these families, one of the two working adults needs to be able to leave work on short notice when a child is sick, or when an aging parent needs care.

Many caregivers are skilled, successful professionals who will only apply to jobs near home because of the ever-present (but rarely invoked) *potential* need to get home quickly on short notice[23]. The distance to the physical office can prevent some caregivers from even applying in the first place. For those who do apply to nearby

---

[22] "Employment Characteristics of Families 2017" by US Department of Labor.

[23] Here are two of many studies worth reading in this field: Mehndiratta, S. & Quiros, T.P. (2014). "Are women 'forced' to work closer to home due to other responsibilities? Does this contribute to gender wage differentials?" and Kwan, M-P (2000). "Evaluating Gender Differences in Individual Accessibility: A Study Using Trip Data Collected By The Global Positioning System, Final Report."

employers and are hired, family emergencies during work hours can limit future project assignments, future promotions, and hence future pay.

How do couples decide who will be the caregiver?

Sometimes the caregiver is the person who earns the lower salary, to minimize loss of income. Sometimes the caregiver is the person whose office is physically closest to home. Statistically[24], and from my personal observations, in a male-female two-income relationship in the US this caregiver role still typically (but not always) falls on the female in the relationship[25]. This means that if a family emergency does arise in the US, it is typically the female who interrupts her work to rush home. I've interviewed caregivers who have tried approaches such as job sharing and gig-economy-style part-time jobs, with hours that accommodate their schedules. These approaches usually involve compromises in career growth and income, so those caregivers continued to experience a career impact—because their job requires a commute to an office. For some, the compromise of career growth and of caregiver role is not worth it.

No wonder 43% of working mothers leave the workforce when they have children[26]. For the 66% of single mothers who work outside of the home[27], there is rarely a choice.

I expect the gender pattern of caregivers to shift as same-sex marriage becomes more widespread and as more dual-income families become dual-work-from-home families. These social

---

[24] Pew Research Center, "Growing Number of Dads Home with the Kids."

[25] The one and only exception that I personally know of is a two-income male-female couple where the female was earning significantly more than the male when they first met. They agreed that he would become the stay-at-home dad when they started a family, because it made overwhelming financial sense. He tells interesting stories of being the only "male mother" at a children's play date with all the other mothers in the neighborhood! More recently, groups like citydadsgroup.com and athomedad.org have formed to connect and support stay-at-home male caregivers.

[26] Hewlett, S. & Luce, C. (2005). Off-ramps and on-ramps: keeping talented women on the road to success. *Harvard Business Review.*

[27] "Single Mother Statistics, 2018" by Dawn Lee.

changes will fundamentally reframe the caregiver diversity discussion.

In 2007, FlexJobs was founded to help highly qualified people find flexible yet meaningful jobs while remote, part-time, or freelancing. FlexJobs is a 100% distributed organization, currently with a 15% male, 85% female gender diversity. As the CEO of this distributed company, Sara Sutton noted that in 2017, 13% of the distributed companies they surveyed had female CEOs compared to only 5.2% of S&P 500 companies[28].

In mid-2016, Toyota announced plans to have a third of their 75,000-person workforce work from home, aiming to improve retention of existing employees who are new mothers or have aging parents.

Some military personnel relocate with their spouse while on tours of duty. These frequent relocations place the spouse in unfamiliar locations, looking for yet another job, where their skills may not be suitable for local employers. Even worse, frequent relocations complicate finding reliable childcare, and discourage local employers from hiring them because of the high likelihood they will move away again soon after on-boarding. No wonder US military spouses have unemployment rates three times higher than their civilian counterparts[29]. Even spouses with Ph.D.'s have a 16% unemployment rate—and those with jobs are paid 38% less than their civilian counterparts.

For every one of these humans, the ability to work in a distributed company is a game changer.

"It is incumbent on every one of us to carry our fair share of the burden of advancing diversity. It's not right to ask the people who are already disadvantaged in their work to also do all of the extra work of advocacy."

Michael Lopp, Author and Senior Director at Apple

---

[28] From remote.co, "Remote Companies Have More Women Leaders, and These Are Hiring."

[29] Military Officers Association of America "Military Spouse Employment Report" (2014).

Environmental Impact

Takeaways

◆ Requiring humans to commute to an office is a management decision that impacts the environment.

◆ Use existing data to automatically "measure what matters."

◆ Share anonymized commute data openly. This helps you get recognition for your work, and helps others solve the same problems.

Measuring the carbon footprint of your organization is an essential first step towards figuring out how to reduce the environmental impact of your organization.

Typically, when organizations talk about reducing their carbon footprint, they focus on things like using more efficient lighting and HVAC systems in offices, reducing paper usage in printers, reducing manufacturing emissions and reducing product packaging waste. Some organizations measure the carbon impact of flights taken for business work meetings or when shipping products to clients.

These are all good things to do, but they overlook an important source of emissions: the recurring impact of humans commuting to and from an office.

The carbon footprint of your staff's regular commute is something your organization can easily and automatically measure. For those working in location-independent roles, this commuter carbon footprint can be reduced simply by encouraging more humans to do what they already want to do: stop commuting twice a day through rush-hour traffic to and from an office building.

The Carbon Footprint of the Commute

In the US, 35% of all carbon emissions come from the transportation sector, most of which comes from passenger cars used in commuting[1]. Within the State of California, the Air Resource Board tracks and publishes detailed emissions data from all sources across California. While all these sources of emissions are worth reducing, in their latest (2019) report[2], the largest source of carbon emissions across the state—28%—was from personal passenger vehicles.

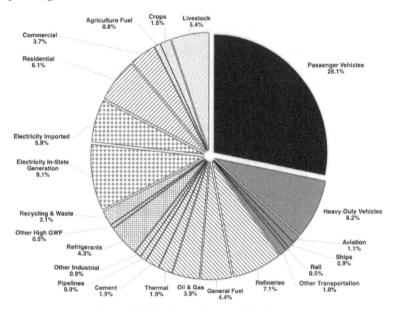

State of California Air Resource Board, 2019

Most of this 28% of emissions came from people driving to and from work. Every workday. Usually in single-occupant cars. Usually in stop-and-go traffic, which is the most inefficient possible way to operate an internal combustion engine.

---

[1] US Energy Information Administration, "State Carbon Dioxide Emissions Data, 2015."

[2] California Greenhouse Gas Emissions, 2000-2017.

Traditional efforts to reduce these emissions focus on encouraging individual humans to change their behavior and reduce "Vehicle Miles Travelled" (VMT). Common strategies include encouraging carpooling by reducing toll fares and creating carpool lanes, discount pricing for commuter tickets on public transit, *free*[3] public transit in specific regions[4], as well as *free* public transit on days with high air pollution[5] or major events[6].

Instead of focusing on each individual human, what if we focus on the organizations requiring those humans to commute?

Leaders in office-based organizations who encourage distributed teams can reduce the frequency of their employee's commute. Conversely, leaders who discourage distributed teams can increase their employee's commute.

One genuinely supported leadership policy can change the commute pattern of many. An example of this is the State of Utah, which now encourages government employees to work from home[7] on days with high air pollution.

The scale of the emission reductions can be rather astonishing— once you figure out how to measure it. Sharing this data across the office-based organization creates measurable incentives for moving towards a distributed teams workforce[8].

---

[3] By "free," I mean "no direct payment by the passenger". Public transit is not "free to operate," and costs money to build, staff, maintain and operate—even when empty. Instead, the costs are paid from local government funds.

[4] freepublictransport.info tracks locations around the globe.

[5] sparetheair.org tracks this for all Silicon Valley / Bay Area government regions.

[6] For example: attendees of New Years Eve events, major national holidays and major sports events.

[7] The "telework on bad air days" policy by Utah's Governor's Office of Management and Budget.

[8] Other helpful metrics to track include financial costs of offices, as well as workforce diversity, hiring, and retention rates. For more on these, see "The Real Cost of an Office" and "Diversity"

"The Chinese expression for 'crisis' consists of two characters side by side. The first is the symbol for 'danger,' the second the symbol for 'opportunity'."

Al Gore

Measure the Commute

Measuring the carbon impact of an organization's commuters sounds difficult, but most employers already have the data they need to start calculating this automatically.

Employers already know where their employees live, because that's where job offer letters, tax forms and other legal paperwork are physically mailed to. This information is not shared publicly, but it is carefully recorded for every human working at the organization and stored in secured HR systems.

Employers know where their employees work. This is tracked in HR desk assignment systems, Wi-Fi access logs, and security door badging systems for office buildings. These systems also record which specific humans worked from which office location—or from home—on which specific days.

Exporting that data from these (often incompatible) systems, and combining them in specific ways creates actionable information.

Take each pair of start (home) and end (office) addresses and upload them into a GIS system to calculate the distance each employee commutes to work. Double this to account for the round trip home after work.

Depending on the location of the physical office building, some employees may be able to walk, bike or use public transit, while some have no choice but to drive. Some organizations I've worked with required all employees to drive to work, because there were no nearby public transit options, bike trails or residential housing. Other organizations caused everyone to commute using public transit, because driving and parking were impractical in those specific downtown large metro regions. Some organizations provide discounted commuter passes if employees pledge to not drive. What matters here is that you can determine the mode of transport used for commuting.

Door badging and security systems tell you when someone enters a building. Wi-Fi logs tell you when someone connects to the internal office network, as opposed to connecting using VPN from home. For this project, you don't care so much what time they arrive or leave. The fact that they were in the office *at any time* during the day means they commuted that day. Organizations that own physical buildings can securely export data from their in-house door badging systems. Organizations that lease parts of buildings sometimes have difficulty getting this door-badge access information from the building owners. Other ways to gather this info is by looking at office Wi-Fi logs to see what days people joined the office Wi-Fi instead of using VPN from home. Another option is to manually note "work from home" days in your HR systems.

You know how many miles each human commutes. You know which specific days they commuted that week. You can make informed guesses on their mode of transport based on the building locations. Verified data on carbon emissions for each different form of transport is readily available. The rest is math. And of course, some work is needed to anonymize the information for privacy reasons.

One organization I worked with, California's Department of General Services ("DGS"), did exactly this. In March 2020, COVID-19 forced the agency to quickly transition from an office-centric culture to a distributed team culture, with over 2,000 people suddenly full-time "teleworking[9]." By September 2020, DGS had created a public dashboard[10] from data in a combination of existing operational systems. This public dashboard automatically—and anonymously—reports real life changes as people join or leave the organization, commute or telework, move house or start work at a different location[11]. Once the dashboard

---

[9] My opinion on the term "telework" is already well described in "Terminology." However, I use the term here because this terminology is common in government agencies, and is used throughout this website.

[10] telework.govops.ca.gov

[11] Another benefit of this approach is that no human is required to manually write an annual report, which is inherently using old information, then circulated to specific audiences. This public dashboard is updated automatically every week with data from existing in-house systems.

was working, DGS started enrolling other State of California agencies. As of January 2021, this public dashboard now tracks telework habits and emissions savings of approximately 8,900 people across 11 State of California agencies—with more agencies being added as I write.

This dashboard revealed some dramatic data. By teleworking at scale, the humans at these agencies have reduced carbon emissions by 408 metric tons in one week. Each week.

That sounds like a lot, but I didn't understand the scale until I did some math. Flying an airplane nonstop from San Francisco to New York City, landing, and then flying nonstop back to San Francisco generates 1.15 metric tons of carbon emissions. These 11 agencies reduced their carbon emissions the same as NOT flying 355 round trip non-stop flights between San Francisco and New York City[12]. In just one week. As these are recurring commutes, these carbon emissions savings happen each week. Or to rephrase: A leadership decision by these agencies to cancel or discourage telework would cause people to commute again—creating the same carbon impact as *adding* 355 round trip non-stop flights between San Francisco and New York City. One flight taking off every 28 minutes over a 24x7 week. Each week.

Deciding to measure what matters and publicly report this data at an organizational level was key. This dashboard shows the value of this strategic leadership decisions on telework policy. The sheer volume of measurable reductions in carbon emissions is impressive. Also impressive is the speed—these reductions started immediately after the leadership policy decision, not years in the future after inventing some new technology.

> *"We are failing, but we have not yet failed. We can still fix this. It is up to us."*
>
> *Greta Thunberg*

---

[12] For those of you reading this in Europe, this is the same as 434 round trip, non-stop flights between Helsinki and Lisbon. Each week. For those in AsiaPac, this is 187 round trip, non-stop flights between Tokyo and Sydney. Each week. For more details, see: carbonfootprint.com.

Organizational Pitfalls to Avoid

Takeaways

◆ If you're not in the same physical location as all of the people you work with, you are *all* remote from *somebody*. This means you *all* have a responsibility to communicate effectively.

◆ When your organization is 100% local—and small—you can get away without crisp organization.

◆ When your organization is mostly local, your remote coworker is the "canary in the coal mine," helping you become aware of preexisting organizational problems.

◆ When your organization is mostly non-local, you *need* crisp organization. This helps remoties, as well as everyone in the local office, work effectively.

Without careful planning and coordination, *any* team can be ineffective—whether the humans are physically distributed or all-in-one-location. This chapter summarizes failures and pitfalls that have happened at other organizations, to help you recognize and avoid repeating these same failures in *your* organization.

All-In-One-Location Model

When your organization is a small startup in a garage, or a rented room in a coworking space, everyone comes to the same physical location every day. Everyone knows each other by name, talks with each other daily, and knows the details of what everyone else is working on. Everyone probably knows a lot about each other's personal lives! It's a small team, and it often feels like a tightly knit family. There are no remote coworkers.

The organization's structure is very flat. There is no org chart. Most communications are unstructured, and formal communication channels are almost nonexistent. Most topics are discussed communally—even the hard scary questions are discussed in public.

Small organization, with everyone in one location

As headcount grows above the Dunbar number[1], things change. Even though everyone still works at the same physical location every day, you no longer know everyone's name. You sometimes wonder what "those people over there" are working on.

The larger physical office also reveals an interesting human trait. As distances between coworkers grow, people become reluctant to walk too far, especially if they need to go up and down three or more floors, wait for slow overcrowded elevators, or walk between buildings in the rain—only to discover that the person they wanted to talk with is not at their desk.

Even though there are no remote coworkers, people start to behave *as if* others are remote. They start to use email, phone, or video instead of meeting in person. MIT Sloan School of Management[2] found that having a team distributed across buildings in nearby cities was *more* effective than having a team distributed on

[1] The Dunbar number is the number of people that one human can interact and maintain social state with, while also keeping track of how each of those people in turn interact and maintain social state with each other. This ability is based on the size and structure of the brain. For humans, that number is around 150. For more on this, see Dunbar, *How Many Friends Does One Person Need?* Harvard University Press, 2010; and the wikipedia.org entry for "Dunbar's number."

[2] Siebdrat, F., Hoegl, M., and Ernst, H. (2009). How to manage virtual teams. *MIT Sloan Management Review*.

different floors of the same building. People working across different cities were acutely aware of the need to organize work communications for their distributed team, whereas people on different floors of the same building felt they were all together—when in reality, they behaved as if they were not[3]. In these less-organized environments, humans on other floors quickly became "out of sight, out of mind" and were treated as if they were in a different location!

The MIT study also found that distributed teams with carefully organized work procedures outperformed all-in-one-location teams. A group's organizational procedures were more important for group effectiveness than the physical distance between humans.

In these scenarios, loosely organized informal communication channels don't scale. Miscommunications start to appear in the cracks. Repeated miscommunications erode people's trust in each other, causing a gradual shift in mindset. You can tell this is happening when "we" statements morph into "us versus them" statements[4] and people become less comfortable about asking hard scary questions in public. People quietly start optimizing for themselves and their own personal career, which may or may not be optimal for the organization.

One early warning signal for these miscommunications is when a human in one part of the organization is working hard to enhance an existing feature, while another human else in another part of the organization is working equally hard to remove that same "unwanted" feature. This tells you that the organization's left hand doesn't know what the right hand is doing.

When this early warning signal is first detected, many companies start building formal communication channels. They create org charts and hire project managers, human managers, and managers of managers. These humans spend the majority of their day meeting humans across multiple teams, orchestrating each team's work in the hope that it will all eventually fit together.

---

[3] In large HQ campus locations, I've found people would avoid walking to adjacent buildings for meetings when it was raining.

[4] For more on this, read *The Tipping Point* by Malcolm Gladwell, specifically the chapter called "The power of context (part two)."

Larger organization, with everyone in one location

Each of these humans acts as a formal communication channel, gathering and spreading information so that each part of the organization knows what is going on elsewhere within the organization. Rebroadcasting everything, unfiltered, is not helpful. Instead, these humans filter everything they see, hear, and read— only rebroadcasting what they feel is important for others to know. This filtering and communicating becomes a job in its own right.

This job is hard to do well, because everyone has a different idea of what is important and what should be excluded. It gets even more difficult as organizations grow, adding layers of management that require additional coordination. Each layer is made up of different humans, with different perspectives on what is important to include and exclude when summarizing the various updates.

The few people I've seen excel at this role have an instinctive ability to quickly figure out what is important from the perspective of the organization, as well as what is important from the perspective of each of their different audiences. Then they communicate that information in ways that each of the different audiences can understand.

In addition to these formal communication channels, you start to see people informally talking in corridors, kitchens and coffee shop areas, trying to fill in the many unspoken gaps that exist in formal communication channels. An informal grapevine, or rumor mill, starts.

Between these formal and informal communication channels, people usually have a good enough idea of what is going on, what needs to be done, and where their work fits into the overall big picture, so they can focus on getting their work done.

Organize-Work-By-Location Model

When your organization grows too big to fit every human into one location, you set up offices in additional locations. To help keep track of the work being done in each location, and to minimize communication delays between the different locations, you arrange work by location.

Work organized by location

For example, a typical software organization could have the CEO, Research and Development, and Sales located at their headquarters in Silicon Valley; localization work based in Dublin, Ireland; and technical support work based in Bangalore, India. In this example, if you live near the Bangalore office and want to apply for a localization job, you would need to relocate to the office where the other localizers work—Dublin!—not the nearby Bangalore office. Likewise, a great sales person in Dublin would be expected to relocate to Silicon Valley to work with the HQ-based sales team. Most major multinational corporations are structured this way. This work-by-location model also applies to mergers and acquisitions, where the newly acquired company initially stays in its existing office to minimize disruption, but over time the organization consolidates some functional teams and relocates humans, so that the newly enlarged company once again has work organized by location. The model also applies to outsourcing, where specific projects are sent to other companies in remote locations.

Informal communication channels between locations are typically slim to nonexistent because of distance and lack of cross-pollination. While you might recognize some of the faces at your location, you don't know everyone's name. You are aware that other locations exist but you don't know many, if any, humans at the other locations. Within a specific location, humans can still get their work done, despite the overhead of internal coordination, by focusing on what's going on in their location and ignoring other locations as much as possible.

In this scenario, there are still communicator-type humans walking around within each location. In addition, you also need more senior communicator-type humans—VPs, directors, divisional managers, and senior project managers—all of whom spend a large amount of time flying back and forth between various locations. As they visit each location they share summaries of what their home location is working on, and they listen to summaries from managers in the other locations. These humans act as slow-moving packets of information in the organization's formal communication channels, gathering, filtering, summarizing, and spreading the news, so that all of the different parts of the organization know what is going on across the organization. This communication between locations is slower (and more expensive!) because it usually involves long drives or flights, travel delays, and other costs.

High-level and mid-level managers working across locations typically generate quarterly or monthly status reports, while lower-level managers working within their own location typically generate daily or weekly status reports. Once a cadence is established, high-level and mid-level managers often start asking for status updates by email or conference call between each on-site visit, hoping to obtain timely information while reducing the costs and human wear and tear due to frequent travel between locations.

For many companies this compromise is good enough, and the organization learns to arrange itself around these slower, more formalized communication channels.

Temporary Travelers and Other Non-Remote Coworkers

If you usually work in an office but intermittently work from home or on the road, it is easy to believe you have "remote work" figured out. However, think explicitly about the types of work you do at each location. If you do solo, focused work at home and collaborative work in the office, you are not location-independent and you are not part of an effective distributed team. Instead, you are using your home as an interrupt-free zone for solo work—as if you were in the office, hiding in an isolated physical meeting room with a Do Not Disturb sign on the door.

Because you are in the physical office most of the time, you are still part of the informal communication channels. You rely on your time in the office for trusted face-to-face updates about "what is really going on" in the organization. A similar problem is described in "The Canary in the Coal Mine."

People who travel infrequently for work (for customer visits, conferences, investor briefings, and so on) can also fall into this category.

You might think that because everyone is in an office, no one is remote. However, it is important to consider that if you work in *an* office with someone else who is in a *different* office, you are *both* remote from each other.

If you're not in the same location as *all* of the other people you work with, you are *all* remote from *somebody*. You *all* share a responsibility to communicate effectively.

Hybrid Model: Remote-by-Role

A variation of the all-in-one-location model is a hybrid model where most humans work in a physical office, except for some humans with very specific job roles.

Examples include claims adjusters at an insurance company, ticket agents at an airline, medical claims processors at a medical insurance company, and traveling sales reps.

Hybrid model: All-in-one-location, with specific role as remote

Hybrid organizations succeed because these specific roles—and the organizational processes around these roles—are very clearly defined to make sure people can work effectively even when remote. Any activities outside of this carefully defined role, such as strategy decisions and new project planning, happen at the office. The remote-by-role humans gather for annual kickoff events, product briefings, and major organizational updates.

Companies that have many remote-by-role humans tend to rely on a combination of carefully organized corporate structure, very carefully defined job scope (to reduce communication overhead), and dedicated in-office humans (area managers, practice area managers, and so on) who act as the primary communication channel between remote-by-role humans and humans at the office.

In these types of organizations, if you change from a remote role to an office role, you typically need to change from working remotely to working at the office.

The Canary in the Coal Mine

When everyone in your organization works in one location except for one remote employee, then you have a "canary in the coal mine." If the remote person hits a recurring communication issue or organizational problem, it is an important alert—an indication of a problem that *everyone* in the organization is quietly struggling with.

A common scenario is when an all-in-one-location organization has a well-respected, long-established employee who wants to relocate away from the office for personal reasons. Every person I interviewed about this did not want their real name used, so for this scenario we'll call the employee Fred. Regardless of the reasons why Fred decided to relocate—a spouse or partner changing jobs, the need to care for aging parents or other family members, the need to buy a house in a more affordable location, or any other major life event—the professional factors are worth noting explicitly: Fred has been an employee with the company for a long time, he likes working at the company, he wants to continue working at the same company after relocating, and he is explicitly *not* looking for a new job at a different company in the new location. Everyone at the company agrees that Fred is productive, trusted, and well respected, so everyone wants to find a way to keep Fred as a valuable employee.

Everyone agrees to give this remote work idea a try. After all, it is the twenty-first century—how hard can it be?

At first, all goes well. Fred continues to work on projects that were already in progress before he relocated. The company retains their long-valued employee, and productive work still happens. It is not yet obvious that communications are broken, and that the situation is only working because of strong momentum from Fred's preexisting personal connections and the fact that he started his current projects before he moved away.

Canary in the coal mine: everyone in one location except for one person

In reality, the organization's formal communication channels have substantial gaps. Even people in the office rely heavily on informal communication channels.

After Fred relocates, his informal communication channels start fading. This loss is gradual, so easy to not notice until it is too late. As his informal communication channels fade, Fred starts relying *only* on formal communication channels. Gradually, Fred notices that he only hears about cool new projects *after* they've been assigned to someone else. After this happens a few times, Fred starts to feel like he's being intentionally overlooked for the types of projects he enjoys—and which he used to routinely be given. Fred starts to feel devalued and sidelined.

Meanwhile, humans in the office start to wonder why Fred is not as proactive as he used to be. He no longer volunteers to take on cool projects (maybe because he hasn't heard about them yet?!) People start to quietly think, "When he was here at the office, he got a lot more done. Now we can't tell. Is he really working?" Over time, his coworkers forget how great Fred used to be, and Fred is perceived as "just average." He no longer gets great reviews or promotions. This makes him vulnerable in future layoffs and reorganizations—and accelerates his feelings of being sidelined.

Over time, this deteriorates enough that Fred feels sidelined to a dead-end job with no career growth prospects. He quits in frustration. Or he begrudgingly decides to put up with having his career sidelined, telling himself that he put his career on hold because career growth is now less important than taking care of his family, his spouse's postgraduate studies, the new home, or the great school district for the kids. Or this formerly highly valued employee is fired, because he is no longer viewed as proactive and productive at his job.

Survivor bias[5] makes it easy and convenient to (incorrectly!) blame these failures entirely on the recently departed remote employee; the surviving humans in the office do not see their own behavior as a contributing factor. It's tempting to find something or someone else to blame. For example, on-site team members might claim, "Our work is so specialized and so fast-paced, we *need* to be physically in one room," or "We move too fast to have remoties!"

It is also convenient (and incorrect!) to think that if working remotely failed for a well-trusted, long-tenured employee, there is no way a new hire would succeed as a remote employee. This can cause humans to dismiss the viability of distributed teams— without questioning what happened, without a postmortem analysis of what went wrong with the canary in the coal mine, and without identifying changes everyone could make to avoid repeating these mistakes with other humans in the future.

---

[5] Smith, Gary (2015). *Standard Deviations: Flawed Assumptions, Tortured Data, and Other Ways to Lie With Statistics.*

This canary in the coal mine scenario is all too common[6], and can give the concept of remote work a bad name. In reality, internal communication for everyone in the organization was already broken. Everyone played a role in this failed miscommunication. The canary in the coal mine "died," revealing preexisting internal communication problems. Unless steps are taken to improve internal communications, the remaining humans in the office will continue to struggle with these ongoing poor communications.

The No-Office Model

When your organization is a small startup that *could* fit in a garage, but all of the co-founders are in different locations, you have a no-office model. Instead of three people in one garage, there are three people working in *three* garages.

Typically, these humans know each other well, and strongly trust each other. They use money saved from office costs to help pay salaries and operate their distributed organization, including periodic group gatherings. Everyone knows each other by name; they talk with each other daily and know the details of what everyone else is working on. It's a small team, and usually feels like a tightly knit family. Everyone probably knows a lot about each other's personal lives! And, everyone is a remotie.

[6] Grenny, J., & Maxfield, D. (2017). "A Study of 1,100 Employees Found That Remote Workers Feel Shunned and Left Out." *Harvard Business Review*.

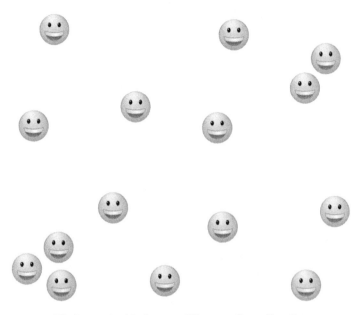

Work organized by human skills, regardless of location

Like the similarly sized all-in-one-location organization in a garage, this organization is very flat and there is no org chart. While communication channels might feel casual, they are typically more crisply organized than similarly sized all-in-one-location companies. These crisply organized communications scale well as the organization grows—reducing the need for additional layers of human bureaucracy and reducing the risk of slowing down innovations.

How

Physical Setup

Takeaways

◆ Avoid making calls from locations where you can be interrupted or interrupt others. This includes open-plan offices, cafes, or a shared room in your home.

◆ Make it easy for others to see if you are ok to interrupt, versus "do not disturb."

The physical structure and layout of offices change how humans go about their work. It's hard to create an office that suits the different, sometimes incompatible, needs of every different human. No wonder so many people complain they can't get work done in the office.

Many offices—especially new "cool and trendy" high-density open-plan offices—are designed in ways that cause unintended negative side effects for distributed teams. This chapter helps you identify these problems, and offers some workarounds.

Home Offices and Coworking Spaces

If you plan to work from home for a prolonged period of time, you need a dedicated workspace.

It might sound cool to work on your laptop while sitting on your living room sofa, wearing pajamas, able to work, eat, and sleep whenever you want. This might be ok in the short term, but will become a significant problem over time for several reasons:

◆ *Physically*, typing on the sofa is a terrible ergonomic posture for your back, neck, and arms. If you intend to work like this for your career—not for just a weekend—poor posture will lead to health issues such as carpal tunnel syndrome and repetitive stress injuries, which can permanently limit your career[1].

♦ *Mentally*, you will gradually look and feel like an amateur slob instead of a career professional. Over time, this will impact your self-confidence and sense of competence, making you less effective at your work. It will be gradual, so you might not notice the transition—but your coworkers will. For more on this, see "Feed Your Soul."

♦ *Socially*, when you're sitting on the sofa, typing on your laptop, it is impossible for others in your house to know if you are interruptible or deeply focused on a complex work problem. When you have no externally visible indicators, even well-intentioned people will need to interrupt you to find out if it is ok to interrupt you! This means your focused work will be interrupted by trivial things like taking out garbage, doing laundry, walking the dog, scheduling social events, and so on. Over time, this impacts your professional productivity.

Don't be an amateur. Be a professional. Think long term. After all, this is your career, which you'd like to be doing for years to come.

Set up a dedicated professional home office space with an ergonomically correct desk, good cameras and microphones, and a door you can close. For more details, see "Phones, Cameras, and Microphones."

To help you focus, make sure that the things you see in your home office space are all work-related, just like a "real" office. This eliminates distractions that can tempt you to procrastinate. You can always do non-work stuff after you "commute home from your home office," but while you are "at work" you need to focus on your work.

---

[1] My doctor noted the sudden increase in RSI related injuries he is treating since COVID-19 hit San Francisco—caused by former office workers now working at home, in poor ergonomic postures, for longer hours while stressed. At time of writing, I was not able to find medical research on this, but this correlates with similar reports and medical research from dentists. For more on this, see "Feed Your Soul."

If a separate dedicated room is not possible in your home, set up a workspace behind a foldable shōji screen in a corner of the quietest room available. I've sometimes run video calls from the passenger seat of my car—sitting quietly parked in my garage with the engine off yet still on my home Wi-Fi.

Working from a spare room in a neighbor's house has become more popular since the start of COVID-19. Older people living alone and isolated because of COVID-19 lockdowns get some socially distant human interaction with a trusted neighbor. Younger neighbors looking for a quiet space to work get a dedicated private room without needing to commute on public transit or exposure to lots of others.

If even that is not possible, rent a desk at a nearby coworking space[2]. Depending on the location and floor plan of the physical coworking space, they follow different COVID-19 closure patterns, so check in advance. Also, be aware, though, that some spaces focus on specific interests or demographics[3]—important to keep in mind when choosing a location where you will feel accepted by your coworking peers. Other popular alternatives are to work from the local library, or your local coffee shop—where you can pay a "per-day membership fee" so that staff will welcome you to work there during the cafe's quiet hours. In addition, some restaurants now let people "rent" seats when they are not serving food and would otherwise be closed[4].

When your job involves communicating and working well with others, put explicit forethought into looking and sounding professional on every single one of your work calls, and ensure that you have uninterrupted blocks of time to do focused work.

[2] The costs of a dedicated home office space or a coworking space membership may be a tax deduction. This depends on the tax laws where you live and the exact nature of your work, so ask a professional accountant about this.

[3] For example, in San Francisco, The Grotto is for writers, ImpactHub is for social innovators, The Assembly is for women, while WeWork has a more "hip vibe."

[4] For examples of "restaurants as coworking space," see: Spacious.com and KettleSpace.com.

Meeting Rooms and Phone Booths

Most offices I've seen in recent years have several large meeting rooms arranged around a large number of open-plan desks. This layout may look impressive, but is not practical. If several people leave their open-plan desks, each to occupy a 10-person meeting room for a video call, the office will quickly run out of available meeting rooms. Anyone else joining a video call will be forced to do so from their open-plan desk.

One solution is to build offices where everyone has their own private office with a door, but this is expensive. Another solution is to build open-plan offices with fewer large meeting rooms, and instead build many small phone-booth-sized rooms. These smaller rooms are designed for solo people attending video calls, or for two people holding a short private one-on-one meeting. Each phone booth room has one or two chairs, a small table or ledge for a laptop, and a power socket.

Small "phone booth" rooms allow more people to have private calls and discussions at the same time, in the same amount of physical office space.

Soundproofing is a real issue. I've worked in offices where meeting rooms were insulated so that the sound of humans talking around a table did not disrupt adjacent meeting rooms. However, when wall-mounted displays and speakers were installed into those same meeting rooms, those speakers resonated through the wall and could be heard perfectly clearly in adjacent meeting rooms. This disrupted adjacent meeting rooms and compromised confidentiality in sensitive personnel meetings[5]. Soundproofing for "phone

---

[5] One company I worked in built smaller "phone booth" sized meeting rooms as part of their office construction. Unwittingly, one "phone booth" had a wall containing all of the internal plumbing for the entire multi-story building. Soon after the office opened, we discovered that when anyone in the building flushed a toilet, the whooshing-water sound in the wall resonated loudly in the small room, and could be clearly heard by everyone on the video call. These distractions inevitably happened at the most inappropriate times in a serious meeting. Over time, I found it best to simply avoid those problematic rooms.

*booth" rooms needs to be even better, to avoid hearing
everything in adjacent phone booths (and having others
overhear you).*

Because of high demand for these "phone booth" rooms,
sometimes even these rooms would all be booked at the same time,
so I had nowhere to hold my scheduled call. After this happened a
few times, I started scheduling my calls so that I could join them
from home (as much as possible), where I was *guaranteed* a quiet
room for professional video calls. I would then commute to and
from the office between scheduled calls—which also helped me
avoid rush hour.

When everyone joins a call from separate locations, it naturally
encourages them all to follow the etiquette of speaking one at a
time, using nonverbal cues and the group chat backchannel. For
more on this, see "Video Etiquette."

Even when joining video calls from a meeting room or phone
booth, pay careful attention to where you sit. Position your laptop
so that your screen is not visible to passersby outside the room,
and adjust your visibility on camera so that you are happy with
your image and what is visible behind you. For more details on
this, see "How Do Others See You?"

Open-Plan Offices

Open-plan offices[6] allow organizations to have more humans-per-
square-foot, which helps reduce recurring office costs. By contrast,
a workplace with each human in their own dedicated room with a
door requires significantly more space and money. Even Dilbert-
style cube farms are now considered too inefficient as furniture

---

[6] The terms open plan, cube farm, bullpen, office landscape, collaborative spaces,
hoteling, and hot desking all describe slightly different types of office
arrangements. To keep things simple in writing, I define "open plan" to be any floor
plan that does not give each employee their own separate room with floor-to-ceiling
walls and a door they can close when needed for focused work and interrupt-free
calls.

designers and office planners continue to find ways to fit more humans into less physical space[7].

Claims that open-plan offices encourage interaction between coworkers frequently ignore complaints about how these informal interrupts make it hard to do any focused, heads-down work[8]. Increased interactions between coworkers sound good, until the continuous interrupts prevent you from focusing on your own work.

Personally, I found that open-plan offices disrupted focused work, and did not take the needs of distributed teams into account—two significant problems for my work[9].

One open-plan office I worked in was so disruptively noisy that I routinely abandoned my ergonomic open-plan desk in favor of standing at the counter in the large, empty, office kitchen area. This was library-quiet all day except during lunch hour, when I would return to work at my desk in the temporarily quiet office.

If you work in an open-plan office, quietly walk around at different times of the day and note how many people sit all day in a meeting room by themselves with the door closed. Some may pretend to be on a call. Some may act as if they just finished a meeting. Others may just blatantly stay until asked to leave because of someone else's scheduled meeting.

[7] "Workplace trends in office space: implications for future office demand," by Norm G. Miller, Burnham-Moores Center for Real Estate, University of San Diego. CoStar Group and CBRE both provide reports on this, by location. A good summary of different open-plan office layouts from 1880s to today can be found on 99percentinvisible.org, "Office Space Time Loop: From Open Plans to Cubicle Farms and Back Again."

[8] Some new offices are being designed not as lively open-plan spaces, but instead as quiet work areas with nearby communal lunch and coffee areas, in an attempt to balance the need for focused work with the need for casual cross-team interactions.

[9] I am not the only one. There is extensive research on this. These articles are a good starting point: Haworth report, "Designing for Focus Work"; and Kim, Jungsoo & Candido, Christhina & Thomas, Leena & de Dear, Richard. (2016). Desk ownership in the workplace: The effect of non-territorial working on employee workplace satisfaction, perceived productivity and health.

These people are using meeting rooms as a substitute for a private office, because they cannot do focused work at their open-plan desk.

If you work in an open-plan office, avoid joining audio and video calls from your desk. Instead, book a meeting room at the same time as you schedule a call. Don't wait until the call is about to start before looking for a free room—you risk being late to the call or end up making the call from your desk, disrupting nearby coworkers. If no meeting rooms are available, and if you can work remotely, schedule meetings so you can attend them from home. This helps reduce the number of calls in the open-plan office. For added goodness, scheduling calls before or after your commute helps you avoid commuting during rush hours.

As a last resort, if you must take a video call in an open-plan office, use an over-the-ear-headset with noise-cancelling microphone. These reduce (but do not eliminate) the annoyance to nearby coworkers. They will no longer be disturbed when others on your call speak; they will only be disturbed when *you* speak. An over-the-ear-headset also reduces background noise for you, which reduces your human tendency to raise your own voice. For more information, see "Meeting Rooms and Phone Booths."

Sensitive business negotiations and personnel matters should never be discussed where others can overhear the conversation.

The cumulative impact of multiple conversations and calls in an open-plan office is worth noting. To compensate for background noise, each human raises their own voice to be heard over the sound of the other nearby conversations and phone calls—making the overall noise levels even worse. Noisy workplaces like this are distracting to the caller, to everyone else on those calls, and to the people sitting at nearby desks who are not on any call or conversation—but might as well be part of all of them.

Finally, if you join a video call in an open-plan office, be aware of what is visible on camera. For more on this, see "How Do Others See You?"

"Do Not Disturb" Etiquette

Communicating "do not disturb" in an open-plan office or at home can be tricky.

In an office, people will walk past Do Not Disturb signs to ask, "Hey, can I interrupt you with a question?"[10] Instead of posting Do Not Disturb signs, wear large headphones.

Large, highly visible headphones communicate to others that you do not want to be interrupted. In addition, large, professional-grade studio headphones are highly visible from a distance and they're designed to be comfortable for long periods of time. These are important advantages over small in-ear bud headphones that can be hard to see from a distance and are uncomfortable over time. Whether you play music or not is irrelevant; it depends on your personal preference. I often wear large headphones without playing any music.

When you're wearing large headphones, anyone considering interrupting you will know in advance they will be interrupting focused work. This will cause them to consider whether their topic is more important than anything you could *possibly* be working on. This shift in mindset is important. Many of the reasons I've been interrupted were not urgent. I could have responded in a brief email during my next break a short time later, after I took off the headphones[11]. This habit of wearing-large-headphones significantly reduced the number of interrupts, and allowed me to do focused work in an open-plan office.

This led to an important culture shift. People started asked themselves, "How urgent is my interrupt?" *before* they interrupted. The wear-large-headphones culture spread across the office organically—not by an imposed-from-on-high mandate—because it was easy to do and had immediate practical benefits.

---

[10] Instead of asking, "Excuse me, can I interrupt?" it would be more accurate to ask, "I know I just interrupted you. My question is more important (to me) than anything you might have been working on."

[11] For more details on the priority of different communication channels, see "Meetings."

When working at home, arrange a nonverbal signal with others to indicate "do not disturb." For example, if you are sitting on the sofa, you are ok to interrupt. If you are sitting in your home office with the door closed, behind a shōji screen or working anywhere outside the home, you signal "do not disturb," just as if you had commuted to a traditional office.

When I join video calls from home, I close my home office door and hang an old hotel Do Not Disturb sign on the door handle. As soon as the call ends, I open the door again. (Sometimes I find sticky notes waiting for me outside the door!) If you don't have a separate room at home for video calls, buy a foldable shōji screen for privacy, and unfold it as a signal to others before you start your calls.

If you have small children, warn the caregiver and then lock the door before starting calls. Adult humans understand nonverbal cues, but small children and pets do not. While there are many personal benefits to working from home, it is a false trap to think that you can work productively from home *and* be a full-time babysitter or pet sitter. You might be lucky every now and then, getting focused work done while baby and dog sleep soundly. However, you might also be unlucky: the dog starts barking, causing the sleeping baby to jolt awake and start crying—midway through your video call presenting the findings of your big project to the CEO. Avoid setting yourself up to fail[12].

Think about how you would handle situations like this if you had to commute to a physical office.

Hire a babysitter to take care of small children during work hours. Or if living with other working adults, negotiate trading who can babysit at what times during the workday. Then lock the office door in case children's natural curiosity causes them to wander in, disrupting your call[13]. Schedule a dog walker to walk your dog during meetings. If you are low on cash, use the money you save

---

[12] Despite careful preparations, things can still go wrong. One coworker, Dan, asked his visiting mother-in-law to babysit while he joined a work video call from home. All went well, until partway through the call when his mother-in-law discovered a snake in the house.

[13] Examples of not taking these precautions have been broadcast on live television interviews with Robert Kelly on bbc.com and Daniel Smith-Rowsey on Al-Jazeera.

by not commuting to pay for this essential help, or take turns babysitting or pet sitting with a neighbor or family member. Figure out this staffing schedule in advance and be consistent about it, so you can consistently focus on your work and join meetings without risk of disruption.

Another essential part of Do Not Disturb etiquette is understanding when, where, and why you do your best focused work. For more on this, see "Morning Person or Night Owl?"

Security Setup

Corporate security is a concern for all organizations. To reduce security risks, some organizations require all office-based humans to use desktop computers with restrictions on user privileges, internet access, and cloud-hosted services. Some organizations prohibit bringing any work out of the office building. Each organization must decide whether these security measures warrant the loss of productivity and if so, how to handle office closures.

As soon as office-based humans bring laptops or work smartphones on business trips or bring them home at night, corporate security is a concern for all. This is a complex field, but here are some essential first steps:

- Require passwords for laptops and phones, on power-up and on login, to deter non-professional hackers who steal laptops or smartphones.

- Use password manager software to define, store, and manage highly secure, unique passwords for each different internet- or cloud-based service you use. Change your passwords frequently. Whenever possible, use two-factor authentication.

- Encrypt all computer hard disks, so that if a laptop is stolen the thieves should not (easily) be able to access your files. This applies to burglaries anywhere: at home, at the office, or from a rental car. Most thieves are looking for a quick resale of stolen consumer electronics, so will simply reformat the device before selling it. However, some thefts are carefully planned acts of industrial espionage. In these situations, encrypting hard disks is helpful, but with enough time, skill, and motivation, most encryption can be decrypted. Storing data in cloud-based services instead of on your local laptop/ smartphone reduces the risk exposure of a stolen device but introduces a different potential risk: weak, insecure passwords on these cloud-based services. Again, password manager software and two-factor authentication can help.

♦ Enable remote lockout and reset capabilities on your smartphone. Smartphones are easy to steal or lose, and their access to email and confidential documents is a data risk.

♦ To avoid risk of data being intercepted while at home, avoid having any IOT devices[14] in your home office. These IOT devices are basically small computers, with an always-on microphone, a Wi-Fi connection and manufacturers who are typically slow to apply security patches.

♦ To avoid risk of data being intercepted while outside your home, avoid unsecured Wi-Fi in public spaces like hotels, cafes and airports. Use your smartphone as a Wi-Fi hotspot to reduce, but not eliminate, this risk. Use VPN software to secure your computer's Wi-Fi connection.

♦ Update software as soon as new security fixes are available. Periodically review all installed software. Uninstall any software you no longer use or which no longer receives security fixes.

These simple security measures are things you can—and should— do today. These are important first steps for everyone, regardless of whether you work at the office, at home, in a shared coworking space, or on the road.

This is obviously not a comprehensive list[15]. Depending on the nature of your work, and the threat models your organization is concerned with, you may need more advanced professional security help[16].

---

[14] Some examples include: Amazon Alexa/EchoDot, Google Nest, Apple Siri/ Homepod, Facebook Portal, Wi-Fi enabled baby monitors and voice-activated "Smart TVs".

[15] I recommend reading "Practical Security for the Prudent American" by Mikey Dickerson and "Surveillance Self-Defense" by Electronic Frontier Foundation.

[16] I trust and recommend the humans at EFF.org and NewDataProject.us. There are others.

Phones, Cameras, and Microphones

Takeaways

+ Avoid most setup problems by using your own cell phone or laptop to join video calls. If a room has shared video/audio hardware installed, simply ignore it.

+ Ask all meeting participants to use their own camera—this makes everyone equally visible, head-and-shoulders, and improves nonverbal communications.

+ Ask all meeting participants to use their individual headphones with built-in microphone. This bypasses most audio setup problems.

How long does it take you to start a video call with a coworker?

Use a stopwatch to measure time from the moment you decide to call someone to when you each have a working video connection, confirmed you can see and hear each other, and can start talking about the topic at hand. If this is more then a few seconds, something is wrong. If delays are caused by a lack of training, learn how to use your tools. If delays are caused by unreliable or overly complex tools, upgrade your tools.

There are many choices of hardware and software available[1]. Learning which tools are reliable and easy to use—and which are best to simply ignore—is an important part of consistently communicating well with others.

When you simplify your tools, you can focus on the *purpose* of your meetings instead of struggling with the tools to *set up* the meeting.

---

[1] Tools change continuously, so I've listed my current personal favorite hardware and software tools here: oduinn.com/book/tools-for-remoties.

Phones

Avoid shared-use, location-specific hardware such as desk phones and conference room speaker phones. This strategy helps avoid predictable hardware setup problems that disrupt meetings.

If you work in an office with speaker phones on meeting room tables, simply ignore them and use your laptop for audio-video conference calls.

If you work in an office with desk phones, forward all incoming calls to your cell phone. Verify that call forwarding is working correctly[2], and then unplug your desk phone and remove it from your desk[3]. This small act helps you respond to calls more quickly, and it streamlines your work—you have fewer places to check for messages. Forwarding your calls makes your cell phone number *more* private, not less[4]. And, if you're moving toward distributed teams, it helps you experience work like a remote person; you become less attached to your physical office.

---

[2] Do not use your cell phone to make this test call. One company I worked at had a PBX switchboard that detected that my cell phone was calling my desk phone forwarding to the same cell phone I was calling from. It treated this as an error. This took me hours to debug, so now I do two test calls: one from another in-office desk phone, and one from someone else's cell phone.

[3] Put the phone in a drawer for safekeeping until you leave the company. Even better, "recycle" the phone by handing it back to your IT team. They're very aware of the purchase cost and recurring maintenance costs of physical handsets. They might even start encouraging others to follow your lead!

[4] When I worked in companies with a desk phone, my voice message typically ended with "...and in case of emergency, please call my cell phone, ###-###-####." Some employers provided a work-issued cell phone to use for all work calls —separate from my personal cell phone. However, some employers encouraged me to put my private cell phone number on my business cards.

After setting up call forwarding, I put *only* my official work number on my business cards. Anyone who called my work "desk phone" was immediately forwarded to my cell phone, keeping my cell phone number private.

When making work phone calls from my personal cell phone, I could either dial into the company switchboard and then dial the client, so the client saw the callerID of my desk phone. Or I could block callerID on my cell phone before calling.

Some organizations I've worked in required me to use a desk phone and a work-issued cell phone for all work calls—separate from my personal cell phone. For these, I redirected my desk phone and only told people my work cell phone number.

By forwarding calls to my cell phone, I made myself more available to callers. This had two interesting benefits that freed up my time: I no longer needed to walk from a meeting room back to my office between meetings to check for voice messages, and I received significantly *fewer* phone calls. People started to self-limit how often they called, because they learned that they would almost always reach me immediately. They didn't want to abuse my availability. They wanted me to answer their calls when they *really* needed me.

Whenever possible, switch from audio-only to audio-video meetings. You will reduce common time-wasting distractions like: "Can you hear me?" or "Did we just lose Fred?" "Is anyone still there?" You will also reduce time spent on the multiple-people-speaking-at-same-time problem, which is usually followed by time spent on "Oh, sorry, after you!" negotiations, typically won by the person with the loudest voice or highest rank.

From a few years of real-world nonscientific measurements, I found hour-long meetings typically became 10 to 15 minutes shorter, simply by switching from audio-only to audio-video. These time savings happened partly because we evolved a nonverbal etiquette to help reduce those common problems. For more details, see "Video Etiquette."

Camera Hardware

Use your laptop camera and headphones when joining audio-video calls.

If you work in an office with wall-mounted screens and wall-mounted cameras in each shared meeting room, simply move the remote control(s) and speakerphone to the side and ignore them. Expensive wall-mounted audio-video systems are well-intentioned efforts to improve interactions with remote people. However, these systems are tricky to install, tricky to use, limit nonverbal communications, and add a location-dependent single point of failure to your meeting that is outside of your control.

Experienced installers will mount the camera, display, and speakers close together on the same wall; this encourages people to instinctively speak and listen facing the camera while looking at the display of other meeting participants[5].

However, this layout quickly hits physical constraints. Mounting the camera at head height of a seated person helps the remote person feel included, as if they are also at the table, but forces the display higher. This raised display can feel domineering to other people in the room[6]. Mounting the display closer to sitting head height helps the displayed remote person be better received by the people sitting at the table, but requires moving the camera. Mounting the camera too low can cause remote people to be visually blocked by the backs of empty chairs in the room, too high can cause remote people to feel they are floating disembodied above the rest of the meeting, and too much to the side can cause remote people to that everyone at the table is looking elsewhere.

Another reason to avoid using a shared video system installed in a specific physical location, is that you do not know what you'll find until you attempt to start the call. Sometimes these systems work fine first time; other times they mysteriously break, derailing your meeting with problems like:

♦ The system is unusable because the physical remote has dead batteries, is damaged, or is missing.

---

[5] I've been in meetings with weird nonverbal dynamics caused when people turned to face the display on one wall, forgetting that they were turning their backs to the cameras mounted on a different wall.

Ceiling-mounted speakers can work if the volume is just right, but they usually turn into a booming voice-from-above, which squashes natural human discussions.

In addition, it's difficult to shout upward to ceiling-mounted microphones, or lean into table-mounted microphones, while trying to look at a camera in another part of the room.

Meeting rooms with large glass windows complicate the installation process.

[6] Even when the remote person is not speaking in a domineering way, the position of the display can cause others to interpret their speech as such. For good visual example of this, see the original Apple Macintosh ad, which used many themes from George Orwell's *1984*.

- The system is updating its software and is unusable.

- The system has been upgraded since you last used it, and the old instructions no longer work. No one has instructions for the new functionality.

- The one person who knows how to start a call on the system is out sick, and the list of instructions on the table is missing.

- The previous meeting is running long, and you can't kick them out because the attendees include the CEO or important clients.

Any of these problems will disrupt your meeting and cause a flurry of last-minute "meeting has moved" messages, followed by people arriving late. Even worse, some of your attendees might not see the update. They go to the original meeting location and disrupt another meeting!

Overall, I've found that these location-specific shared systems make things worse, not better. After several failures, I now consider any problems caused by location-specific systems to be self-imposed problems from choosing to use shared-use, location-specific, hardware in the first place. Even when I am in an office meeting room with expensive equipment installed on the walls, I find it safer and more reliable to have everyone join the audio-video conference call using their familiar laptop and headphones.

Sidestep all of these problems by using your laptop and headphones for video calls. The hardware and software are under your control. You choose when the software is upgraded, so there are no last-minute surprises as you attempt to start the meeting[7]. A missing or broken handheld remote is not an issue. You use the same instructions to join a video call from home, from the office, or

---

[7] Every time you change laptop hardware; upgrade software; or change your physical desk, room, or lighting; do a quick test call to verify that your new setup still works. Test immediately, while you remember what you did and still have time to fix it before your next meeting. Waiting until the start of your next video meeting to discover any problems is only setting yourself up to fail.

Doing a test call with a friendly coworker is quick, and it avoids embarrassing disruptions of important meetings. Doing test calls, and encouraging coworkers to do the same, raises awareness across the team that professional communication is an expected part of working well with others.

from a hotel. If the previous meeting runs long in a physical meeting room, you simply walk into any other available meeting room (ignoring any wall-mounted systems that might be there), and use your laptop with headphones to join the call on time. Cross chatter in a big meeting room is not a problem, because everyone is in separate locations; any cross chatter happens in the meeting-specific backchannel or it's coordinated with the meeting moderator. For more on this, see "Meeting Moderator."

In addition to technical and business issues, there is another factor to consider. These wall-mounted systems limit important nonverbal human communication, slowing down meetings significantly. For more on this, see "How Do Others See You?"

Microphones

When using your laptop for video calls, never use your laptop's built-in microphone and speakers. They cannot handle crossover chatter from others talking in the meeting room, from nearby calls in open-plan offices, or other background noise. This is disruptive for everyone. Even on high-quality laptops, some microphones pick up the sound of the video call coming out the laptop's speakers. This causes everyone on the call to hear themselves with a slight time delay—or they hear audio feedback loops until you get the settings just right. Other laptop microphones pick up the sound of laptop fans. This is noticeable to everyone in the meeting *except* the person causing the problem.

Avoid table-top microphones. These usually work fine when only one person talks in a quiet room, but they cannot handle multiple humans talking at the same time. In a crowded meeting room, multiple sidebar discussions are temptingly easy to start—and once they start, it is impossible for remote callers to hear or understand *anything* being said in the room.

To make things worse, small noises on the meeting table resonate and are clearly picked up by table-top microphones. This means remote listeners hear sounds like typing-on-laptop, pen-tapping-on-table, and impatient-human-tapping-fingers-on-table drown out the sound of any humans talking in the room.

If you are fortunate enough to have a dedicated room for all your calls, set up an external boom-arm mounted microphone and speakers. Otherwise, buy a good headphone with microphone to use for all audio-video calls. It does not need to be expensive. Wearing in-ear bud headphones work great, they're cheap, and they're easy to travel with, but they can become irritating after multiple hours of calls per day. Full over-the-ear headphones with a microphone also work great, are very price-conscious, and are more comfortable for multiple hours of calls per day. Some models fold down for easy travel. Find what hardware works well for you and then use it consistently.

If you have no choice but to take a video call in an open-plan office, a cafe or an airport lounge, use an over-the-ear headset with microphone. Others nearby will still be disrupted when you speak, but will at least be spared listening to all the other people speaking in your meeting. These headphones will also cut down the background noise from others to *you*, which will in turn reduce your human tendency to raise your own voice. This helps reduce noise pollution for others nearby—whether they are coworkers trying to do their own focused work or strangers in the airport trying to not be included in your meeting.

How Do Others See You?

Takeaways

♦ For video calls, sit with your back to solid walls or whiteboards—not glass walls, windows, or mirrors.

♦ Look in your "rear-view mirror" when joining a video call. Can people clearly see expressions on your face? Are you happy with what people see behind you? If not, reposition your camera, your lighting, or yourself.

♦ Move the window for your video software as close as possible to your camera, so that you naturally look more directly into the camera when talking to people.

♦ Learn cinematography tricks for camera positioning, background framing, and lighting.

Laptops and smartphones have cameras with resolutions high enough for decent quality video calls. However, the art of using the camera is frequently overlooked. The following cinematography tips will improve the speed and effectiveness of your video calls.

Look at Yourself

Many camera and lighting problems are easy to fix immediately— once you are aware of the problem.

When joining a video call, look at your "rear-view mirror"[1] and make sure you are happy with how others see you. If not,

---

[1] This thumbnail rearview mirror of yourself is available by default on almost all video call software. If your software does not have this feature, switch to a different product.

reposition yourself, your camera and your lighting until your face is uniformly and naturally lit.

Professional photographers and movie directors pay a lot of attention to "setting up the shot": deciding where to position the camera; how the person is lit; and where the light source is placed relative to the camera, the human, and the visible background. They know that even a slight change in camera position, lighting, humans, or the background can completely change the mood of the entire picture—even before the first word is spoken.

While cinematography is a specialized field, some simple tactics can significantly improve the ambient nonverbal tone of everyday audio-video calls[2]. Here are several basic tips that I've found helpful for audio-video calls:

- *Adjust your camera to eye level.* If you place your camera below your neckline, pointing up, the camera will exaggerate your mouth and cast your eyes into dark ominous shadows. This was a common technique in old black and white horror movies. It can also make you self-conscious about people looking up your nose or thinking you have a double chin. To fix this, raise your laptop or lower your chair so that your camera is at eye level.

- *Add lighting nearby.* If you're in a dark room, your screen or monitor will cast a weird blue light that makes human skin look unhealthy, and hence less trustworthy. Wearing glasses complicates things further, with reflections that prevent others seeing your eyes, and at same time let people see reflections of what is on your screen. To fix this, turn on a nearby desk lamp for a more natural, healthy, skin coloring. Position the lamp so it doesn't cause you to squint due to bright glare in your eyes or reflection on your screen.

- *Diffuse nearby lighting.* If you have a bright light or an outside window on either side of your head, the camera will emphasize a one-side-stark-bright, one-side-dark-masked appearance. Cinematographers use this technique when showing people going through traumatic emotional or mental

---

[2] These also improve communications with deaf, hard of hearing and DeafBlind users. For more details, see "Video Conferencing Platforms Feature Matrix" by National Association of the Deaf, 2020.

change, especially in old black and white "film noir" movies. To fix this, reposition your lamp to reflect light on nearby walls, creating a softer ambient light. Close window curtains, and move your chair until your face is uniformly lit.

◆ *Avoid backlighting.* If you have a bright light behind your head, or if you're sitting in front of a bright sun-filled window, the camera will show a silhouetted "witness protection program" look. This makes it impossible to see facial expressions, which eliminates most nonverbal communication and reduces trust. To fix this, turn off or move the light, close the window blinds, or move your chair.

◆ *Position your video call window near the camera.* If your eyes are not looking at your camera, others on the call will perceive you to be distracted, focusing elsewhere instead of focusing on the video call. For example, if your laptop camera is on your desk and your video call window is on an external display next to the laptop screen, your gaze will be directed to the side of the camera. To fix this, move the window for your video call software as close as possible to your camera. This will help you maintain eye contact, because you will instinctively look towards the other person (on your screen) when talking and listening. You will notice any video problems very quickly—if you are no longer visible on camera, if your lighting has changed, or if someone else freezes on their video window.

The following images show examples of ineffective and effective video camera use.

Clockwise from top-left: Person unaware they are not visible on their own camera —and showing a NotSuitableForWork poster to everyone on the work video call. Messy room with door visible that opens directly on camera and is not locked, so family can accidentally walk into video call. "Witness protection program" look caused by sitting in front of bright window. "Darth Vader look" caused by face obscured by hat, and poor lighting masking facial expressions. Video call in cafe or open-plan office—with distracting people in background unaware they are visible on camera. Wall-mounted camera in a crowded room, where the collection of small humans around the large table makes it impossible to see any facial cues and cross-chatter in the room makes it impossible to hear what anyone in the room is saying.

Everyone has good, even lighting and a calm professional background. Each person is using their own laptop camera and is head-and-shoulders visible on the video call, so facial cues are visible. Clockwise from top-left: Active listening in a relaxed professional setting. Listening while note-taking. Nonverbal cue for "ok, I agree." Nonverbal request to ask the next question. Nonverbal cue indicating an audio problem. Nonverbal cue for "Stop speaking, there's a problem."

As a meeting moderator, I look at each person as they join my meeting to verify that I can see their head, shoulders, and the expression on their face. I welcome them with a casual question, which encourages them to speak and also serves as an informal audio check; for example, "Hi Kevin, thanks for joining. Can you move to another spot? We can't see you because you are backlit." To keep things lighthearted, I use terms like the "witness protection program" look, the "Darth Vader" look, and the "crazy mountain man" look.

Doing this as each person joins the video call gently raises awareness for all participants. Soon people start checking their own rear-view mirror and audio as they join the call, or when they hear you asking someone else to adjust their video or audio.

It is too late to ask people to do this after the meeting has already started, amid an unexpectedly tricky moment in discussions—when the missing nonverbal cues would be very helpful.

Look Behind You

Now that your face is clearly visible, consider your background. People see everything that is visible to your camera, not just your face. Be aware of what people see behind you[3].

Position your chair and laptop so that you have your back to a wall, whiteboard, or other solid surface. This will reduce lighting and reflection problems caused by glass walls, mirrors, windows, or doors behind you, as well as social hazards like:

+ Curious people stop outside the room to see who you are meeting with, unaware that they are visible to others on your video call. This can also happen with people outside of street level windows.

+ Practical jokers play rabbit-ear-finger-games behind your head. You might not notice, but everyone else on your call sees them.

+ People stop to chat in the corridor to talk with others, talk on their cell phones or socialize at the water cooler, unaware that they're visible in the background of your video call.

+ A coworker fidgets at their nearby open-plan desk, unaware they are visible on your video call. This is unfair to the coworker, and distracting to everyone on your video call.

+ Someone accidentally walks in the door of your room, and is immediately in full view of the camera. This is especially hazardous if you are at home, joining video calls from your bedroom.

---

[3] I've had to call people back immediately after a meeting ended and ask them to take down a not-suitable-for-work poster hanging on the wall of their home, which they did not realize was clearly visible on the video call. The legal requirements here are complex and evolving, but a good rule of thumb is this: If it might not be suitable to display in a physical office, it should not be visible on a work video call.

If you have no choice but to join a video call from a large open-plan office, make sure your camera is positioned so that others nearby are not visible in the background of the call. Alternatively, reschedule your recurring meetings so you join them from the privacy of your home office—then commute to and from your open-plan office.

These types of distractions might be merely annoying for an internal video call, but they can be damaging during an important call with clients or others from outside the company.

Position your laptop so the screen is not visible to passersby outside the room.

Usually, it's fine if other people see who you are meeting. However, privacy is essential for complex or emotional calls like negotiating a company merger, planning a company reorganization, resolving an interpersonal conflict, or handling formal disciplinary situations. If you arrange your seating, check your screen placement and check your rear-view mirror as an explicit habit before starting every call, you will automatically do this for calls where you need privacy the most—when tensions are high and you are already distracted.

Make this your routine habit for all video calls.

Camera Shy

When I first started advocating for video calls, I believed the claims that video calls were more complex or error prone than audio calls. After all, some of the audio-video software at that time was overly complex. Setting up a video call *was* more complex than setting up an audio-only conference call. As software usability and reliability improved, though, these technical reasons disappeared.

Only after we had reliable audio-video technology hardware and software available did I discover several non-technical reasons for using audio and video during conference calls.

Sometimes people are reluctant to join video calls because they do not want to be visible on camera. No one likes looking bad on camera, and some people are more self-conscious about their image than others. Reactions to passport photos or ill-timed social photographs are good examples of this. The same is true for video calls.

Lighting and camera position can help address this concern. Poorly positioned cameras with poor lighting will make *anyone* look bad on camera, no matter how photogenic they might be in real life. Ask people to move their camera position and adjust the color and position of their lighting; these quick fixes can make a world of difference. Encouraging others do this will help them feel more comfortable about being visible on camera[4].

Even if they don't say anything at first, people who don't like being on camera will notice if anyone else in the meeting avoids turning on their camera. The meeting moderator needs to be constantly vigilant about this, ensuring that all attendees are visible on camera during an audio-video call. Usually a quick comment will suffice: "Hey Fred, thanks for joining—we can hear you but cannot see you. Did you forget to turn on your camera?"[5] Repeat offenders might need a separate private discussion. If not addressed quickly, attendees who *do* turn on their cameras will lose faith in the meeting moderator. Over time, more people will start "accidentally forgetting" to turn on their cameras. This eliminates the benefits of a video call and downgrades the entire meeting to a slower, lower-quality, audio-only conference call. For more on this, see "Meeting Moderator."

---

[4] Even if your video software allows you to start an instant video call with one click, you should always ask the other person before starting a video call. For more on the etiquette of impromptu video calls, see "Video Etiquette."

[5] This is less challenging than a more direct "Hey Fred, turn on your camera."

Video Etiquette

Takeaways

◆ Understand the hidden tax of audio-only meetings, compared with the hidden tax of audio-video meetings.

◆ Schedule every meeting as an audio-video call. Audio-video meetings are faster than audio-only meetings.

◆ Use group chat backchannel and nonverbal communication to speed up video calls.

◆ If someone's microphone is not working, don't verbally tell them. They are having audio problems, so they may not be able to hear you! Instead, use nonverbal communication or the group backchannel.

When you work with others, communicating is part of your job. Learning the correct use of video hardware and software is just one part of holding effective meetings. This chapter covers etiquette and nonverbal habits that help make video calls more effective—and faster. This chapter assumes that you have already read "Physical Setup" and "Phones, Cameras, and Microphones."

Improving audio-video meeting efficiency is not sexy, and culture change is hard. However, in many organizations the bar is so low that radical improvements can be made very quickly, giving your entire organization immediate, significant, recurring benefits.

If you work in a large organization, quietly focus on making your own team hyper-efficient on all audio-video calls. Once your team routinely has efficient, well-run video calls, others will soon notice. Inevitably, a peer will ask, "We work in the same company, using the same tools. Why are your video calls so efficient while our video calls are so disruptive?" Use this cue to help change culture and improve efficiency in other teams, showing them that the tools work just fine when humans use them correctly.

Hidden Tax of Audio-Only Meetings

People sometimes use the term "hidden video tax" to describe extra setup time for a video call. The term is usually followed by a comment like, "Video is too slow, let's just use a conference call; it's faster." This line of reasoning conveniently ignores the hidden "audio-only tax" of audio-only calls.

In my experience, audio-video calls are faster, higher quality and more productive than audio-only calls. We routinely shortened 60-minute meetings by 10 to 15 minutes *solely* by moving from audio-only to audio-video[1] Where do these time savings come from?

During a meeting, I usually finish talking about an agenda topic by asking, "Does anyone have any questions?" I then pause and wait, quietly counting to five seconds. These pauses would feel awkwardly long in an all-in-one-location meeting, but during an audio call they were longer out of necessity—other attendees needed time to realize that I'd finished talking, and then press their unmute button and start talking.

Typically, multiple people would unmute and start talking at the same time, talking over each other until they all noticed. Then they stopped talking about the topic at hand so that they could negotiate who should speak next[2]. This was frustrating, wasted everyone's time, and distracted us from the purpose of the meeting.

If after five seconds all I heard was silence, I'd ask, "Is there anyone there, or did I get disconnected?" I would then wait another five seconds for a response. Meanwhile, I sent chat messages to specific humans I knew in the meeting, in case they could hear me but I could not hear their response.

---

[1] As we organized further, with meeting agendas and meeting moderators, meetings became even faster and more productive. For more details, see "Meetings" and "Meeting Moderator."

[2] When the meeting was relaxed, we wasted time on a familiar "Ah, sorry, after you"; "No, no, after you"; "No really, you were first, after you." refrain. When tensions were high, these collisions further elevated the already high tensions, with more assertive humans just talking over others.

Worst case, I'd discover that I'd lost *my* connection to the meeting and was unaware that I had been talking into a dead microphone for the last few minutes. No one heard anything I said. Others were distracted, trying to figure out how to let me know. When this happened, sometimes the attendees would announce "It sounds like we lost John," and continue the meeting without me. Other meetings would stop, forcing all attendees wait for me to reconnect, remember what I'd said, and then repeat it all again—a frustrating experience for everyone.

Another common audio-only tax is when a person is animatedly talking and asking questions, not realizing they're muted. Later, after they figure out why no one is answering their questions, they unmute and interrupt the current topic, with "Sorry, I was accidentally muted earlier. Can we go back to the earlier topic?"

Of course, technical problems happen with audio-video calls, as with audio-only calls. However, audio-video has important advantages. When everyone is head-and-shoulders visible on a video call, nonverbal cues immediately tell you if the video connection is broken, or if someone is dropped from the call or is speaking while muted. Less time is wasted talking into a dead microphone, or asking questions of someone who lost their connection. When everyone is on head-and-shoulders video, you can use nonverbal communications to speed up meetings even further—for more on this, see "Nonverbal Communication."

Now, whenever someone says, "We don't have time to set up an audio-video call, let's just do a conference call," what I actually hear is, "I know how to use the *audio* conference tools, but I still can't use the *video* tools well enough to run a video call quickly and reliably." Whether caused by substandard tools, a lack of training, cultural resistance, or something else, this inability causes recurring inefficiencies—and it impacts their ability to do their job. If you work in finance and don't know how to use a spreadsheet, you don't switch to a pencil, paper, and a calculator—you learn the tools of the trade. Software engineers learn tools for developing software in a team: code repositories, code reviews, bug tracking systems, CI/CD systems[3], and so on. Sales people learn tools for building customer relationships and tracking sales: customer relationship management systems, sales target tracking

---

[3] Continuous Integration / Continuous Deployment

systems, and so on. Accountants learn tools for handling expenses, payroll, and tax filings. Humans who coordinate work with others need to be reliably comfortable using the latest communication tools.

When humans learn how to use video software efficiently, they speed up meetings, reduce the video meeting tax, and eliminate the larger audio-only meeting tax. These recurring improvements save your organization time and money, increase productivity, and help humans work better together in each meeting.

Specify a Group Chat Channel for Each Meeting

The effective use of group chat tools is complex enough to be its own chapter (see "Group Chat Etiquette"). However, one aspect of group chat is important to cover here, as part of video call etiquette.

Everyone attending a meeting needs to use the same group channel. To help make this happen, when you create a calendar invite for a meeting, decide which private group chat channel should be used by all attendees. Explicitly list that channel in the calendar invite. This designated channel is commonly called a "backchannel," because the stream of texts is secondary to the video and audio streams for the meeting.

If meeting attendees are from different teams, you could create a new channel just for backchannel chatter in this meeting. If all meeting attendees are all from the same group, the existing group private channel might suffice. Regardless of which channel you use, specify it in the invite. All meeting attendees, especially the meeting moderator, will know to watch this backchannel constantly throughout the meeting.

Backchannel conversations help meetings move smoothly in several crucial ways:

- ◆ When a meeting attendee loses video or audio, use backchannel to debug the problem while the meeting continues. (If group chat is also down, your internet connection is probably down. If group chat is still available, your video software is probably having problems.)

◆ When multiple attendees lose video or audio, use backchannel to coordinate rescheduling the meeting.

◆ When attendees have questions during a meeting, they can raise their hand on camera or type "/me raises hand" into backchannel. The moderator is responsible for watching the backchannel, maintaining a queue of pending speakers, and ensuring that people get to speak in the correct queued sequence.

◆ When meetings are lively with lots of people asking questions, the moderator can use backchannel to keep track of who speaks next: "ok, Bob had his hand up first, then Jane next, and then Ted," or "Let's start queuing up everyone in backchannel."

◆ When someone waiting in the queue hears their question being answered, they can take down their hand and (in backchannel) tell the moderator "never mind, my question has been answered." This is faster and less disruptive than waiting for people to unmute, verbally say that their question has been answered, and re-mute. This helps the moderator make time for others.

◆ Attendees can type side comments into backchannel without blocking the entire meeting. For example, people can support the current speaker ("I agree with Jane," or "+1") without taking up valuable time in the meeting.

◆ Attendees can ask and answer quick questions in backchannel without interrupting the current speaker or the moderator. For example, a question like "Did Jane just say $15k or $50k?" can be answered by anyone in backchannel without disrupting the meeting.

Sidebar backchannel discussions happen in all-in-one-location meetings and in geographically distributed meetings. When you use backchannel in these ways, meetings run more smoothly and you save time, whether attendees are in one location or distributed.

For large meetings, or for meetings with formal speakers presenting to an in-person audience and remote attendees, the presenters might not be able to monitor backchannel. In these situations, have a dedicated meeting moderator or "remote advocate" who watches the backchannel for remote questions and audio/video issues. This advocate should be introduced to the presenters and audience beforehand, and have technical privileges to mute anyone who does not know they are unmuted and evict uninvited gatecrashers who "zoom bomb" your meeting. When in the same physical room as the presenters, the advocate should sit within arm's reach, and—if the venue is large enough—have their own microphone.

Presenters should give priority to questions from this one human, because he or she represents multiple remote attendees. To keep everyone aware of the remote attendees, and to help the advocate feel comfortable asking awkward questions, the advocate should start all questions by saying, "Question from group chat" or "Question from remotie." For more details, see "Meeting Moderator."

Some video products have a built-in group chat feature of their own, with a backchannel created automatically so that all meeting attendees can message each other during the meeting. If you work in a team without existing group chat, or if your video call is with humans from different organizations, this can make sense. If you already use a group chat product routinely, I find it better to ignore (and, if possible, disable) the video product feature for several reasons. Firstly, an additional group chat product confuses matters, causing some humans to use their normal chat channels in the normal chat product, while other humans use the video product chat channel. Secondly, if the video software freezes or crashes you will lose the video connection and also the backchannel, making it harder to coordinate how to resume the meeting. Lastly, the video product group chat typically disappears at the end of the video call, so any important text messages will be lost before they can be added to the Single Source of Truth.

Troubleshooting

Technology glitches can happen with audio-only and audio-video calls. The quicker you can detect, isolate, and resolve any connection issues, the less disruption and lost discussion. With an audio-only call, it's hard to tell when someone drops off the call—or if you yourself are disconnected. Video calls give you more ways to detect problems. This makes them much more efficient than audio calls.

In video calls, nonverbal communication can be very helpful for identifying and resolving connection issues.

Connection issues on video calls are instantly noticeable: humans have evolved to notice when they see other humans suddenly stop moving on camera. Even humans who sit very still when they're listening will fidget, blink, or otherwise move just a little.

If one human freezes on camera for more than a few seconds, you'll know that they are having video problems. If *all* humans freeze on camera for more than a few seconds, you'll know that *you* are having video problems.

When someone's image freezes on a video call, quickly point it out to them—not on video, because you already know they are having video problems. Instead, use an unrelated communication medium: the group chat backchannel for that meeting. Sometimes the person will already know about the issue; other times they will be surprised, and thank you as they scramble to reconnect.

If you see someone's lips moving but you can't hear them speaking, either you or they have audio problems. If you are the only person signaling that you can't hear, you know that the others can hear just fine; the problem is with *your* setup.

If multiple humans signal that they can't hear, the person speaking has audio problems. Don't bother saying, "We can't hear you." Because of their audio problems, they might not be able to hear you either. Instead, use nonverbal communication. If their video is still working, point your finger horizontally toward your ear while gently shaking your head—or hold the palm of your hand in front of your camera like a traffic cop signaling "stop," and keep it there until they stop talking. You can also type a message in backchannel, making sure to explicitly mention them by name so they are notified. Sometimes people can't be heard because their microphone is on mute. Most of the time they realize this quickly, and unmute with an apology.

If you notice a problem, do this immediately. It is frustrating to stop speaking and fix your audio, but it is *far* worse to give a status update for five minutes, only to discover that no one could hear anything you said, forcing you to delay the meeting while you scramble to resolve the issue and repeat your entire update.

Nonverbal Communication

In addition to helping troubleshooting issues, nonverbal communication speeds up all communications in meetings.

Nonverbal communication can reduce or eliminate speaker collisions, which happen when one person finishes talking and multiple people unmute to speak at the same time. Best case, everyone wastes time doing a verbal "oh no, after you" negotiation to decide who should speak next. Worst case, more assertive personalities dominate the meeting, excluding others from speaking. In meetings that are already tense, speaker collisions can further increase tensions.

Speaker collisions can be eliminated by developing a culture of using nonverbal techniques. For example, when one attendee is speaking and another attendee wants to speak next, the attendee who is waiting can quietly hold their hand up beside their head, visible on camera, as if raising their hand in school[4]. The meeting moderator watches for hands and keeps track, saying things like "ok, I see three hands just went up. Alice you were first, then Bob, then Charlie."[5] Specifying the sequence of speakers lets everyone know they've been seen, speeds up transitions between humans, and eliminates verbal speaker collisions.

---

[4] Some video conferencing products include electronic ways to signal a raised hand, but I prefer to see people raising their physical hands. It was always easier to see, and it worked with every video software tool we used. Culturally, people are accustomed to taking turns asking questions in schools and large community meetings, so it was interesting to see this habit spread to large all-in-one-room meetings.

[5] As people became accustomed to this behavior, people would self-correct if the meeting moderator accidentally got the sequence wrong: "Actually, Alice had her hand up before me, so she should go before me. Go ahead, Alice."

When attendees are familiar with this process, further improvements can evolve.

Instead of handing the "verbal baton" back from one human to the moderator, who then hands it to next human, attendees can hand the baton directly to the next person in line. In the previous example, instead of Alice returning control to the moderator, who would then say, "Thanks Alice. Bob, you were next," Alice can conclude with, "...and that's it from me. Bob, you were next."

The meeting moderator must actively ensure that everyone who raises their hand has a chance to speak in turn. In the preceding example, if Doug jumps in to say something as Alice finishes speaking, the moderator needs to interrupt: "Hold on Doug, you can go after the others who already asked to speak. Bob, it's your turn, please start. Next, it's Charlie. Doug, after that it'll be your turn."

When I first worked with coworkers from many different cultures and backgrounds, individuals who were louder, more outgoing or more assertive usually dominated the speaking time in meetings. This combination of active moderators and nonverbal communications helped speed up our meetings. In addition, I discovered an unexpected benefit: humans who were unwilling to interrupt others were no longer routinely sidelined in meetings. Because of the active moderator role and nonverbal communications, they were able to speak during meetings. This is especially important in culturally diverse organizations, and it did not lengthen our meetings. Instead, different perspectives kept our meetings lively, led to higher-quality group decisions, and resulted in fewer follow-on meetings—crucial concerns were discussed during our meetings, not quietly raised afterwards.

Another meeting speedup occurred when a person droned on and on about minutia. On an audio-only call, people were usually reluctant to interrupt and say "please speed up." It's too easy to sound rude! On a video call, people were more comfortable signaling "speed up" using nonverbal communication.

To let the speaker know they should speed up or skip over some minutia, nod your head rapidly while waving your hand on camera in an encouraging circular speed-up beckoning motion. This encourages the speaker to pick up the pace or even jump to the end of their presentation in a socially graceful way, speeding up the meeting for everyone.

When humans have differing levels of understanding about a topic, it can be difficult to decide how much detail to cover in a meeting. The speaker might feel it's necessary to give a detailed background, so all attendees have the same understanding. However, if everyone in the group start signaling "speed up," the speaker can safely speed up, saying something like, "It looks everyone already understands the context, so I'll skip ahead to the punchline. I think we should ship Wednesday instead of Friday. Thoughts?"

All of these time-saving tips help speed up audio-video calls—making them faster and more efficient than audio-only calls.

Brainstorming

Physical whiteboards are great for collaborative brainstorming. They make it easy to convey ideas and collaborate on complex work problems. The same need exists in distributed teams.

Some audio-video software packages include whiteboard functionality, which allows users to draw diagrams as if they were standing side by side at a physical whiteboard. In practice, all of the software-based whiteboards I've tried were too complex to be useful—I always lost inspiration or forgot concepts while I struggled with the tools. The tools got in the way of the brainstorming process.

Instead, use familiar tools that everyone can use reliably.

If you suddenly need to draw diagrams while brainstorming on a video call, simply turn your laptop, so the camera faces the nearest whiteboard. Ask remote viewers to tell you the maximum area they can see on the whiteboard, and draw a box on the whiteboard to show these camera limits. Move your seat, so you can still be seen on camera. Now, brainstorm and draw on the whiteboard like usual, staying within the box. Use dark-colored markers for maximum contrast. Avoid pastel colored and faint, nearly-depleted markers—these are hard to see in person, and even harder to see on a video call.

If there is no whiteboard nearby, draw diagrams using a dark pen and a piece of paper, and then hold the paper up in front of your laptop camera for others to see.

When the meeting ends, use your cell phone to photograph the whiteboard (or the scrap of paper) and share with everyone in the Single Source of Truth. For more on this, see "Single Source of Truth."

Impromptu Video Calls

Before starting an impromptu video call, first ask if it is ok to interrupt your coworkers. Don't start a video call without any warning.

Even if your video technology is always running on everyone's machines (so that technically you can start a call instantly), you should always ask first. They might be free to talk, or they might resent a surprise intrusion disrupting another call or some complex higher-priority work. You won't know unless you ask first. For more on this, see "Choose Communication Channels Carefully."

Just as importantly, be aware of the social dynamics of suddenly appearing without warning on their screen (or psychologically in their home) uninvited. Even if you don't mind people calling you without warning any time of day or night, others may not be comfortable with this. Be respectful of their personal space.

Most humans would be uncomfortable walking in the front door of a coworker's home unannounced. Think of a video call as arriving at someone's home, knocking on their door, and waiting to be invited in.

The request can be quick. Send a chat message like: "Hey, got a minute for a quick video call about...?" This gives them a chance to decide if your topic is more important than their work-in-progress, and if yes, then save their work, mentally switch gears, and close their home-office door before joining you on the call. If they reply "Yes," immediately start the video call.

One engineer I worked with, Brian, was always having camera problems with his Linux laptop during group calls. At the start of the meeting, he'd say, "I can hear and see you just fine, and you can hear me fine. It looks like my linux camera software is broken again. I'll fix it after." When I talked with him about this after each group meeting, he assured me he'd get it fixed before next week's meeting. This went on for weeks. At one point I noticed that his systems consistently worked well for our one-on-one video calls, and consistently did not work for our group calls, so I started saying "that's what you said last week. Please fix it, or I'll ship you another computer." Eventually, I quietly shipped him a Mac Mini and a web camera.

When it arrived, he was surprised—and we finally got to the truth. His existing camera and software worked fine. The problem was not computer hardware or software; the problem was human culture. Our group video calls felt like a jarring intrusion into his home.

When he turned on his camera and joined a video call, he felt that all of his coworkers were suddenly physically in his home. This was a new home with his new girlfriend; his home was very important and personal to him. Although he genuinely enjoyed spending time with coworkers at group gatherings, Brian was a very private guy. To him, it felt like we were ringing the doorbell and—without waiting for an invite to enter—promptly walking through his front door directly into whichever room he was in.

After some discussions, we came up with a plan. For the short term, during their remodeling project, we tested a setup where he could sit in a corner of the kitchen with the camera facing towards him, the blank kitchen wall behind him, and his camera on for meetings. The longer-term plan was to designate a spare bedroom with a door as his home office. He'd close the door during video calls as a signal to his partner, so she could safely remain off camera. The rest of their home was safe from prying eyes.

Own Your Calendar

Takeaways

- Keep your calendar accurate, including all non-meeting events. This helps others schedule meetings with you without calendar haggling.

- When calendar haggling, reduce back-and-forth emails by suggesting three possible times that work for you, in order of your personal preference.

- Use time zones by default when speaking or emailing about times. Encourage others to do the same.

- Experiment with different cadences and durations of meetings. Find what works best for you and make that your default. For me it works well to alternate "meeting days" and "maker days." On meeting days, each meeting is 30 minutes long with 30-minute gaps in between.

- Experiment with different calendar reminder times. Find what works best for you and make that your calendar default. For me, 10-minute reminders work best. When the reminder goes off, join the meeting early.

Owning your calendar, instead of reacting to inbound events from others, is good discipline when humans all work in one physical location—and it's essential when they work in different locations. Make sure that everything important to you is on your calendar, so others can tell when you're available. Reserve time for your own work, food, travel, and so on. Before you accept incoming invites, understand why you are being invited and make sure it's an appropriate use of your time. These small steps help you have time and mental headspace for the work you are responsible for.

When I first became a manager, I was surprised how many meetings I was suddenly invited to. Not knowing any better, I accepted each meeting invite—even if I didn't know why I was invited or the objective of the meeting. After all, the meeting invites rarely had any agendas and everyone else seemed to accept the invites, so I thought this was a normal part of my new life as a manager[1].

It turned out that some people were inviting me to meetings simply because *they* thought I *might* want to attend—regardless of whether I was needed. There was rarely an agenda, and meeting descriptions were vague, so it was hard to tell what exactly would be covered in the meeting, or if it would be a good use of my time. If the organizer considered me optional for the meeting, it was rarely specified in the invite. Sometimes the organizer was clearly surprised that I had reshuffled my busy calendar to attend what they considered to be an optional, non-critical meeting. Others invited me in a laudable attempt to encourage cross-team communications, not realizing I would have been happier to read meeting notes later—if notes existed. Still others invited a wide range of people to their meetings, simply because they had not figured out who was needed. They preferred to invite too many people, to avoid discovering mid-meeting that they were missing a key individual. Their mindset was "Let's just get everyone in a room and figure out what we want to meet about—and then if you are not needed, you can leave!" They conveniently ignored the disruption this caused across the organization.

This was frustrating for everyone, and made me resent future invites from the organizer.

A subtle yet disruptive side effect was that people asked me to attend meetings at a time of their convenience, regardless of the impact on my schedule. If the time was inconvenient for me, I found myself in the awkward position of asking them to reschedule their meeting just for me—and sometimes found myself responsible for finding a new calendar time that suited all of the other invitees of their meeting.

---

[1] It is not just me. In large organizations, managers spend 75% of their time in meetings and meeting-related activities. For details, see "Manager-Led Group Meetings: A Context for Promoting Employee Engagement" by Allen & Rogelberg and "Meetings, Manners, and Civilization: The Development of Modern Meeting Behaviour" by van Vree.

Over time, I realized I was reacting to my own calendar, running late between poorly timed meetings (if there were no gaps), and helping other people find alternate times for their own meetings. I was disrupting my own work at the whims of others. Even working more than 80 hours a week, I was unable to finish my own work in the poorly timed, awkward gaps between meetings. Simply running faster or working more hours does not solve this problem. I know, I tried.

When I found myself routinely lamenting "I started work early this morning, I've been in meetings all day, it's now 9pm, and my to-do list is longer, not shorter," I knew I had to stop reacting to my calendar. Instead, I needed to own my calendar.

Plan Your Week

The tension of balancing time between "meeting work" and "maker work"[2] is not new. Each organization I've played a role in had its own cadence for recurring meetings, but they all had patterns of recurring "heartbeat" meetings: cross-group planning meetings, project status meetings, company-wide planning status meetings, one-on-one meetings with direct reports, one-on-one meetings with managers, and so on. I had control over scheduling some of these meetings; others I did not. These recurring meetings formed the structure of my work week, around which I had to find time for meetings I ran, as well as my own non-meeting work.

If you work in an organization like this, take time to experiment and find what works for you. Then create a premeditated structure for your week.

I tried mixing meeting work and maker work throughout the day, but the context switching and interrupted time blocks quickly proved this to be unworkable. I tried having all meetings together at the start of my day, so I would then have uninterrupted focus time afterwards—but that didn't work for coworkers in certain time zones. Moving all meetings to the end of my day didn't work for coworkers in certain other time zones.

---

[2] Hat tip to Paul Graham for writing "Maker's Schedule, Manager's Schedule": paulgraham.com/makersschedule.html.

In another experiment I scheduled all of my meeting days together at the start of the week, so that the rest of the week could be meeting-free maker days. This seemed like a good idea, but in practice it did not work. Something always came up on a maker day that could not wait multiple days until my next meeting day. Despite my best efforts, my maker days were routinely interrupted by urgent meetings. Annoyingly, most of these urgent interrupts could have waited a day if the very next day had been a meeting day—but they couldn't wait multiple days.

I also found that after a few adjacent meeting days it was harder to start productive work on a maker day, because it took me significantly longer to rebuild mental context from my last maker day.

After more experimenting, what worked best for me was to schedule alternate meeting days and maker days. At one company, my meeting days were Monday, Wednesday, and Friday; my maker days were Tuesday and Thursday. At another company, my meeting days were Monday, Tuesday, and Thursday; my maker days were Wednesday and Friday.

Of course, every week brings surprise issues, requiring ad hoc meetings and unexpected work. The ratio of meeting days to maker days could fluctuate each week as my workload changed, but it was important to alternate days. If the need for an emergency meeting arose on a maker day I had a quick two- or three-minute chat for immediate advice. I found that most urgent meetings could wait until the next day—a meeting day! For more on surprise meetings, see "Handling Surprise Meetings."

Alternating meeting days with maker days in a predictable way had unexpected benefits. With designated meeting days it became easier to schedule meetings with humans in different time zones. It reduced mental meeting fatigue caused by multiple days of back-to-back meetings. It became much easier to plan my week, and each day was more predictable. Each night, when preparing for the next day, I prepared differently for meeting days or maker days. This helped me wake up in the morning mentally prepared for what I would, and would not, be focused on that day.

Whenever possible, schedule meetings on similar topics near each other to reduce mental context switching—with short gaps in between. For more on this, see "Schedule 30-Minute Gaps."

Keep a Realistic Calendar

Keeping your calendar accurate sounds obvious. Keeping your calendar 100% accurate, with blocks of time for your own individual work and life, is less obvious—yet crucial.

If you know that a meeting will start late because someone said they would be late, update your calendar to match the new reality. Similarly, if a meeting runs long, update your calendar afterwards. Both of these steps are easier and less confusing than sending an email or group chat message with the revised time, while leaving the original now-inaccurate calendar invite unchanged.

When you keep your calendar accurate like this, it's easier to notice patterns when attendees are consistently late, or meetings consistently run long. This allows you to adjust future meeting invites and avoid predictable "surprises."

In addition to meetings, schedule pseudo-meetings for all essential events that occupy time in your day. This adds clarity to your workdays, and communicates the reality of your availability to others. Here are several examples of pseudo-meeting entries:

- ◆ If you work from home some days and commute to an office on other days, create a pseudo-meeting called "Commute" for the times when you will be commuting.

- ◆ If you are on vacation or sick, don't just create an all-day event in your calendar. All-day events typically appear as a small item at the start of a day, so people can miss it when scheduling meetings. Instead, create meetings from 08:00[3] to 18:00 called "PTO" or "Vacation," to block any attempts to arrange meetings while you are out.

- ◆ If you need an uninterrupted block of time for focused work, create a meeting called "Do Not Disturb" or "Get Work Done."[4] I reserve blocks of time around upcoming deadlines.

---

[3] For more on speaking or writing about times, see "Writing Dates and Times."

[4] For example, one company I worked at had a weekly company-wide directors' meeting at 10:00am every Thursday. For several weeks in a row, I was late to this meeting because a coworker added a last-minute "urgent" 9:30 to 10:00 meeting to my calendar. Their meeting ran long, causing me to be late for the 10:00 meeting. In

When my calendar is an accurate plan of record with *everything* on it, I gain several unexpected benefits:

◆ I spend less time negotiating meeting times. People can schedule a meeting with me while I am doing other things. They don't need to ask if I am free at a specific time, and then wait while I email back and forth about when to meet. If anyone asks to meet me, my immediate response is "My calendar is accurate. Just pick a time that is free and works for you. What's this meeting for?"

◆ Over time, people learn that it's ok to add things to my calendar without having to ask me first. For anyone who does not have access to my shared calendar, there is still some calendar haggling involved. For more on this, see "Calendar Haggling."

◆ It's easier to triage urgent requests. Instead of dropping everything to address the latest emergency-of-the-day, I pause briefly to look at my realistic calendar. I ask myself, "Is this emergency truly more important than what I was scheduled to do, or can it wait until my next meeting day tomorrow? Is this something I can delegate?" If it is a real emergency, I reschedule or cancel other meetings.

◆ I am able to give more helpful responses when emergencies arise. I gradually stopped responding with "I'm sorry, I can't help you. I'm busy (on unstated work)," or "I have nothing on my calendar, and my own work is invisible, so I am free to drop everything to help." Instead I respond with "I'm sorry, I can't help you right now because I'm busy working on xxx. Let's figure out who else can help," or "I'm free for 20 minutes before I'm supposed to do xxx. Let's see what we can do in that time." Or, "This is more urgent than my work on xxx; give me a minute to tell others, and then I can start helping."

◆ When I have an unexpected opening in my day, I no longer sit at my desk thinking about how to fill the gap. I find it easier to prioritize work. My personal productivity has increased substantially.

---

frustration, I created a recurring "Prepare" meeting from 9:30 to 10:00. I was never late to the 10:00am meeting again.

♦ When people invite me to their meetings without explanation or agenda, I politely decline the invite, stating that without more information I believe my other existing work commitments are more important. The meeting host is welcome to give me more context, or they might agree that I'm not needed. Sometimes they ask if I can send a representative instead.

Treat your calendar as an accurate Single Source of Truth record of where you spend your time. For more on this, see "Single Source of Truth."

Schedule 30-Minute Meetings

Change your calendar settings so that all meetings default to 30 minutes long.

I used to schedule one-hour meetings by default, without really thinking about it. It was the default on my calendar, and it was what I saw others doing. The few times I even questioned it, I'd tell myself that it was better to be safe than sorry. If it turned out we didn't need the full hour, we could always end the meeting early.

This is a trap.

Some teams are disciplined enough to say, "ok, we've covered everything, let's end the meeting early." This is rare. Usually, whenever I did try to end a meeting early, someone would inevitably say, "Hey, while we are all here and have spare time, can we talk about...?" Meeting "hijackings" like this meant that meetings usually expanded to fill all available time[5]. For more on meeting hijacking, see "Meeting Hijacking and Coming-To-Meeting-Just-In-Case-Itis."

People remember the frustration when a meeting ends late, but— interestingly—tend to forget how time wasted at the start of a meeting contributes to the late ending. Several companies I've worked with had one-hour meetings that would wait 10 minutes for all invitees to join, followed by a few more minutes tracking

---

[5] Parkinson, C.N. (1955). *Parkinson's Law.*

down the last late-but-critical person. Once the last stragglers joined, we spent a few minutes constructing a meeting agenda. As a result, the meeting usually started 15 to 20 minutes after the official start time. This left only 40 to 45 minutes of scheduled meeting time, and left me frustrated trying to figure out how to cover everything in the remaining time.

Left unchecked, this became self-perpetuating. Punctual people gradually stopped showing up on time because they knew that the first 15 minutes would be a waste of their time.

With an active moderator and a prewritten meeting agenda, you can minimize wasted time at the start of a meeting. The moderator can also prevent meeting hijacking, which helps eliminate wasted time toward the end of a meeting. Suddenly, your 30-minute focused meeting is not much shorter than the 40-usable-minutes-in-60-minutes meeting.

If there are too many topics to realistically cover in 30 minutes, ask yourself if you need all of the same people for the entire meeting. If some agenda items only need a subset of people, split them out to a separate 30-minute meeting. If there really is a need for the same set of people to be in one longer meeting, consider breaking it into two separate shorter meetings with a break to refresh and check email. This will also help constrain agenda items to their allocated time slots.

The trick is that 30-minute meetings help everyone focus on meeting efficiency. Shorter meetings require crisp organizational skills. Even if your hour-long meetings are efficient, changing to a default of 30 minutes is a great catalyst for further improvement. It takes planning to start meetings on time with an accurate agenda, the correct list of invitees, and an active meeting moderator. The recurring goodness is worth the effort. For more on this, see "Meetings" and "Meeting Moderator."

Schedule 30-Minute Gaps

On meeting days, it is helpful to schedule gaps between meetings. A 30-minute gap between meetings worked best for me.

It took a lot of trial-and-error experimenting to find what did and didn't work for my calendar. Likewise, you should experiment to find what works best for you. In case it is helpful, here's a summary of what I tried and why each did or didn't work.

I first attempted to schedule all of my meetings back to back immediately after each other. I wanted to attend all of my meetings for the week as quickly as possible, so that I could then focus on "real" work for the rest of the uninterrupted week. However, this turned out to be impractical for several reasons:

◆ If one meeting had an unexpected emergency or ran long, it had a ripple effect, causing all other meetings that day to also start late. This happened so often that people started to object to mid- to late-afternoon meetings with me, because I'd been late every week for the last few months. Sadly, they were correct. Even worse, they had data to prove it!

◆ Being late to a meeting never sends a good signal to others, and it is rude. If a meeting was likely to be tense, the simple act of showing up late increased the tension before the meeting even started. This extra tension took time to defuse before we could start to address the initial topic. This caused the meeting to run even longer.

◆ The domino effect of delays meant that I frequently found myself joining one meeting late, while trying to reschedule the remaining meetings later in the day—meetings that I knew I had no hope of attending because of the compounding calendar slippage. It was hard to find new times for rescheduled meetings, so I ended up agreeing to new meeting times in a rush—meetings that were just as likely to get rescheduled. All of this was happening while I was supposed to be paying attention to the people in the meeting I was currently in. This was rude and disrespectful to others, stressful to myself, bad for my own time management, and 100% self-imposed.

◆ If any of my meetings required me to actually *do* something— send an email to a client, schedule a meeting, or check budget numbers—I never had time to do it during the day because I was in back-to-back meetings. Instead, I would start a growing list of urgent follow-up items, which I could only start to deal with after the last back-to-back meeting ended. This was typically after everyone else left the office at the end of the day. After dealing with the follow-up items, I could finally start to address my own to-do list.

- ◆ To make matters worse, during this sequence of back-to-back meetings I could not keep up with my own emails. At the end of the day I would open my email inbox for the first time in hours, only to discover that I'd been unaware of several urgent email threads that were waiting for my response.

This was clearly not working. I continued experimenting.

I tried scheduling back-to-back meetings only in the morning, with no meetings for the rest of the day, so I could have longer focused time for the rest of the day. This was better, because I could follow up on morning meetings and keep track of my email inbox. I also had a better chance to do some of my own focused work. It meant, however, that every single day had meetings. Even worse, some of these meetings could not be held in the morning due to time zones differences. I couldn't restrict meetings to mornings, and I found it hard to do focused work in the morning when I knew tricky meetings were coming later in the day.

I tried scheduling a few back-to-back meetings in the morning, followed by a multi-hour gap, followed by a few back-to-back meetings in the afternoon and a multi-hour gap afterwards. This was better, because I could now deal with action items from the morning meetings quickly. I was better able to keep track of my email inbox. It was still not great. The few-hour gap in the middle of the day was long enough to give me false hope of getting focused work done, but it was too short to do any real focused work. I was also far too easily interrupted whenever someone discovered I was not in a meeting. This in turn caused me to become frustrated because I expected to do real focused work in that multi-hour gap, but I was never actually able to get anything done.

I tried scheduling a gap of 15 minutes, but this was too short: a meeting overrun could easily use up that time, and I'd lose the chance to check email or do anything else before the next meeting. Similarly, a cadence of 25-minute meetings with five-minute gaps did not work for me. Also, I think people expect meetings to start at the top of the hour. It's difficult to explain meetings that start at 30 minutes past, but it's doable. Scheduling meetings at 15 minutes past or 45 minutes past is more difficult.

A gap of 30 minutes worked well as a buffer for me. If a meeting runs long, my next meeting can still start on time. When a meeting ends on time I can use the 30-minute gap to handle action items from the previous meeting, quickly check my email inbox (using speed tips from "Email Etiquette"), and reply to any hot issues. Sometimes I can even handle an item or two from my own to-do list and still have time for a bathroom or coffee break before my next meeting[6].

These 30-minute gaps have a surprise benefit: I do not expect to get focused work done in that short amount of time, so I am less frustrated when someone interrupts me. By contrast, a gap of an hour or more between meetings led me to believe that I might get focused work done between meetings—causing me to feel personally frustrated when I was interrupted. Quick interrupts are a valid part of working with others, so I need to be available for them. Fine-tuning the cadence of these meetings helped me help others.

Handling Surprise Meetings

When you keep your calendar 100% accurate, you gain several non-obvious yet crucially important benefits.

In the heat of an emergency I typically don't have the time or mental bandwidth to pause and remember unwritten calendar exceptions. With a 100% accurate calendar, I can scan my calendar with confidence and make scheduling decisions very rapidly, *knowing* that my calendar is 100% accurate.

If something is urgent, people can always double-book a meeting —but this should be very rare[7]. If someone double-books me into a meeting, they need to email or direct-message me, explaining why this is important enough for me to reschedule my existing meetings. If the need is not clearly stated, I'll decline the new double-booked meeting—noting that if their need is truly urgent,

---

[6] These transition times are also important mental and emotional breaks. For more on this, see "Feed Your Soul."

[7] Some people booking meetings assume that their need is always greater; they expect you to adjust your calendar to match their needs, even though most calendar scheduling programs will let you see what times others are available. This is a human (not technical) problem, best addressed in person or on a video call.

they should clarify why this new meeting request is important enough for me to cancel my preexisting meetings for them.

If there is a real emergency, do what you can to help your coworkers. After all, you work together at the same organization. It is important to remember, though, that an emergency for someone else is not automatically an emergency for you. When asked to help on an emergency, pause for a quick, cold, hard assessment.

- First, decide as objectively as possible if you think this is a genuine emergency or a storm in a teacup, while keeping your focus on your scheduled priorities.

- If you decide to help, be clear about how much time commitment is likely needed. If this will impact your preexisting work commitments, ask stakeholders for permission to delay (or reassign) your scheduled work, so that you can help with the emergency.

- Get agreement *before* you start helping. Set clear new expectations with everyone. Sometimes the need for help is self-evident and gains a speedy rubber-stamp approval. Other times, however, undeclared priorities may surface, showing why your scheduled work is more important. Maybe others can be reassigned to help with the emergency. Asking *after* you have fixed the emergency is a poor choice. This leaves other stakeholders with an unpleasant surprise: their scheduled work is now late, and they have limited time to help mitigate this.

- After an emergency is resolved it is all too easy to forget about it. There are plenty of new emergencies to worry about. People forget the urgency and the downstream cost of work that was dropped in order to help. Stakeholders might pressure you with comments like, "I know you worked late fixing that emergency, but we still need your project finished on time. Can you work late again?" Over time, this will lead to burnout and feeling under-appreciated.

From a broader career perspective, if you repeatedly drop everything to help fix other people's emergencies, you might unwittingly be making a significant career choice. You risk building a reputation as a firefighter: the person who always saves the day. There is nothing wrong with this; you are helping coworkers fix something important for the organization. Some people thrive on high-pressure situations like this. The next time anything goes wrong, however, people will tend to come to you first for help. You fixed the last emergency, so you are a natural choice to help with this new emergency. Over time, you can find yourself spending so much time fixing other people's emergencies that you cannot complete *your own* scheduled work on time. This can create new emergencies for you and the organization.

If a delay in your scheduled work creates an even bigger emergency than the emergency you just fixed, your good intentions can actually make things worse. If your scheduled projects are consistently late because you are always helping other people fix their emergencies, you risk building a reputation as someone who cannot complete their own scheduled work on time. New projects will start being assigned to people who *can* reliably complete their work on schedule, not those who are consistently late on scheduled work because they are fixing (other people's) emergencies.

In summary, make clear decisions about where to spend your time and effort. Sometimes it's important to help out in an emergency. Other times it's appropriate to not help—instead, remain focused on your scheduled work, and flag the emergency to that person's manager so that they can find help. This may be the best way for people to learn from these teachable moments, especially if it is a repeated pattern of behavior.

These decisions are important for your professional reputation and career. An accurate calendar helps you keep track of how you choose to spend your time—and hence whether you are honoring your own career priorities.

Calendar Haggling

An accurate, shared calendar helps other people see when you are free to meet. They can schedule a meeting without interrupting you, or with minimal interruption.

Without an accurate, shared calendar, you face a traditional dance of phone calls, voice messages, or emails back and forth to find a time that everyone will be available. I call this "calendar haggling." Sadly, I've seen many occasions where calendar haggling for a meeting took more time than the actual meeting.

Being intentionally efficient when you are calendar haggling—with only one or two rounds of negotiation— is useful when you work together in one office in one time zone. It is *essential* when you work with people across multiple locations in different time zones.

There are tools available to help schedule meetings with people outside your organization, or others who do not have access to your calendar[8].

In keeping with the mindset that different communication channels have different response expectations (see "Choose Communication Channels Carefully"), and to reduce miscommunications, I rarely do calendar haggling live in a meeting or on the phone. Instead I use email, and I reduce the time spent on calendar-haggling with meeting requests that look like this:

```
To: Adam, Ben
From: John
Subject: Meeting about Project Snoopy
Hi Adam, Ben:
I'd like to meet later this week about Project Snoopy
before the board meeting on Friday evening. When should we
meet?
To start the calendar haggling, here are a few times that
work for me, in order of my personal preference:
* Thu 08:00-10:00 PT range
* Fri 09:30-10:00 PT
* Thu 11:30-12noon PT
* If none of those work, can you suggest a few times that
work for you? Once we have date/time agreed, I'll send the
calendar invite with video link.
John
```

I list a few times that I am available to meet, sorted in order of my personal preference. If I list only one possible time, I'd likely find myself dealing with multiple back and forth emails, each counter-proposing a new alternate time—exactly the interactions I want to avoid. Listing more than three possible times takes too long for me

---

[8] I can recommend calend.ly and timetrade.com, but there are others.

to figure out, and often causes decision overload for others. In my experience, three possibilities work best.

By explicitly stating that the three times are listed in order of my preference, I'm reminding people that they do not need to accept the first one in the list—any of the times work for me, they can choose whichever is best for them. In case none of the options work for the other invitees, I make it explicitly safe for them to counteroffer with multiple alternative times of their own.

I also note that we are doing calendar haggling, negotiating about *when* to meet. We are not discussing the topic that requires a meeting. This distinction can be important depending on how tense you expect the meeting will be. It can also raise awareness of the invisible costs of meetings: In the time it took to schedule this meeting, could I have resolved the problem by email, without needing a meeting?

After starting this habit, most of my meetings are scheduled in one back-and-forth email. Sometimes it can go up to two emails. Either way, it is a vast improvement.

When all the proposed times are in the same current week, I specify the day without date—like in the example above. However, when the proposed dates are in future weeks, or over multiple different weeks, I specify the day and date, for example: "Thu 04feb". I avoid phrases like "this Thurs" and "next Thurs," which mean different things in different cultures. If anyone uses these phrases with me, I rephrase and reply using explicit dates—which causes me to look at a calendar. These habits catch errors often enough that I now do them consistently. Detecting and fixing errors during scheduling prevents more serious frustrations later.

Set Calendar Time Zones

Make sure that your calendar time zone is set correctly. If your calendar defaults to one time zone and you are physically working in another time zone, you force other people to keep track of where you are and do time-zone math every time they want to schedule a meeting with you. Even worse, you set yourself up for surprise meetings outside normal business hours if someone makes a mistake in their time-zone math or misunderstands your location. This is 100% avoidable. All decent calendar programs support time zones. Find and set your time zone appropriately when you first set up your computer, and every time you travel[9].

It is easy to convince yourself that because you have a small team who are all in fixed locations, you can remember the local time for each of them—so you can do the time-zone math in your head. After all, you are smart and math is easy, so you can do that math perfectly, most of the time. Consider, though, that clocks are moved forward and back every year as part of daylight saving time (DST) changes. To add to the fun, every government in the world makes their own decision about when to do this. Over a few weeks in the spring and a few weeks in autumn, countries[10] around the world change their national clocks on different days[11].

Don't be surprised by daylight saving time changes. You know there will be two periods of disruption every year, so you might as well prepare for it. It's impossible to keep all of this straight in your head, so don't even try. There are free tools that solve this problem. Find tools that work for you, and use them consistently[12].

You'll know that your team has mastered this skill when someone travels for work or schedules an interview with a candidate in

---

[9] After you set your correct time zone, remember to change your time zone when you travel to different time zones for work, and then remember to change it back again when you return home.

[10] In some cases, different regions *within* a country handle DST differently.

[11] Avoid planning a work trip that involves crossing the dateline during one of these daylight saving time change flurries. I thought I had time zones and daylight saving time well under control, so I did not even think about it on my first working trip to Japan in 2006. As a result, my first few days of meetings and phone calls were disrupted by daylight saving time changes. While recovering from jet lag, I would get up in the middle of the night to join a video call an hour early and adjust for DST. The next day I would discover I was an hour late because yet another country had changed DST—all because my trip overlapped the flurry of activity when different countries were changing their daylight saving time. Never again.

[12] I use and recommend WorldTimeBuddy.com, FoxClocks (a free add-on for Mozilla's Firefox and other browsers), and TimeandDate.com.

another time zone—and you quietly notice that no one was confused by the time zone differences.

Writing Dates and Times

Different parts of the world have different conventions on how to write dates and times. The date "10/11/15" means the 11th of October 2015 in the US, the 10th of November 2015 in Ireland, and the 15th of November 2010 in Japan.

Don't write dates and times in a format that works for your location and expect everyone else to do the mental juggling correctly. To avoid confusion, everyone should write in a format that is obvious to people in all locations.

I once had a schedule surprise on a project I was working on, because I was traveling between countries and sending project dates to people in multiple locations. I learned the hard way how important it is to use a date format that could not be misunderstood. By anyone. Since then, I write dates in DD-mmm-YYYY format (for example, "11-nov-2015") or DDmmmYYYY format (for example, "11nov2015"). This habit eliminates confusion, and it requires typing only a few extra characters[13].

Unless you work in a pure 9-to-5 company where everyone is in the same location and time zone, you need to be careful about assumptions with times. To prevent confusion, I write time in a 24-hour format instead of using am or pm—for example, I use "13:00" instead of "1pm." All humans I've worked with understand this, and some countries and industries use 24-hour format by default[14]. If you prefer to use 12-hour format, explicitly state "am" or "pm." For all but the most casual situations, include the time zone.

I also find it helpful to clarify times that people easily confuse, such as 12am and 12pm. For example, "We'll announce at 12

---

[13] This DD-mmm-YYYY format still requires non-English speakers to translate the name of the month, but it significantly reduces the risk of miscommunication across all languages.

[14] Japan uses a 24-hour format for times, with an extra twist. You can indicate 2am as either 02:00 when you are getting up very early, or 26:00 when you stay up very late!

o'clock Friday" is unclear. "We'll announce at 12am Friday" and "We'll announce at 12midnight PT Friday" are slightly better. Instead, I prefer to use "We'll announce at 23:59 PT Friday."

Explicitly do not use casual, imprecise descriptions like "first thing in the morning," "lunchtime" or "close of business," as these mean different times to different humans. Instead specify the explicit time you had in mind: "9:00 PT," "1pm PT (or 13:00 PT)," or "18:00 PT" to prevent miscommunications with people who start work early or leave work late.

When you consistently write dates and times like this, you eliminate the possibility of confusion. This is crucial when working in distributed teams across multiple time zones, when people travel for work, or when a team is working yet another late night.

Change the Default Reminder in Calendar

Change your default reminder to 10 minutes in your calendar program. The default was trivially easy to change in my calendar software, and the consequences were significant for me.

When my 15-minute default calendar reminder went off I would dismiss the alert, thinking "I still have time to do just one more thing before the meeting starts." That one more thing always took longer than expected, and I would suddenly discover I was late for the meeting. This happened repeatedly, and it was a completely avoidable, 100%-self-imposed failure on my part.

I experimented with changing my default reminder to five minutes This helped with meeting punctuality, but it had negative side effects. If I was halfway through an important email when the five-minute alert sounded, I'd rush the end of the email to be on time for the meeting—or I'd stop immediately, leaving the draft email unfinished until I rediscovered it hours later, still unsent! In addition, if there were any problems with physical setup or video call connections, the five-minute reminder did not leave much time to fix the connection before the meeting was scheduled to start.

Changing the default reminder to 10 minutes works great for me. When this reminder goes off, it allows me a minute or two to calmly finish whatever email I am writing, yet feels too short for me to consider starting anything else. I dismiss the reminder, finish that email, refill my coffee cup, and then join the video meeting or walk to the meeting room—*early*. Worst case, if I have any problems with meeting setup (room still in use, hardware or software issues, and so on), I have time to find another room or resolve the technical issues, and still be on time for the meeting. After I join the call, I quickly re-skim the shared agenda for any last-minute additions or comments. Sometimes, everything I want to add to the agenda is already there, because I added things to the agenda *when I thought of them* during the week. (For more on this, see "Meeting Moderator.") If I still have time before others join, I minimize the window and continue to handle email while I wait. When others join the meeting, the notification as they enter the meeting prevents me from losing track of time and being late— after all, I'm already in the meeting, even if I might be doing something else while I wait. This helps meetings start on time, which in turn helps meetings *end* on time.

Being consistently early as a leader communicates clear expectations, and encourages the same behavior in others. Meetings usually start and stop on time, improving the effectiveness of the overall group.

For events that require extra travel time, such as offsite customer visits and doctor appointments, override your default reminder to allow for travel time. For example, when flying, I have reminders set four weeks ahead (to make sure I did actually buy tickets and check passport expiry dates), 24 hours ahead (to check-in online and get serious about packing), and two hours ahead (to get to the airport).

Meetings

Takeaways

♦ Before organizing a meeting, stop and ask, "Does this topic actually need a meeting? Is a meeting the most appropriate choice for this particular topic?" Sometimes an email to the group is more appropriate and faster.

♦ If a topic does require a meeting, ask yourself a few additional questions: "How will I know if the meeting was a success? What is its purpose?" Will I use the meeting to broadcast a product decision or company announcement? To announce a product decision, and then lead a prolonged discussion with feedback? To brainstorm an idea? To introduce a new hire?

♦ Be very intentional about which invitees are required, and which invitees are welcome-if-curious.

People complain about wasting time in unproductive, sloppily organized meetings that prevent them from doing their job. Sadly, they are right to complain—this shocking waste of time and effort is all too common. The negative impact of these poorly-run meetings is even more profound for people who are physically remote.

By contrast, people rarely complain about useful, informative, productive meetings that help them do their job, and remote attendees find these meetings particularly helpful.

Coordinating meetings effectively, while aggressively limiting the number of meetings, requires intentional focused leadership. This is an area where you can lead by example.

Aggressively Limit the Number of Meetings

There are many different ways to communicate and coordinate amongst people; meetings are just one option. When appropriate, having meetings is fine. Well-run, properly planned meetings can be a great help. However, unprepared meetings with no agenda and no clear desired outcome are just an expensive waste of time for everyone involved[1] and for the company[2].

Phrases like, "We have too many meetings," or "Why didn't anyone tell me about this—was there a meeting about it?" indicate that an organization is having problems with meetings, and with internal communications in general. I've worked in companies that have way too many meetings—where engineers continually bemoan unproductive meetings that prevent them from getting work done. I've worked in companies where meetings were routinely called without knowing what the meeting was to achieve, who should attend, or (afterwards) what had been decided. Sadly, I've also worked in places where irreversible decisions were made in meetings that—accidentally or intentionally—did not include all of the necessary people. These situations meant that some people were out of touch with what others were doing, sometimes with serious consequences—people in one team were busily working on improving a project while another team was busily killing off the same project. Each of these miscommunications had serious consequences—to the revenue of the company, as well as the morale and trust of everyone involved.

Before you set up a meeting, make it your habit to pause, take a deep breath, and ask yourself "*Why* do we need to meet?" and "Is a meeting the *best* way to deal with this?"

---

[1] One idea I've played with was to use costofmeetings.com to figure out the cost of a meeting. I would then require anyone who called a meeting to "pay" for the meeting on a corporate credit card, and then display that "cost" in the calendar invite so that all attendees would be aware of the financial cost of this meeting. At the end of the month, anyone who organized a meeting would need to justify the cost of these meetings to their boss as part of the "reimbursement" process for those costs.

[2] Personally, I also think it is disrespectful of other people's time.

If a meeting is the right format, great. Go ahead and set up the meeting, after reading the rest of this chapter as well as "Meeting Moderator." Also, make sure to ask yourself questions like, "Who exactly should be there?" For more on this, see "Identify Need-To-Attend vs. Welcome-If-Curious."

Well-run, productive meetings can help people do their jobs; they are well worth the cost.

If a meeting is *not* the right format, then it is important to consider the many alternatives that might work better. A few seconds of premeditated thought will weed out many useless meetings, which will save your organization a lot of wasted time and money. This is particularly important if your group is not all in the same physical location. A nice side effect is that you free up time and mental focus for meetings that *are* genuinely needed.

At Mozilla, for 18 people in 14 cities across four non-adjacent time zones, we experimented with several ideas. We eventually settled on a cadence of four required meetings a week:

◆ The entire group met for 30 minutes (sometimes 45) once a week, on Monday.

◆ Group members who were involved in recent or upcoming software releases met for 30 minutes once a week, on Tuesday. (At first, most of the group attended. This shrank to a small subset as we streamlined how we worked.)

◆ Each person met one-on-one with their manager for 30 minutes once a week, every week.

◆ The entire group met for a weekly social—on video—on Friday. For more on this, see "Organizing Weekly Social Events."

Some individuals also attended meetings called by people in other parts of the company—for company status updates, cross-group project updates, and so on. There were also meetings with external vendors and clients. Attendance and cadence of those other meetings varied. Individuals working together on a project could choose to meet with others on the project if and when they thought it was helpful. These meetings varied from week to week, and were initiated by each other—not "the boss."

Despite this small number of team meetings, everyone was tightly organized. We knew what our coworkers were working on. Clear consistent use of this mindset *reduced* the number of meetings we needed, without reducing how tightly interconnected and well informed we were.

I've worked with people who thought that the best way to deal with an urgent issue was to call a meeting on short notice, inviting anyone physically sitting nearby. Sadly, they did not stop and ask, "Who can best help?"[3] They also did not ask, "Are the people I see here already working on something that is as important—or more important—than the new hot topic that I'm calling a meeting for?" In my more cynical moments, I wondered if they were more interested in *being seen* to do something, instead of doing what was best for the latest emergency or for the overall organization.

When you take a moment to ask if there might be a better way, you'll notice that a lot of urgent, short-notice meetings are not needed and are, in fact, counterproductive. Yes, it is easier to call a meeting for everyone in the group: no advance planning, no risk of omitting the person who will have the best idea, and no risk of no-shows if you are the boss. However, in some cases it is faster to phone one other person, reach a decision, and then email the decision to the group: "This is the problem as we see it. Here is what we propose as a solution. Is there anything we missed before we proceed?" This helps make sure you have framed the problem correctly, and it forces you to explain what you are proposing to do (and why). The entire group can quickly read this, looking for gaps or missed assumptions. If any are discovered, you might need a quick meeting with a few carefully chosen people on those specific points, while the rest of the group continues working on other things without interruption.

In some cases you *will* need to meet with the entire group, but I've found that with this limit-the-number-of-meetings mindset, the need to meet with the *entire* group is rare.

Once you have this habit of asking yourself these questions before you organize a meeting, you can quietly start to spread this mindset and raise awareness in other parts of the organization. If

---

[3] Inviting all humans sitting nearby is a clear indicator of an "out of sight, out of mind" mindset. This is a serious problem in any geo-distributed organization.

you are invited to a meeting and you aren't sure what the objective is, why you are needed, or whether it really requires a meeting, discretely ask the organizer these questions. The organizer might still hold the meeting, or reduce the invite list to be more realistic, or maybe realize that there is a better way to solve the problem, and cancel the meeting! Either way, you've just raised awareness.

Technology makes it easy and inexpensive to schedule meetings—maybe too easy. Technology also makes it possible to meet with people in other locations and other time zones without requiring weeks of planning. It's hard to picture a time when human messengers carried a written agenda on horseback, asking attendees to travel to a meeting several weeks in the future. As humans, we need to evolve our thinking to match new technical and social realities. If your default response to each new burning issue is to call a meeting or start phoning multiple people, consider that you might be harming—not helping—the group's ability to respond.

Develop and practice this mindset continuously. Managers typically call most meetings, but anyone who calls a meeting can be a role model for this behavior. Lead by example.

> *"Walk out of a meeting or drop off a call as soon as it is obvious you aren't adding value. It is not rude to leave, it is rude to make someone stay and waste their time."*
>
> *Elon Musk*

Choose Communication Channels Carefully

Today's technologies offer a bewildering and growing range of communication channels. Every communication medium has a different implied level of social urgency and a different expectation of responsiveness. Human social etiquette is still evolving to catch up with the social changes these new technologies bring, but we need a baseline. Here is my summary of prioritized communication channels, ranked from most to least urgent:

- ◆ Meeting in person, by video, or with an audio-only conference call

- ◆ Cell phone
- ◆ SMS (text messaging)
- ◆ Group chat
- ◆ Email to recipient
- ◆ Email, Cc recipient
- ◆ Email from a bug tracking or project ticketing system
- ◆ Emails about changes to watched pages on an internal wiki or website

An emergency meeting or conference call is most urgent. A cell phone call is almost as urgent. An update from a project ticketing system or website is least urgent.

Next time you want to contact someone, try asking yourself, "What is the urgency of this situation, and what's the appropriate communication channel for it?" This requires thought—if you misjudge and use the wrong channel for the level of urgency, you set yourself and others up for failure.

This awareness of channels is also useful when deciding whether a meeting is needed. Before scheduling a meeting, ask yourself where the topic fits on this prioritized hierarchy. As mentioned in "Aggressively Limit the Number of Meetings," first figure out the urgency of the communication. *Then* decide which communication channel fits best. Here are some examples:

- ◆ *Scenario*: "The CEO is going into a board meeting in 30 minutes, and is urgently looking for an explanation on that $1 million budget overrun." *Recommended channel*: Phone call to find me quickly, even if I'm not at my desk, and then switch to video. Don't use email or ticketing system, because I won't see it in time.

- ◆ *Scenario*: "We're changing the version of the Java Development Kit supported in the next release shipping at the end of the financial quarter, which means we need to rethink project xxx by the end of next week." *Recommended channel*: Posting in ticketing system should be fine. If recipients haven't responded after a few days, send a gentle reminder email. If recipients haven't responded and time is running out, then a phone call is justified.

♦ *Scenario*: "Your best engineer just told me that she is going to quit." *Recommended channel*: Phone call to find me quickly, even if I'm not at my desk, then switch to video.

♦ *Scenario*: "We need to brainstorm how our group can help implement a new company directive." *Recommended channel*: Probably a meeting, with any advance work clearly specified so people come prepared. Decide in advance who will be the meeting organizer and moderator.

Take a moment to assess urgency, and then choose the appropriate medium. Don't set everyone up to fail by emailing about the CEO budget drama or the ready-to-quit engineer. Likewise, don't interrupt coworkers' meetings to call them about a low-priority issue, such as a product change that won't happen for a few months.

The first time someone contacts me on an urgent channel for a less-urgent message, I ask them why they thought it was urgent enough to interrupt me. If they repeat this mistake too often, I'll never answer their calls in a meeting—which means I will not answer their call when it *is* a genuine emergency.

When I have an impulse to use an urgent channel—a phone call—for a quick question ("Oh, I'll just call Fredda and ask; she won't mind and it'll be quick!"), first pause for a moment. I have no idea what I'm about to interrupt. If I do call her, I'm deciding that my call is more important than anything she *might* be doing. When her phone starts ringing, she has no idea how urgent it is, so she can't tell whether to interrupt what she is doing to answer my call or to ignore my call. If I *know* that this is the most urgent thing for *both* of us, the call is appropriate. Otherwise, I'll review other communication channels and choose one that is more appropriate.

After our group stopped reacting to artificial, self-imposed emergencies, life became a lot calmer. People had more time to work. Interestingly, when a real emergency did arise, we dealt with it more effectively because we had less mental fatigue due to false emergencies.

Identify Need-To-Attend vs. Welcome-If-Curious

When setting up a meeting, I used to invite everyone in the group —or everyone on the email discussion—in case they were interested or might have useful information. I cast the net wide so I wouldn't forget to invite that one critical person.

After noticing how big and inefficient these meetings were, and hearing complaints about too many meetings, I started focusing on who *needed* to attend. Jeff Bezos at Amazon is famous for making meetings more effective with his "two pizza rule,"[4] which is supported by research from Bob Sutton at Stanford[5]. With this in mind, I tried an experiment. I ran a few meetings where I only invited those who I thought *needed* to attend. These meetings were faster and more focused, so I thought this was an improvement.

Then I was surprised by complaints from coworkers who weren't invited: "Why did you exclude me from that meeting?" I responded, "I thought you wouldn't want to attend. It was about Project Snoopy, which you are not working on and you've complained bitterly about having too many meetings." They agreed, but said they would still like to be invited, "because... well... because." Some felt excluded; others felt like they needed to be there "just in case." For more on this, see the discussion about Coming-to-Meetings-Just-In-Case-Itis in "Meeting Moderator."

After further experiments, I identified two groups of attendees: need-to-attend (required) and welcome-if-curious (optional).

Identifying need-to-attend and welcome-if-curious attendees takes time and premeditated thought; carelessly bulk-inviting an entire group is certainly faster. However, this dual-invite approach has several advantages that help meetings go faster:

◆ The process of deciding who was need-to-attend versus welcome-if-curious forced me to be intentional about the reason for the meeting and what I hoped to achieve in the meeting. This focus helped others decide if they were truly needed or not. It also encouraged them to have the organizer invite others who were not yet invited yet were interested in —or critical to—that discussion.

---

[4] Bezos argues that meeting size should be limited so you could feed all attendees with only two pizzas.

[5] See Bob Sutton's article on his "Work Matters" blog, "Why Big Teams Suck: Seven (Plus or Minus Two) is the Magical Number Once Again."

◆ Anyone who needs-to-attend but doesn't know *why* they are needed, will notice when they receive the invite, not when the meeting starts. They will ask why they are needed. Maybe they are crucial, but did not know until they asked. When they understand *before* the meeting why they were invited, they still have time to prepare for the meeting. If you made a mistake and someone should be optional (or dropped from the meeting completely), you can do that—again, before the meeting. Maybe you've invited the wrong person, and you need to invite someone else instead. Far better to discover that a crucial human is missing from the invite *before* the meeting instead of *during* the meeting, when you'd need to cancel and reschedule.

◆ Welcome-if-curious attendees are optional; it becomes *their choice* whether to attend. This is important. If welcome-if-curious people attend, they don't feel pressured to talk. They can also choose to skip the meeting, read the meeting notes afterwards to confirm that nothing interesting happened. This reinforces their decision to not attend and builds trust.

◆ It's easier to schedule a smaller meeting. As you invite more people to a meeting, it becomes more difficult to find a time when everyone is available. This becomes even more complicated if your invitees are in multiple time zones. Instead, a reduced list of need-to-attend people, separate from welcome-if-curious people, makes scheduling easier. You can focus on finding a time that works for those who need-to-attend. If you can find a time that works for most or all of the optional people, great—but they are optional; you *need* the required people.

◆ If you, as a manager, set up a meeting outside normal business hours (18:00 Friday, 08:00 Monday, or even 15:00 Sunday), people will grumble, but usually show up—especially if they report to you. This is a sociocultural thing. People want to do what their boss asks them to do. They don't want to upset the boss, nor do they want to appear as if they don't care about the project. "If I don't attend, I'll be seen as somehow not doing my job," is a substantial social pressure. Very few people feel comfortable asking their boss, "Can I skip your meeting?" Even if the invitee knows they have nothing to contribute to the meeting, they will accept the invite and attend anyway, simply because their boss invited them. To make sure their attendance was noticed by the boss, they will often find reasons to say something—anything—in the meeting. Sadly, this causes meetings to take more time.

◆ Meetings with a lot of need-to-attend humans tend to take more time, because they can feel tempted to say something in the meeting simply to appear engaged and useful. Even if their comments are of no value to the meeting or the organization, they can feel compelled to justify the fact that they were need-to-attend. On the other extreme, some need-to-attend humans who were not needed might begrudge the fact that they were not needed, despite being told otherwise. Remember: you invited them.

Mechanically, it's easy to let people know if their attendance is mandatory or optional. When you create a meeting invite in your calendar, mark all optional invitees as "optional" in the calendar software[6]. When you create an invite in email, send the email "To" the required attendees, and "Cc" the optional attendees. To make sure everyone clearly understands this distinction, start the email by listing the required and optional attendees:

```
To: Adam, Ben
Cc: all@...
From: John
Subject: Project Snoopy meeting
Hi Adam, Ben: (cc-ing others who are welcome-if-curious)
As promised, I've set up a quick go/no-go status meeting
on Project Snoopy for Friday at 17:00 PST. Adam, Ben, John
needed, others are welcome-if-curious.
Agenda (and notes) at: ...
Video info is at: ...
John.
```

Too many people skip this step and jump straight to "let's all meet and start talking," without thinking about the desired end result or the wider organizational cost of holding the meeting[7]. Spending

---

[6] For example, in Google calendar, when creating a calendar invite, click on the human silhouette beside the person's name. It will change from black (required) to white (optional).

[7] When stuck in a useless, unproductive meeting, one popular pastime is to calculate the cost of a meeting, usually by figuring out the hourly salary of all attendees. costofmeetings.com is just one example of a website that will help you

time to make sure the right attendees are invited to meetings will be repaid many times over by shorter, more focused, more productive meetings.

Calendar Haggling

I already talked about calendar haggling in "Own Your Calendar," but one point is worth repeating. I've heard people say, "We need to meet, because meetings are faster and email is too slow." This might or might not be true. Yes, in-person communication has much higher bandwidth than text-only email. For some topics this is the right way to go.

However, this assumes that everyone is free to meet right now, and that they're interruptible because whatever they are working on is lower priority. In reality, I've seen calendar haggling (deciding *when* to meet) take longer than the actual meeting. If you factor in the calendar haggling, sometimes meetings are *slower* than email.

Instead of sending a flurry of emails back and forth to negotiate a time to meet, consider whether an email about the *topic* could resolve the situation faster than an email about *scheduling time to meet* about the topic. You might find that you can resolve the topic with fewer emails—and no meeting!

Calendar Invite Essentials

Keep your use of "To" and "Cc" obsessively accurate: as you add and remove attendees, update your meeting invite. This helps invitees know who else is attending—and be notified of any last-minute changes to the meeting time, location, or agenda.

If you've ever been on a video call waiting for others to join—only to eventually discover that the meeting was rescheduled or everyone else is in another video room wondering where you are —you know how frustrating this is.

---

do this math. Note that these costs are lower than reality because they don't include the cost of the physical room, or the opportunity cost of what else those same people could have been working on instead of coming-to-meeting-just-in-case.

To help meetings start on time, include this additional information in your invite:

Here is additional information to include in your invite, to help meetings start on time:

- The link to the video call.

- Last-minute changes to the video room (update this in the invite, so all attendees will be notified).

- A link to the shared document containing the agenda (and later, the shared meeting notes).

- The name of the shared group chat channel used for backchannel. For more on this, see "Video Etiquette."

Adding these details to your calendar invite turns it into the Single Source of Truth for the meeting. Changes to the agenda, times, and invite list are all handled in the invite.

When the calendar reminder pops up, people have all of the information they need to quickly join the meeting, without needing to search emails, group chat or ask their coworkers.

Start (And Stop!) On Time

One reason meetings run long is because they didn't *start* on time. Starting a meeting on time means that the right people are invited, they're all punctual, and they're ready to start, using an accurate, complete agenda. This is harder than it sounds.

Advance preparation is key. For more on preparing an agenda in advance and inviting the right attendees, see "Own Your Calendar." After that, the last big question is: How to encourage people to actually show up on time?

Starting meetings on time because "the boss *said* meetings should start on time" nearly always gets pushback or is gradually ignored. I tried that a few times in different organizations without much success. Then I attended a meeting where I heard this:

> *"It's three minutes past—we're starting the meeting now, out of respect for those who were punctual."*
>
> *Thomas Arend, Ph.D.*

I love this. I never liked playing the bad cop, chasing people to join meetings on time. Instead, it is much nicer to play good cop, respecting the majority of people who *do* show up on time or early. This "Three Minute Rule" is a more positive, respectful, and classy interaction[8].

To change a culture where meetings always started late, I pre-planned my approach with the routinely punctual folks. I thanked them for being punctual, and asked them to be especially sure to attend on time for the next few meetings because I wanted to try an experiment to make our meetings more punctual. They were frustrated by waiting for habitual stragglers, so they were delighted to help.

In our next meeting, I started with the following:

> "ok, it's meeting time. Thank you Alice, Bob, and Charlie for being on time. As usual, we'll wait three minutes before starting."

> "Meanwhile, if you haven't already done so, please add any last-minute items to the agenda. Oh, and Charlie, can you move your camera to fix the backlighting?"

> *[...sound of quiet typing with occasional social chit-chat]*

> "ok, it's three minutes past. We'll start the meeting now, out of respect for those who were punctual. First on the agenda is Alice—looks like you added an item about quarterly goals."

> *[...continue down the agenda...]*

Following an agenda in strict sequence encourages a healthy group meeting culture. People quickly learn that if they want their topics covered early in the meeting, they need to add them to the

---

[8] This is also importantly different than saying "We'll wait a little longer for enough people to join". Setting an explicit time limit lets those who were punctual know exactly how much mental-break transition time they have. For more on this see "Creating Transition Times."

agenda well before the meeting starts, and arrive on time. (This has a nice side effect: others can see what will be covered in the meeting, so they can prepare in advance.)

If an agenda item can't be covered because of a missing attendee, move that agenda item to the *end* of the agenda and keep the meeting going. Do not halt the meeting while you track down the missing person. When the latecomer finally arrives, do not jump to their item as soon as they arrive; this encourages a mindset that "it's ok to arrive late just for my items." Their item was deferred to the end of the agenda because they were not there earlier, so they need to wait their turn—no special treatment or enabling of their disruptive behavior.

Attendees who add agenda items late or during the meeting, or who arrive late, will learn that their items will be covered later. They (not I!) might need to ask people to stay longer, to cover their last-minute additions. Latecomers quickly discover it is socially awkward to arrive late, add last-minute items to the agenda, and then ask punctual people to stay after the scheduled end of the meeting. The unpopularity of this with peers can be a great motivator. In our group, people quickly learned to be more punctual. Another nice side effect was that the responsibility shifted: the latecomer (not the meeting organizer) was seen as the reason why the meeting ran late. Peer pressure helped latecomers become more punctual, and agendas more organized, for the next meeting. Over time, meetings became more efficient. The benefits were clearly appreciated by everyone in the group, especially when group members rotated into the meeting moderator role. For more on this, see "Meeting Moderator."

If a latecomer complained that the meeting started without them, I'd simply state, "You were late; we waited three minutes as usual, and then started out of respect for everyone else who was punctual. We don't have time to recap everything now, but you can read the notes. I'm happy to talk with you after the meeting and go over the details of what you missed."

If people with deferred agenda items don't show up, conclude the meeting. If a key person doesn't attend and the meeting cannot proceed, cancel the meeting. In both situations, state that the item cannot be dealt with because "not everyone who said they would attend, did in fact attend." Ask the group, "Do we need to schedule another meeting, or can we deal with this topic in a different way?" No need to list names. Everyone in the meeting knows who didn't show. The person who missed the meeting knows they look bad to the other attendees. They might apologize or provide an excuse, but they will make more of an effort to attend the rescheduled meeting on time.

One of the most egregious cases I dealt with was "Steve." He would routinely miss meetings he agreed to attend, and was habitually 15 minutes late to the meetings he did attend. Upon arriving, Steve insisted on discussing his items immediately, even if they were not on the agenda. He would leave the meeting as soon as his items were covered, even though other items on the agenda warranted his input. Steve believed that his time was more valuable than all of the other attendees. He thought the purpose of the meeting was for him to tell people what they needed to do, and for them to answer any questions he might have. He had, quite simply, not considered the idea that the meeting was also for others to raise topics to him. His disruptive behavior impacted interpersonal dynamics and caused personnel issues with other meeting attendees. It had never been corrected.

In his defense, that series of meetings had been poorly run, with no agenda or clear intentions. Once I started running those meetings and posting an agenda, Steve's tardy pattern continued with, "Oh, I was too busy to read the agenda. Can you forward me the link?" I repeatedly asked him to be punctual, without success. When I instead started the meeting without him "after three minutes out of respect for those who are punctual," he was surprised and vocally very unhappy at first—yet within a few weeks, he was on time. He started adding his items to the agenda. It took a few months of careful watching to ensure consistent behavior, but his new habit eventually stuck[9].

To maintain awareness of punctuality, for the next month or so I thanked everyone for being punctual—only when everyone was punctual. When the meeting ended early, I would explicitly mention that ending early was only possible because we all started on time. I then thanked everyone again for being punctual at the start of the meeting. Just this change alone shortened a 60-minute meeting to around 40 minutes!

---

[9] ...even though he continued his old habits in other people's meetings.

Meeting Moderator

Takeaways

◆ Set up a shared, editable agenda in advance, and have everyone *append* items to the agenda.

◆ Cancel meetings in advance if all required people cannot attend, or if the shared agenda is empty.

◆ Ask each attendee to post notes for their agenda item into the shared editable agenda during the meeting.

◆ Take turns being the active meeting moderator.

After you decide that a meeting *is* needed and you follow the setup steps in "Meetings," you'll need an active moderator. The moderator will make sure that the meeting starts and ends on time, follows the posted agenda, and that the attendees follow remote-friendly etiquette. To accomplish this, the moderator must be focused, friendly, efficient, consistent, fair, and—when the situation calls for it—hard-nosed.

Clearly identify the moderator before the start of the meeting.

A good default is to ask the meeting organizer to be the moderator —they have a vested interest in the meeting being productive. If the organizer cannot be the moderator, someone else needs to agree to do it—ideally before sending the meeting invite—so that the substitute moderator can make sure that all of the required attendees will attend and have their advance preparation work done, to make the meeting useful.

If you think having an active meeting moderator is optional or too much work, try hosting meetings with and without a moderator. Each time I've done this, the value of the moderator role was strongly reinforced.

Meeting Hijacking and Coming-To-Meeting-Just-In-Case-Itis

An important part of the moderator role is to prevent meeting hijacking[1] and a related corporate disease called "coming-to-meeting-just-in-case-itis."

Sometimes people attend meetings not because of what's on the agenda, but because of *who else* is attending. They notice that everyone they want to meet with about a new product is attending someone else's upcoming budget meeting. So, instead of setting up their own meeting, they attend the budget meeting, intending to discuss their new product feature first. Once the budget meeting starts, they hijack it[2] until their product decision is reached, and then they allow the scheduled budget meeting to continue in the remaining time. This causes people to not trust meeting agendas, even if they exist.

Other times, people attend meetings because they are afraid others in the meeting will raise topics (not on the agenda) that will disrupt what they're working on. They believe that the best way to avert potential disruption is to attend the meeting "just in case." Taken to an extreme, they attend every meeting they hear about, purely for defensive reasons. This reflects a very unhealthy work environment, and I've seen it in multiple companies—it is not as rare as I would hope. Best case, nothing happens during the meeting and they "only" waste expensive time coming-to-meeting-just-in-case.

I first became aware of meeting hijacking and coming-to-meeting-just-in-case-itis after a meeting that I moderated:

---

[1] "Meeting hijacking" is when someone prevents a meeting from covering scheduled topics until their (unscheduled) topics are covered first. This is an unfair waste of time for other attendees, who need to sit through a long discussion about a surprise off-topic item, understandably frustrated because this off-topic item is preventing them from discussing the on-topic agenda items they care about.

[2] An example of a common ploy would be to hijack a finance meeting with, "We don't know what the cost for this project will be until we finish this design decision. Fred, Mary—we're all here now, what design do you think we should use?"

As usual, I asked: "...ok, has anyone got anything else before we end?"

Someone replied: "Hey John, yes, there is one last thing. You asked a few of us to figure out a design for this new [unrelated] project. We've looked at a few different ways of doing this, and we think the best approach would be to do it this way. We just want a formal ok from you as the boss, so we can start work. Are you ok with using this approach?"

I asked some questions to sanity-check technical concerns, and it all sounded reasonable. "Looks good to me. Is there anything I need to be worried about, or anything you need me to help with?"

"No, we have everything we need, we just need your approval to start work."

"ok, yes, I formally approve."

The meeting ended and everyone left happy.

Until the next day.

I didn't realize that three out of four engineers on the project really wanted one design for this project, while the fourth person strongly wanted a different design. The three engineers were in that meeting; the fourth wasn't at the meeting because this topic wasn't on the agenda. Later, the three people told the fourth person, "We met with John, and he decided we should do it our way." The fourth person, clearly very frustrated, called to ask why I vetoed his approach (which I wasn't even aware of) in a meeting that he didn't attend (because this topic wasn't on the agenda). By making this decision without his input, he thought that I must not value his professional opinion. He said that the episode destroyed his trust in his coworkers and in his management—me! To prevent something like this happening again, he now intended to attend all future meetings, regardless of what was on the agenda, just in case something else came up that might impact him.

He now had coming-to-meeting-just-in-case-itis. And it was my fault.

Once I understood what happened, I took immediate action to stop this disease from spreading. I apologized for bypassing the fourth person, and I promised to fix the situation immediately. I met with the three engineers and made sure they understood why their behavior was toxic for the entire group—never to be repeated. Then I called a separate meeting with all four engineers, so we could *all* agree on the approach for this disputed project.

This important lesson changed how I moderated meetings.

To be clear, I'm ok discussing unscheduled off-topic items in meetings. Sometimes life happens like that. Whenever new items come up, though, I insist that the item be added to the *end* of the editable agenda, like everything else, and we will get to it in order. This ensures that off-topic items are published in the agenda, for others to see afterwards.

The change for me as moderator, was this: When we get to any off-topic items added to the agenda, I ask, "Is this quick, and are *all* stakeholders here?" My next steps depend on the response:

- If everyone is present and it is quick, then we discuss it.

- If we are missing any stakeholders, I firmly but politely say, "Sorry, you cannot do it here. You need to call your own separate meeting, inviting all of the right people." Then I remove the item from the agenda, out of the current meeting. Sometimes the simple act of asking, "Is everyone present?" is enough to persuade people to retract their end-run attempt and do the right thing, calling their own separate meeting with everyone involved.

- If everyone is present but the discussion will take a long time, I move the item to the very end of the agenda. When we get to it, I say, "ok, now the only thing left is xxxxx. This last item will take a while, so only those who care about this topic need to stay. Everyone else is welcome-if-curious, but if you have anything better to do, feel free to drop off now." Depending on the situation, I might even drive the point home further by indicating that this is the end of the scheduled meeting, and then dropping off the call myself.

Your job as meeting moderator is to be hard-nosed and consistently fair. Active meeting moderation is important to do, and it's also important for attendees to *see* it done consistently.

Done well, meeting moderation builds trust, prevents coming-to-meeting-just-in-case-itis, and frees up a lot of time for a group. You will need to continue to be hyper-vigilant, because this disease starts small, spreads quickly, and undermines trust. It soaks up a disproportionate amount of time in the group, because everyone feels the need to attend every meeting they hear about, just-in-case. If you see early warning signs, move quickly and decisively to stop this disease before it has a chance to spread.

Sharing an Editable Agenda in Advance

We all know that creating an agenda in advance is good. The catch is *how* you do it.

Don't ask people to send *you* agenda items in advance. This puts pressure on others to send you an email with details of *everything* they need covered. It takes work to sort that out, and it leaves people feeling like you might approve or reject their meeting items without warning or explanation.

For meetings held on short notice, this process simply does not work. For meetings further in the future, you create time-consuming busy work for yourself—merging emails and casual phone or corridor comments into an organized agenda. This takes *your* time, and it can get quite hectic as the meeting approaches. You might even find yourself unpopular for forgetting something in the last-minute flurry.

To address these issues, I started accumulating a list of items I wanted to cover in each meeting. At the start of each meeting I asked, "Does anyone have anything for the agenda?" People told me what they wanted to add, and I added my list too. Then we'd start the meeting.

Even though we had an agenda, this process didn't work for several reasons. Because the agenda wasn't available in advance, it was impossible to tell if a meeting could be safely cancelled without getting everyone together. Forming the agenda in the meeting like this enabled louder or more politically powerful humans to add their items to the agenda first; quieter individuals added their items later, or sometimes not at all if they accurately decided there would not be enough remaining time. Attendees had no time to prepare for last-minute agenda items. And, some people used my open-ended agenda question to hijack the meeting by saying, "As we're all here anyway, can we talk about…?"

At some point I realized I could make things better for me and for others, simply by adding items to the agenda *when we thought of them, before the meeting started.* I created the following process, which avoids recurring busy work for every meeting. This was important as the group grew, and it worked for all meetings going forward.

Create a shared document containing a template agenda[3]. Keep the agenda format very, very simple. After multiple experiments, here's a format that works well for me:

```
Dial-in/video/room info: [link]
Date: [dd-mmm-yyyy time-with-timezone]
Attendees:
Upcoming Vacations/OOO:
*

Agenda/Roundtable:
* release date for security fix (john)
* update on project snoopy (charlie)
* review of budget numbers (mary)
*
```

In your meeting calendar invite, add a link to this shared document. Make sure that all invitees can edit the agenda in the shared document, then send out the calendar invite.

Now, if someone asks you to add something to the agenda, remind them that the calendar invite has the link to the editable agenda; they can add it themselves. Be consistent. For some humans, it is typical to send agenda suggestions to the boss, so it might take them a few iterations to get used to the culture change of adding their own agenda items.

Over time, people learn to add items to the agenda without asking the meeting organizer to do anything. I find they quickly prefer it. After all, adding something to the agenda yourself is less work than writing an email asking the meeting organizer to add it, and

---

[3] We preferred etherpad.org for this, because of their highlighting and line numbers, but you can also use Google Docs with "suggestions" enabled. We found that Evernote and wiki did not work for this, because of how edit conflicts were handled. We also found that asking people to send emails didn't work, because it forced the meeting organizer to do a lot of organizing with last-minute emails, and was hard to keep track of new items once the meeting started.

then following up to make sure the item was correctly added to the agenda.

Set up your calendar invite to send reminder emails (with the agenda link) to all attendees 24 hours in advance, one hour in advance, and 10 minutes before the meeting start time. If someone sees the reminder and wants to add an item to the agenda, they can easily add it themselves, using the link in the reminder email.

The agenda is now a shared creation by everyone in the group—no one person is stuck doing it. The only rule is that everyone *appends* their items to the agenda. Each meeting will follow the order in which people have added items to the agenda[4]. This approach guarantees that introverted people, or people from cultural backgrounds who avoid speaking over louder speakers, are able to discuss their items in the meeting. The range and sequence of items covered in the meeting is more inclusive and healthier for the entire group.

If someone adds an agenda item that requires people who haven't been invited, you can suggest inviting the missing people—before the meeting starts. Alternatively, if a lot of attendees are not involved with a topic, you can ask the person to remove their agenda item and create their own meeting for that topic.

This is also less work for the meeting organizer. The one-time setup work is minimal, and the process is great for recurring meetings. You no longer need to maintain lists of items for upcoming meetings. No more last-minute flurries, adding items to the agenda while joining the call. Others can see agenda items in advance, and sometimes even prepare beforehand. You can cancel a meeting beforehand if there is nothing on the agenda. At the start of a meeting, you no longer need to stop and ask, "What meeting am I going into, and what did I want to cover?"

People show up at meetings a lot more prepared, because the agenda is available in advance, allowing them to prepare beforehand. They can add comments or thoughts to other people's agenda items, which speeds up discussion during the meeting.

---

[4] Any exceptions to this, such as moving items due to topic length or relation to other items, should be explicitly called out at the very start of the meeting and agreed by all involved.

Sometimes an agenda item can be resolved before the meeting starts—great! (When this happens in my meetings, I don't skip the item. Instead, I take a few seconds to read the summary, making sure that everyone was aware of the decision, and then I thank everyone involved for helping speed up the meeting.)

When agenda items are ready before the meeting starts, you spend more of the expensive meeting time on the *purpose* of the meeting, instead of discussing *why* you are meeting. This helps meeting moderators and makes meetings more efficient for everyone.

Cancelling Meetings

As meeting moderator, there are several situations that might require you to cancel a meeting; for example:

- ♦ One or more need-to-attend people are not planning to attend the meeting.

- ♦ The group-generated agenda is empty.

When you get the first calendar reminder, 24 hours before the meeting, review the responses to the meeting invite. If any need-to-attend people have not accepted the invite, ask them to confirm their plans by accepting or declining the invite. If any need-to-attend people cannot attend, this is your last reasonable chance to reschedule or cancel the meeting without wasting other people's time. Cancelling meetings on short notice is not great, but it is better than having people join the meeting only to discover (after 10 minutes of frantic phone calls, text messages, and group chat messages) that some of your need-to-attend people will not attend, forcing you to reschedule. When this happens, you've wasted the time of the humans who did show up, and as meeting moderator, you've damaged some of your own reputation.

When you get the 10-minute reminder, check the invite responses and the agenda one last time. If there is nothing in the agenda, contact the invitees. Ask if the meeting can be cancelled because there's nothing on the agenda.

Sometimes this gets no response, and after five minutes I cancel the meeting (amid quiet "thank you" emails from people who wanted to get other work done, and avoid meeting-for-the-sake-of-meeting). Sometimes, however, someone will add something to the agenda, and we end up holding the meeting after all—which is fine.

If you do this consistently, people soon learn to put things on the agenda long before the meeting starts. Over time, this reduces the need for public nudging, and it avoids last-minute flurry of activity[5]. It also helps people view meetings as something they all have some control over, by helping decide whether to cancel or hold a meeting. Meetings are not just called by the boss—an important mindset change.

If you cancel a recurring meeting a few times in a row, investigate carefully why that series of meetings was created, and whether it is still needed. The trick is to not cancel a series of *useful* meetings, even if they are not needed for a week or two. Before you cancel a recurring meeting, ask the attendees these questions:

- ◆ Is the recurring meeting still needed, but you expect it to be dormant for a few weeks or months because of external factors? If so, when will the external factors change; when should the meeting series be revived?

- ◆ Is the recurring meeting now obsolete; can it be safely cancelled?

- ◆ Have circumstances changed enough that the cadence of the meeting should be reduced from once per week to once per month or once per quarter?

- ◆ Could the same need now be addressed via email, instead of an actual meeting?

- ◆ Has the need for the meeting changed enough that you should cancel this recurring meeting and create a new recurring meeting, with a revised set of the attendees and a revised, refocused agenda?

Cancelling unproductive meetings in advance is an important tool at your disposal.

---

[5] You know you have succeeded when someone else does this to you!

Taking Notes in the Group-Editable Agenda

Everyone thinks meeting notes are great, but no one wants to be the dedicated note-taker.

Note-taking is a thankless, potentially high-risk chore. The note-taker can't fully participate in the meeting, because they are busy trying to take accurate notes. After the meeting ends, they spend time cleaning up the rough notes into something useful, before sending the notes to everyone.

Most people ignore or delete emails with meeting notes—until there is a problem. At that point, they dig through meeting notes in detail, looking for evidence supporting their recollection of events. Disagreements can easily become the fault of the note taker; no wonder no one wants to take notes in meetings. Rotating the role across team members helps share the risk, but it does not fix the root of the problem. The traditional method of note-taking in meetings is set up to fail.

One way to avoid the note-taking role is to avoid taking notes entirely, and instead rely on human memory. Sadly, this was typical in several companies where I've worked. This approach might work some of the time, but I've found it to be sloppy and error-prone. Reconciling different understandings in human memory was painful and time-consuming, and it usually needed to be done in tight, time-pressured situations. All of this is suboptimal for humans in the same physical office; it is even more disruptive for humans on distributed teams.

Despite these challenges, notes are important. Imagine yourself leaving a meeting where everyone agreed on a project deadline of Friday. As you sit down at your desk, you realize that you don't remember if the group agreed on a deadline of Friday 09:00, Friday 17:00, Friday 23:59, or Monday 09:00[6]. Or which time zone will be

---

[6] To some software developers, 09:00 on Monday is the same, and importantly more useful, than 17:00 on Friday. To someone working with external journalists who have weekend print deadlines, or embargoed press releases, the difference is crucial.

used[7]. You try to reach others who were at the meeting. If you hear back and there still isn't clear agreement, you'll need another meeting to figure out the disconnect. This wastes a lot of time. An even worse scenario is when no-one notices this avoidable disconnect until sometime Friday.

Instead, share the note-taking responsibility by asking everyone to take notes together, in real time. Jointly written and jointly reviewed notes are more accurate. They also eliminate miscommunications—and are easier if you follow some key tips:

◆ As soon as each agenda item is finished, the person who added the item to the agenda immediately writes the notes in the shared, editable agenda document. They should add the notes to the line following their agenda item, and indent the first line. In the meanwhile, everyone else in the meeting starts discussing the next agenda item.

◆ Because everyone keeps the agenda open during the meeting, they can see the notes as they're being written. If anyone sees something missing, or if they disagree with what was written, they can say so immediately. We then go back and revise the shared notes. This is very quick to do, because we are all still in the meeting and the context of the discussion is fresh— after all, we just finished talking about it a minute ago.

◆ End the meeting with "ok, that's all. We covered a lot, so before we drop off, let's take a quick look at the notes. Anyone see anything we missed? Anyone have anything else?" (*Wait in silence while people read and revise notes as needed. This is very fast—usually under a minute.*)

◆ At the end of the meeting, copy the entire agenda-with-embedded-notes into your group's official Single Source of Truth. In some organizations, it might culturally also be important to email the document to a group mailing list[8] or

---

[7] For distributed teams working across multiple timezones, it is easy for a tired person working late on a rapidly approaching deadline to make assumptions about using their local time, or guessing the wrong timezone, unless a timezone is explicitly listed.

[8] When emailing notes, I simply compose a new email, address it to everyone who was invited (and sometimes a few wider distribution lists), add a subject the line with the date and name of the meeting, select-all the agenda-with-inline-notes, copy-paste it into the body of the email, and click Send.

post it on a wiki server[9]. Personally, I think posting to a wiki server is better, because future new hires can read what was covered in meetings prior to their start date.

◆ Replace the shared agenda (and notes) with a new, blank, agenda template, ready and waiting for the next meeting. This keeps the agenda link consistent in the calendar invite, and across all instances of the recurring meeting, so people can immediately start adding items to the agenda for the next meeting.

These shared notes are high-quality and very accurate—and no one is a dedicated note-taker.

Continuing the earlier example about an unclear project deadline, here is an example of shared note-taking: After the group agrees on a project deadline of Friday, the person who added the agenda item adds notes about this decision as they understand it: "Ship by 17:00 Friday." If no time zone was discussed, someone in another time zone will usually ask about that. If someone else in the meeting understood the deadline as 9am Friday or sometime before 9am Monday, they'll immediately ask. Everyone is still in the meeting. Everyone still has the context, because they just talked about it. Everyone is still present, so they can quickly go back, resolve the question, and adjust the notes immediately.

Here is the agenda from "Sharing an Editable Agenda in Advance," updated with notes[10]:

```
Dial-in/video/room info:...
Date: [dd-mmm-yyyy time-with-timezone]
Attendees: [as people join the meeting, they add their own
names here]
```

---

[9] Manual wiki markup is time-consuming. To avoid spending time on wiki markup after every meeting, we found it best to put the wiki syntax into the agenda template. At the end of each meeting, we could select-all and copy the entire agenda-with-inline-meeting-notes, including the preexisting wiki markup. We would then create a new page on the wiki server and hit Save on the new wiki page. Do this consistently over time, and you will build a repository of your meeting notes over years.

[10] This example is shown in wiki markup format. When published on a wiki server, each asterisk appears as an indented bullet point.

```
Upcoming Vacations/OOO:
* Charlie: will be off Friday for car repair work
* Mary: potential jury duty next week.
*  ...
Agenda/Roundtable:
* release date for security fix (john)
** needed before Friday 5pm PST, details in bug#1234567
* update on project snoopy (charlie)
* review of budget numbers (mary)
** looks good—but Mary+Tom to check budget for new
firewall hardware.
* possible dates for Christmas Party (john)
** hold Christmas Party after the big December release
deadline
** 20dec works for everyone; John to confirm date of Dec
release.
*  ...
```

This process requires consistent action. Post notes immediately—at the end of the meeting—before you get distracted by something else. This process is especially crucial for meetings where welcome-if-curious people did not attend. They will probably read those notes after one or two meetings, to make sure nothing unexpected happened. Once they trust the consistent pattern of complete, accurate notes, they will be clearer about whether or not they need to attend a future meeting. If they decide not to attend, they'll be able get other work done. This is success!

Watching the Clock

To help meetings start, run, and end on time, the meeting moderator needs to watch the clock very closely. All. The. Time.

Join the meeting when the 10-minute reminder goes off. Start after three minutes "out of respect for those who were punctual." If the rationale for any of this is unclear, please go back and reread "Meetings."

At the start of a meeting it can feel like there is lots of time to cover agenda items. Somehow, though, after the midway point I find myself focusing on the dwindling time remaining.

My awareness is not enough—*everyone* needs to be aware of the dwindling time. One easy way to do this, as part of wrapping up one agenda item and starting the next agenda item, is to remind attendees how much time is left: "ok, that's done. We have 10 minutes left. Next on the agenda is..." This short verbal nudge reminds people that you are trying to keep the meeting on schedule, and it encourages people to stay on focus. If time runs short, people will volunteer to remove low-priority items from the agenda—either deferring them to a future meeting, or moving them to an off-line discussion.

If the meeting runs long despite your best efforts, explicitly say: "We're 10 minutes over, but I think we're finally done. Thanks everyone for staying late, and we'll do better next time."

If the meeting ends early, explicitly note that too, saying, "We're all done. Early. Everyone gets 10 minutes of life back. Thank you."

Being a Traffic Cop

When I'm the meeting moderator, I watch for the following:

- ◆ Nonverbal cues from the head-and-shoulder video of everyone attending. If someone freezes or disappears (a lost connection), raises their hand on camera (requesting to speak), or moves lips without sound (accidentally muted), I can respond quickly. For more on this, see "Video Etiquette."

- ◆ Messages on the pre-agreed group chat channel for the meeting. When someone is speaking in the meeting, related chatter in the group chat backchannel can speed the meeting along without interrupting the speaker. If we *all* lose video connection, this backchannel lets us know what is happening. Also, people could show support for an idea by commenting in backchannel without needing to take time as a verbal speaker in the meeting.

- ◆ Items added or removed from the shared editable agenda.

- ◆ Note-taking in the agenda.

- ◆ The clock!

Watching all of this while participating in the meeting requires mental focus. However, the improved overall effectiveness of *the many* (the meeting attendees) is well worth the effort by *the one* (the meeting moderator).

Sharing the Moderator Role

Once a recurring meeting has a regular rhythm, it is time to start sharing the moderator role with others. Quietly ask a few group members if they would be willing to run the meeting with your support. After a few different volunteers have run the meeting successfully, roll out a rotating schedule across the group.

When I started sharing the moderator role, I found that asking people to moderate one meeting each did not work. Everyone was able to try moderating more quickly, but they did not have time to learn from their mistakes and improve their moderating skills before it was someone else's turn. Instead, it worked well to have each person moderate a handful of meetings before passing the moderator role to the next person on the schedule. This cadence allowed them to get comfortable moderating the meeting a few times in a row, with increasing success. The cadence also allowed everyone in the group to have their turn and rotate back into role *again* before they forgot how to moderate. For a once-a-week meetings, having each person moderate for a month worked well. For daily meetings, asking each person to moderate for a week worked well.

Sharing the moderator role is important for several reasons:

- ◆ Everyone in the team learns the mechanics of running meetings. As a leader, it is important to avoid being a single point of organizational failure. If you are the only person who knows how to set up and moderate a crucial meeting, things could get messy if you are out sick or you take a vacation. The meeting structure should be familiar to everyone who's been attending the meetings, but being the moderator is very different to attending a meeting that someone else runs. For this, practice makes perfect. Having others learn to moderate, while you are present, helps you mentor them to become successful moderators. When several people are comfortable moderating, those important meetings can continue in your absence without any disruption.

- ◆ If there are vocal meeting critics in your organization, moderating a series of meetings is a great way for them to "walk a mile in your shoes" and experience what it is like to run the exact same meeting themselves. After moderating a few meetings, they tend to have a new appreciation for the moderator role and become less critical, especially when something goes wrong. After I started rotating the moderator role, one of my most vocal meeting critics quietly told me, "I used to sit in your meetings, complaining how bad they were. Now I realize how hard it is to run a good meeting. I don't know how you have the patience for it."

◆ It's good delegation. Setting up a rotation reduced my constant need-to-moderate-and-drive-meeting focus. When the role rotated back to me, I was fresh again after my break. For anyone considering moving into a manager role, learning these meeting moderation skills in advance is helpful.

An unexpected surprise was watching how differently everyone handled things. After people ran a few successful meetings in a row, they started to change things—removing things from the meeting that irritated them, or adding things that they thought would improve the meeting. Many of the improvements outlined here were initiated by others rotating into the moderator role.

If someone changes part of a meeting and you have concerns, talk with the person after the meeting, *privately*. Do not undermine these moderator experiments in public in the meeting. Maybe they see a change that you never thought would be useful. Maybe you will need to explain a previously unstated requirement of the meeting. Either way, rotating the role means it can evolve over time; almost every time the rotation came back to me, the meeting format had changed. Again. And again. As far as I can remember, these changes always improved the meetings.

After everyone learned the mechanics of running meetings, I noticed a more subtle, broader impact. Members of our team attended meetings run by others elsewhere in the company. With their new skills moderating well-run meetings, they now noticed poorly run meetings and would quietly ask their friends: "Hey, we improved our meetings, why don't you improve yours?" and discretely offer suggestions to improve their friend's meetings.

Over time, this culture of quiet improvement spread virally, raising the standard of meetings across the company far more effectively than any edict handed down from upper management.

Single Source of Truth

Takeaways

+ Agree where to write things down, define it as your Single Source of Truth, and then be obsessively consistent about using it!

+ When you need information, look in the Single Source of Truth first, before asking a human.

+ If someone asks you for information that you know is already in the Single Source of Truth, don't repeat what is already written. Instead, respond with the link to that information.

+ If someone has questions after reading your Single Source of Truth, immediately update it with your response, so that others will not need to ask you the same question.

+ As a leader, encourage others to follow these steps when they respond to requests.

In today's world it's easy to get overwhelmed just trying to keep up with discussions and updates. Humans have discussions, ideas, and lively conversations whenever and wherever it suits them: in hallways and meetings, over the phone, via chat or email, and through collaboration on formal documents such as project plans. This creative brainstorming is healthy and productive.

The downside? You need to search numerous channels—email, chat, wiki, and so on—to find and track information you're interested in. It can take a while to find the latest update for a project. How many places do *you* need to look? And how confident are you that you are looking at the latest, most up-to-date details?

This chapter describes an effective approach for consolidating important business information: the Single Source of Truth ("SSoT"). An SSoT makes it quick and easy to find information. It facilitates decision-making; reduces time spent giving status updates via email, phone, and in meetings to folks across the organization looking for status; and reduces time spent sorting through iterations of notes, trying to figure out which is the latest version. When people know where to find the SSoT and trust its contents, they can check it anytime: at night, throughout the day, or on short notice during a crucial high-drama meeting—without being seen as interruptive or a micro-manager. They can even share the SSoT with other leaders across the organization. An SSoT can streamline communications and reduce confusion during emergencies. An SSoT even makes it easier to bring newcomers up to speed on a project.

The productivity gains are substantial.

What is a Single Source of Truth?

Single Source of Truth ("SSoT") is about fostering a shared human mindset and culture where everyone obsessively tracks all information for a given project or task in one well-defined location. When done consistently, the SSoT shares information rapidly and accurately to any interested humans across the organization, while allowing the humans doing the actual work to spend more time doing their work—not spending time talking to all of the different humans asking for status.

If you believe that your team needs to be in the same office so that you can tap someone on the shoulder for status at any time, your organization has no Single Source of Truth ("SSoT"). Lack of SSoT hampers growth, because what works for nine people in a garage will not work for 90 people in a large garage, or nine people in nine garages. Lack of SSoT also exposes your organization to miscommunication errors—the children's game of "telephone" is a sobering example of this, where updates change in subtle yet important ways with each retelling. Lastly, lack of SSoT introduces risk of communication disruption if a key human quits, is out sick, or is unable to get to the office.

Your SSoT should have the following characteristics:

- It is located in a trusted, reliable electronic storage area.
- It is easy to access, search, and update by everyone who needs the information.

- It clearly highlights and timestamps each individual change, so that it is immediately obvious who changed what since you last looked.

- It always contains the latest copy of all important information for a specific project. It might include project specifications and plans, group chat records, relevant snippets from a long email thread, a short summary of a verbal discussion, and links to relevant information in other systems (sales tracking, bug tracking, and so on).

The SSoT is the only reality that matters. Anything written down or stored elsewhere is, by definition, nonessential (and possibly out of date). If you discover other records or documents with contradictory information, the SSoT is always the final authority.

A useful, accurate SSoT requires a specific organizational mindset. Simply saying "write things down" is not enough[1]. Here are several crucial guidelines for creating and maintaining a useful SSoT:

- With your group, agree in advance where to locate the SSoT.

- As a group, be *obsessively* consistent about keeping the SSoT 100% up-to-date. Whenever you hear or discuss something that is important enough to tell others, add it to the SSoT *immediately*. Your work is not finished until you update the SSoT.

- Don't write a thesis. You don't have time for that, and others don't have time to read it. Instead, keep it short. Very short. Use bullet points. Aspire to write the shortest update you can, covering all pertinent facts, accurate to the best of your knowledge. Using the fewest words. I find it helpful to imagine reading this on my smartphone.

- If your updates need to contain detailed notes for humans directly involved with the project, then periodically also post a brief summary for stakeholders who don't need to know or understand all of the minutia. A short one- or two-sentence summary will suffice—focused on any changes relative to their business needs. If they want more information, they can

---

[1] The movie "Office Space" has become a cultural meme on the topic of pointless written "TPS reports," which are then ignored.

read the details in the same SSoT. These updates are a good way to communicate status to different stakeholders—and they remind everyone working on the project how their work is visible across the entire organization.

♦ When you add information about a decision, call it a decision and note who made the decision. This makes it easy for others to follow up with them directly if they have any questions.

♦ If you don't know some of the details, simply say "unknown." If you know who is resolving unknowns, add their names next to the associated unknowns. If no owner is known, say that.

♦ When plans change, update the SSoT with the new information as soon as it comes in.

It's surprisingly quick to update an SSoT using this process. I found that updating the SSoT *saved* me time, by reducing the number of status meetings I had to attend, and the amount of time I spent responding to phone/email requests for updates. I replied to these requests immediately, with a link to the most recent update.

The specific tool you use for an SSoT is less important than simply having an SSoT. Choose a tool that works well for your organization[2]. Mozilla uses Bugzilla. 37signals uses Basecamp. Automattic uses P2. New Relic uses email discussions that end with a human requirement to email a summary. Emergency dispatchers use CAD (Computer Aided Dispatch) systems. Medical doctors use Electronic Medical Record systems[3]. The US Navy uses standing orders. What matters is that everyone across the organization uses the *same* tool; they all have access, know

---

[2] I carefully limit use of cloud based services like Google Drive, Microsoft Office 365, Dropbox, Sharepoint, or other shared file servers. I also avoid long email threads sending Microsoft Office files back-and-forth, with versioning enabled. For all of these, I find it hard to quickly and confidently tell who changed what when. Instead, I find myself relying on human memory to notice changes between what I see now and what I saw last time—a mental tax with risk of human error—which defeats the entire purpose of SSoT.

[3] Sometimes called Electronic Health Records, these electronic systems replace old paper folders of hand written notes taken by the medical doctor.

where to find it, and how to use it; they can easily see who made exactly what changes at exactly what time, and they are 100% dedicated toward keeping the SSoT accurate.

When a team writes and stores clear, concise, timely updates in a prearranged location, their coworkers can quickly access these updates at a time of their choosing, without having to interrupt anyone. This is important for all organizations, especially distributed ones.

Encouraging Culture Change

Creating the technical structure for an SSoT is only part of the work. To realize all of the benefits of an SSoT, it is also important to develop cultural support.

Here is an example of an interaction that will reduce the effectiveness of your SSOT: A senior person asks a junior person for a detailed status update. The junior person stops their work immediately, to give a verbal update.

People are smart. If you ask them to write things down, then you ignore what they wrote and ask them to tell you what they already wrote down, they will notice. Pretty soon, people will stop writing things down because they correctly believe it's a waste of their time.

Instead, if a senior person asks a more junior person for a status update, the junior person should feel comfortable and be encouraged to *not* give a verbal update. Instead, they should politely reply with something like the following: "The SSoT is in ticket#1234. Let me know if you need any other info." If the question was written—in email or group chat—then reply with a clickable link that goes straight to the relevant comment in the SSoT.

Over time, the requester will learn to read the SSoT *before* asking questions or requesting an update. After reading the latest updates, if they still have a question, they should ask for an update! At that point they are usually asking *new* questions, so their question and the new answer should be posted to the SSoT.

In this interaction, both the requester and the recipient have important roles in the culture change. Interactions like these are not disrespectful or unhelpful. They represent the best and fastest way for the person doing the work to give a well-thought-out, accurate summary and for both parties to get back to work quickly.

Culture change is hard. As a leader, consistently model this behavior:

- ◆ Across the group, agree in advance how to handle requests for status updates that are stored in the SSoT.

- ◆ Instead of asking, "What's the status of ...?" try asking, "Where is the latest SSoT for ...?" If someone offers to *tell* you the status, politely stop them and say that you'll let them know if you have questions after you read the SSoT.

- ◆ If you have new, unanswered questions after reading the status in the SSoT, ask them to update the SSoT with the answer, or offer to do it for them. If you have no additional questions, which is ideal, say so—this positive reinforcement is important when forming new cultural habits!

- ◆ Do not assume that silence is good. If you don't hear back after sending the link to the SSoT, follow up to ask if all of their questions were answered. If yes, great. If no, you can answer those new questions immediately, thank them, and let them know that you are updating the SSoT with their question and your response, so anyone else with the same question will see the response.

Watch for reactions when first introducing culture change like this. Initially, people might perceive SSoT-based responses as a brush-off or avoidance. You might need to remind them of the advantages (to them and to the organization) of the SSoT[4]. Similar

---

[4] I've seen people in leadership roles refuse to even *open* the SSoT, insisting, "I don't have time to read your ticket—just tell me the latest update." The SSoT had a concise, up-to-date summary of the info they wanted, but they were used to verbal updates—in the past, written updates were out-of-date.

Once, during an emergency, when a stressed C-level executive snapped at me on the phone, telling me that he wanted status and didn't have time to read the SSoT, I opened the ticket myself and read the most recent entry over the phone—verbatim. His response: "Oh, perfect, that's just what I needed to know, thanks." After the emergency was over, I showed him how I read that update to him from the SSoT,

to the phrase "Don't give someone a fish, teach them how to fish," I think of this as "Don't give someone a status update, teach them how to get their own status update."

Experiment: To measure how well this is working across the organization, find someone outside your group shortly before they make a major irreversible decision. Ask how confident they are that they have the correct, latest status update from your group—without needing a status meeting.

Growing a Shared "Borg" Mindset

How do you know what others are working on, thinking about, and talking about?

One approach is to hold daily status meetings and, between status meetings, ask people to tell each other the latest update. There are several disadvantages to this often-used approach:

- Daily status meetings only work if you are all in the same time zone, your commutes are coordinated, and you have similar workday focus patterns. Those criteria are rarely met, so daily status meetings are often held at times that are convenient for some but disruptive for others.

- Repeated storytelling is time-consuming and location-dependent.

told him how often we updated the SSoT during emergencies, and described how his call disrupted the recovery work.

I also emphasized that the SSoT was available whenever he wanted it, allowing him to get timely information without worrying that he was disrupting humans working on the problem by asking for too many status updates. This is important— I've seen organizational leaders make suboptimal decisions for a project in crisis because they didn't want to ask people for yet another status update between their cadence of hourly calls looking for status.

Changing this mindset takes a pattern of consistent behavior over time across an organization, but as trust grows, an SSoT quickly become indispensable.

◆ As your organization grows, re-telling status for multiple projects to more and more humans simply does not scale.

Instead, clearly communicate status when it is convenient for you, and read everyone else's updates when it is convenient for you.

Start every day by reading your team's private group chat channel in full. Scrolling back through all the messages in this channel is a good way to find out what the other humans in your team have been doing since you were last at your keyboard. This helps build a shared "Borg"[5] mindset with the entire team. For more on this, see "Group Chat Etiquette."

In addition to your team's private group chat channel, there might be a lot of other channels you could read[6]. It is not possible to follow all group chat in all channels all of the time, so don't even try! Instead, treat all group chat as transient and simply ignore any past discussions that might be there. If anything meaningful came up in those random chat discussions, it is the responsibility of those involved to update the relevant SSoT.

This includes you.

Once you know what people are thinking and talking about, there might be new ways to share information. For example, you might publish a saved search query for a ticketing system, to ensure that everyone can quickly find the same set of important tickets for their set of projects. If you are in a management role, regularly review all updates to the tickets. Pay attention to tickets that have *not* been updated in a while—you might need to nudge assignees or reassign the tickets to someone else.

Don't expect everyone to memorize the details of everyone else's work, for every minute of every project. Instead, everyone should have a *rough* idea of what their coworkers are working on, and know where to quickly find the SSoT—confident that it has accurate, up-to-date, detailed status.

---

[5] With apologies to the Borg from Star Trek.

[6] For some reason, I usually find the number of channels at an organization is typically around three times the number of humans?!

To track how this culture change to SSoT is progressing, use your calendar. The tips in "Own Your Calendar" should help your calendar accurately track where you spent your time. This has an important benefit—it lets you look back to see how much time you spent in what types of meetings. Have a look back over the last few weeks and see much time you spent in "tell me status" meetings vs. other types of meetings like one-on-ones, brainstorming/deciding something, coworking. As this SSoT mindset becomes the cultural norm, you'll gradually notice you are attending fewer status meetings, the ones that remain are shorter—and everyone across the team still knows what's going on.

Being Efficient During Emergencies

One way to evaluate how well a team communicates internally is to notice how the team communicates during an emergency, when fast, accurate, efficient communications are essential.

Emergencies usually start with little advance warning. Whether it is someone in support noticing a spike in customer complaints, an operations engineer responding to a production outage, or a first responder arriving at a fire, they start tackling the newly discovered problem while also raising the alert for additional help.

Each new arrival is a welcome relief for the first responder: reinforcements have arrived! However, each new arrival is also an interrupt: they need current status. As more and more help arrives, the first responder with the most current information will spend more and more time on repeated requests to answer the same status questions again and again: What was originally broken? What (if anything) has been done so far? What steps have already been tried? Sometimes new arrivals will ask other recent arrivals or jump to their own conclusions—possibly leading them to work on the wrong thing, add to the confusion, and unintentionally make the situation worse.

Compare this to teams that habitually use a Single Source of Truth in normal day-to-day work. These teams also rely on their SSoT during operational emergencies—when crisply organized communications are essential:

- When the first responder notices an emergency, they create a ticket, log the issue, and describe what they're doing to fix it. The description can be super quick, like "investigating production down" and assigning the ticket to themselves while cc'ing others. This ticket is now the Single Source of Truth (SSoT).

- The ticketing system is connected to the alerting system, so other team members are automatically notified.

- As the first responder continues discovering additional information and trying different fixes, they continue adding brief one- or two-line updates to the SSoT. Nothing fancy or time consuming. Even one-line copy-and-paste commands from their console will be helpful to others when they arrive.

- New arrivals announce their availability when they arrive, and then briefly pause to read the SSoT and understand what has already been done. They do this without needing to interrupt the busy human first responder.

- New arrivals can, in turn, tell later arrivals about the SSoT[7]. After reading the SSoT, new arrivals are now fully up-to-date with accurate information, and they are ready to help. Importantly, any questions they ask now will be *new* questions!

During production outages I've had people across my organization call my cell phone in a panic, looking for status. They called believing it was the best way to get timely status information—without considering how they were complicating my work by taking me and others away from the emergency. Some wanted to know how to help. Some wanted status about uptime. Others wanted to know how the outage would impact ongoing commitments. In each case, I would read them the latest update from the ticket—our SSoT for the outage. Then I would "Cc" them on the ticket, so they would be automatically emailed

---

[7] If you have a pre-agreed group chat channel for emergencies, you can pin this ticket number to the "topic" of the channel. Depending on the system in use for the SSoT, you might also be able to include the ticket number in messages that are sent asking for help.

when we made future updates—reducing the need for them to call me for future updates. If anyone called asking a *new* question, I would add their question and my answer to the same ticket. Similarly, if people asked me questions in email or group chat, I would copy and paste their question and my answer into the ticket.

This habit quickly reduced the number of interrupts from others for questions that had already been asked—and it kept the first responders aware of the visibility of the problem, as well as the value of the "air cover" shielding them from interrupts so they could remain focused on recovering from the outage.

Using a Single Source of Truth like this is *less* intrusive to everyone working the emergency. It reduces the amount of time spent giving status updates. It reduces miscommunications caused by secondhand stories. To do this well in an emergency, the SSoT needs to be a familiar process for everyone—hence the importance of habitually using SSoT for normal work activities.

After the emergency is over, the automatic timestamps in the SSoT have an additional benefit: Each update shows the timeline of steps taken during the emergency work. This makes postmortems[8] easier, more accurate, and more productive. It also helps ensure that the people who resolved the problem get credit and recognition for their urgent recovery work.

Out of Sight, Out of Mind?

Recognizing humans for doing good work can be a challenge regardless of whether the organization is all-in-one-building, spread-across-one-campus, or distributed-with-no-office.

When you and your team do good work, it is important that other humans recognize your work. Instead of feeling a need to brag (and possibly airbrushing over any mistakes), be truthful and tell the good with the bad. When something goes well, say it. When

---

[8] It is important to meet after each emergency is over to figure out what went well, and what could be improved. Depending on your organization, these may have slightly different formats, and be called Postmortem, After Action Hotwash, RCA (Root Cause Analysis) or similar.

something goes wrong, be equally vocal letting others know about the problem, what steps were taken to fix it, and what steps were taken to make sure it never happens again.

Making sure that your work, and the work of your team, is clearly visible can be difficult: gender, race, and culture are some of the many human factors that limit our willingness to publicize our work. For more on this, see "Diversity." I struggle with it daily. For years, I focused on quietly doing work, assuming that others would notice my accomplishments and reward me appropriately with pay increases, bonuses and promotions. Sometimes that happened. Usually, however, I was disappointed when others claimed recognition and reward for work I had done. When I started leading teams, I wanted the work of humans across my teams to be visible to me. As part of this, I started thinking about how to make sure our work was visible to others—in an easy self-documenting way that did not get in the way of doing the actual work.

Instead of the more traditional "Management by Walking Around," newer approaches like "Management by Objective" and "Results Only Work Environment" focus on the work people are expected to do, and hold them accountable to their commitments. It did not matter how many hours they sat at their desk (in the office, at home or elsewhere). The basic idea is that you each agreed what to do and you each agreed when the work was done in an objectively measurable way.

I found a helpful twist to these new(ish) philosophies was to write down updates in one place *as you work*. Consistently updating your Single Source of Truth lets others easily see your work *as you progress*. These updates show exactly who has been doing the work, so stakeholders across the organization can correctly credit the human who did the work. These updates also remind everyone that their work is visible across the entire organization.

> *"If people write up what they're working on, then others will have a greater appreciation for the work they're doing. Writing things down isn't just for other people—it helps people replay their day themselves and keep a log of their work."*
>
> Jason Fried, CEO Basecamp/37signals

Email Etiquette

Takeaways

◆ Archive email by year so you don't need to waste time thinking about which folder to save email in—or later, remembering which folder to look through.

◆ Create filters to color-code the importance of each incoming email, and then deal with each email based on priority.

◆ When sending email, make sure the "To" and "Cc" fields are accurate.

◆ Adjust the email subject before replying, when appropriate.

◆ Use "just fyi" and "tl;dr" when appropriate.

Distributed teams tend to use written communication a lot, so it should be no surprise that being more effective with email helps you be more effective at your job. For me, the surprise was *just how much* of an immediate and recurring improvement this made.

After experimenting with ways to improve how I handled email, I now spend less time *every day* on the recurring mental tax of simply operating my email. I experienced much less stress about the possibility of missing urgent emails. My coworkers spent less time waiting for me to reply to them.

Your email settings—and how you handle your email—is 100% in your control. Start improving your email efficiency today.

Is Your Email System a Friend or Foe?

"I get too much email!" is a very common complaint these days. Email is a pervasive part of our lives, yet how often do we step back and think about how to use it more efficiently?

When you improve email efficiency, you gain immediate benefits when working with people all in one location. These improvements become even more essential when working with people in different locations.

In my last few jobs, I got a lot of email from internal stakeholders, coworkers, and (usually only unhappy) external customers. In addition, I got computer-generated emails from production monitoring systems and ticketing systems—emails that I (or anyone else in the company!) thought I needed to see. It was not unusual to receive a few thousand emails a day, with only a slight dip on weekends and holidays. Email arrived in a never-ending stream: urgent customer escalations, production outages (some of which had already self-recovered), CEO requests for revised budget numbers, administrivia about new HR policies, requests to reschedule routine meetings, personnel issues, external vendor contacts, details about company parties, and announcements of upcoming vacations.

Before I could delete an email I had to ask myself, "Am I certain I will *never* need this email in the future?" Some emails were clearly not important and could be deleted immediately. Others were crucial and needed to be kept for years due to legal requirements, such as personnel decisions, or potential liability issues around product tradeoff decisions made when shipping a product. Most were in an annoying gray zone.

It took time and focus to weed through this sheer volume of email, looking for anything urgent that needed quick action. Sometimes an email was urgent enough that I dropped everything and ran to address it[1]. In general, though, the signal-to-noise ratio was low for emails I wanted to keep. After a few minutes of intense focus, it was easy to lose concentration for a few seconds—just long enough to accidentally delete an urgent email.

The need to make so many keep-or-delete decisions throughout the day was intrusive, mentally draining, and stressful. I

---

[1] On bad days, I would find and immediately deal with emergency #1, only to return and discover that there was an unrelated emergency #2 waiting for me further down in my inbox. On even worse days, while I was working on emergency #1 I'd get a phone call interrupting me to ask me about emergency #2, which I had been blissfully unaware of.

continually wondered if the next email would be an emergency. Reading my email became a never-ending, full time job—never mind *doing* anything as a result of what I found in my inbox, or even writing a thoughtful response back!

When I returned from a no-laptop vacation, it took so much dedicated focus time to catch up on my vacation backlog—while also dealing with new incoming emails—that by the time I caught up on my email, I felt like I needed another vacation. Later I tried taking my laptop with me on vacation, so that I could spend a few hours a day keeping up with email[2].

How I handled email was hampering my work. I spent too much time dealing with the *mechanics* of my email, and not enough time dealing with the *contents* of my email.

It wasn't just a matter of working harder; I was already running fast, keeping up as well as I could. No matter how much faster or longer I worked, I was never going to get ahead of the never-ending stream—so I started experimenting with how I handled email. This chapter summarizes a few years of trial-and-error experiments, describing what did and didn't work—and why.

Using these techniques, I no longer missed crucial emails. When someone emailed me they got their answer more quickly, and I started getting emails that started with, "Thanks for the speedy response!" If they needed more details, the topic was still fresh in both of our minds; we still had mental context and could resolve it quickly. Responding quickly to important emails also had a strange side effect: people tended to respond faster *to me*, helping *me* be more effective at my job.

I had fewer impromptu meeting interrupts—people found that it was faster and easier to reach me and get a response in email instead of calling a meeting. This was especially helpful for people in other physical locations. Sometimes we still needed a meeting, but a lot of smaller items no longer needed a meeting. This freed up time for the items that did merit a meeting.

---

[2] Another approach I saw was to take vacation without a laptop. On the first day back at work, they deleted their entire inbox and sent one email saying, "I'm back and declaring email bankruptcy. If there was anything urgent while I was away, please resend." For more about this, see "What Did NOT Work."

What Did NOT Work

When I started rethinking how I handled email, I found of a lot of suggestions on the internet and in books. My friends offered suggestions too. I tried anything that seemed halfway reasonable. Here is a summary of experiments I tried that did not work for me —and why:

♦ *Sort inbox by date, oldest first*: Reading emails in the sequence they arrived (oldest first), helped me see how a discussion progressed. By the time I reached the last email on a thread, I had full context and could give a well-informed response. However, every so often I sent a response, only to find a response from someone else later in my inbox—my response was out of date. Annoyingly, sometimes I would finally read the last email on the thread to discover that the issue had been resolved, there was nothing for me to do and I could have deleted the entire thread.

♦ *Sort inbox by date, newest first*: I tried sorting my inbox in the opposite direction (newest first), which was a slight improvement. I would find the email saying the emergency was over before I found the email saying there was an emergency, which was an improvement in terms of my own time and focus. I saw the most recent response first, which was often enough to understand the situation. One drawback was that if someone trimmed out some of the discussion, I needed to find an older, more complete email in the thread, so that I had full context before I replied.

♦ *Open emails one at a time, in a full window with email preview disabled*: I thought this approach would help me handle each email faster, because adjacent emails would not be visible so it would help me focus. Instead, the load time for each email took slightly longer—enough to be intolerable when dealing with so many emails. Even worse, when I later opened an email that was part of a thread I'd already replied to, I needed to figure out if this email was after my reply (and needed further attention), or before my reply (and could be immediately archived). I also found that the one-at-a-time view meant that I couldn't see the current email within the context of other email in my inbox. Was it part of a hot-and-heavy thread with 50 responses in the last hour? Were there multiple concurrent threads on the same topic? I quickly abandoned this approach, and switched back to using email preview mode.

- ◆ *Create folders for specific topics, and manually move emails from my inbox into these folders after reading them*: This sounds easy, but some emails cover multiple topics, so could correctly go into multiple possible folders. Deciding which folder to use became yet another decision, adding to the decision fatigue. Months later, when I looked for an old email I needed to figure out where I moved it. I found myself scanning multiple folders, only to find some emails for a topic in one folder, and other emails for the same topic in a different folder! This caused me to doubt myself: I wondered if I was really looking at the latest email, or if I should keep looking for a more recent email in yet another folder.

- ◆ *Create filters to automatically and immediately move incoming emails to predetermined folders*: With this approach I expected to have more time, and better focus, because my emails were automatically organized by topic or source. I created folders called *boss*, *customers*, and *bugmail* (for automated emails from our ticketing system); several folders for mailing lists I was on (such as a folder called *release-drivers* for all emails on the "release-drivers@" mailing list); and a folder called *alerts* for all alerts sent by our production monitoring systems. My filters automatically moved new email from my inbox into one of these folders, leaving a smaller set of emails that did not meet any of my filters. It was much easier to read through my inbox. However, while my emails were now nicely filtered into different folders, I didn't actually open any of those folders to read them—I had an "all done with inbox, now get back to work" mindset, and I rarely had time to catch up on all folders. Only when someone asked me about an emergency-in-progress would I open that relevant folder— and find a long series of emails that I'd been blissfully unaware of. There were also problems with emails about multiple topics being filtered into the wrong folder.

- ◆ *Rely on the sender of the email to correctly indicate if their email is urgent*: To mark an email as urgent, a sender might include the word "urgent" in the subject or set the priority flag in their email client. Relying on these indicators did not work, for two reasons: First, most people send email without taking the time to set the priority in their email client. (Some might not even know their email program has that option—and some email programs make this rarely used feature intentionally hard to find.) Second, some people specify "urgent" to get the recipient's attention, even when their email is not urgent[3].

◆ *Declare email bankruptcy*: This might sound tempting when circumstances are unexpectedly difficult. However, like crash diets and financial bankruptcy, this extreme step isn't a long-term solution—the person also needs to change underlying habits that got them into the situation. Until I had a way to handle the volume of email flowing into my inbox, I brought my laptop on vacations to avoid declaring email bankruptcy when I returned after each vacation.

While many of these ideas helped, I still spent too much time dealing with the *mechanics* of my email, and not enough time actually dealing with the *contents* of my email. The remainder of this chapter describes ideas that helped me be more effective with email, freed up a lot of my time, and helped me be more productive.

Color Coding Emails Automatically

Define color-coding filters to mark the importance of each incoming email. When email messages arrive in my inbox, my filters leave them in my inbox, and color-code the messages based on three simple rules:

◆ *VIP* (red): The email is "To," "Cc" or "From" someone on a list of very important people. Examples include: my boss and anyone else at the CxO level, external customers, investors, and their assistants. My immediate family members and close friends are also on this list.

◆ *Important* (orange): The email is "To," "Cc" or "From" someone on a list of people I think are important in another

---

[3] Over time people learned to ignore "URGENT" from that person, so when a *real* emergency happened, the sender had to use "URGENT URGENT URGENT!!!" to get attention. Declaring a false emergency impacts how people react to you if a genuine emergency arises. If you're tempted to send emails with the word "Urgent" or "Emergency" in the subject, re-read Aesop's fable, "The Boy Who Cried Wolf."

way. Examples include: VPs, managers in different areas of the company, and point-people working on crucial projects.

♦ *Maybe Important* (green): The email is addressed "To" or "Cc" me *and* the sender is someone I know, or there is mention of my name "joduinn" in the body of the email[4].

All other email messages are left uncolored (in black text).

When I open my inbox, I read all of the red emails first. If necessary, I reply and then archive or delete each message. After I have handled all of the red emails, I handle any orange emails. If I only have three to five minutes to check email, this is all I do. Then I stop—with peace of mind. I've handled all of the emails I deem most important, so my risk of missing or deleting an important email is significantly reduced. If I have more time, then I do the same with any green emails. If there are no more red, orange, or green emails in my inbox, I start reading the remaining (black) emails.

This experiment started gradually, adding one person to a color filter whenever I had time. As more people were added, it quickly proved useful. For this to work, it is critically important that the color-coding filters continue to be accurate over time. If I find an email that was incorrectly left black when it should have been red, orange, or green, I fix the filter immediately. Then I verify that the email now appears red, orange, or green.

I only leave a red, orange, or green email in my inbox when I need to do something with it as soon as possible. I reply to most email within minutes of leaving my previous meeting; it is rare that I still have any red or orange emails by the end of the day.

Some mailing list software includes extra header information that you can use when setting up your filters. For software that does not have this information, you can prevent extra highlighting by using a variation of your address—for example, using the following address:

---

[4] I tried to use the color green for any email that mentioned "John" or my surname, but there are too many people called John, and too many people mistype my surname, so the filter didn't work well. My Unix login ID of "joduinn" is a unique string that worked well with my filters.

yourname+mailinglist1@yourcompany.com. Most email servers will still send that email to your usual email account, so all emails will correctly show up in your inbox.

Your red, orange, and green filters will leave those mailing-list emails color-coded black, not green. This is much less intrusive when scanning your inbox for red, orange, or green emails. Of course, if someone adds you to the "To" or "Cc" field, the red, orange, and green filters will highlight it as usual.

Using Archive Folders

It's confusing and time-consuming to search through different email folders to find an old email. Instead of creating folders for different topics, and later wondering where to look, create an archive folder for all emails. You can then use fast, full-text search to quickly skip figuring out where you manually stored an email.

Hosted email providers like Google Gmail and Microsoft Outlook (in Office 365) have no operating system file limit, so you can save all emails in one "Archive" folder. To find an email in this (large!) folder, use full-text search.

For email stored on your laptop, keep in mind that each operating system has limits on the size of a directory. After hitting this limit once, I now archive all email on my laptop using a separate archive folder for each year. For example, at time of writing, my archive folder is called Archive/2021.

- ∨ ✉ **john@oduinn.com**
  - ☑ **Inbox (277)**
  - ◁ Sent
  - ☐ Trash
- ∨ ☐ **Local Folders**
  - ▤ **Drafts (195)**
  - ∨ ☐ Local-Archives
    - ☐ 1996
    - ☐ 1997
    - ☐ 1998
    - ☐ 1999
    - ☐ 2000
    - ☐ 2001
    - ☐ 2002
    - ☐ 2003
    - ☐ 2004
    - ☐ 2005
    - ☐ 2006
    - ☐ 2007
    - ☐ 2008
    - ☐ 2009
    - ☐ 2010
    - ☐ 2012
    - ☐ 2013
    - ☐ 2014
    - ☐ 2015
    - ☐ 2016
    - ☐ 2017
    - ☐ 2018
    - ☐ 2019
    - ☐ 2020
    - ☐ 2021 (140)

Archive all email, one folder per year.

I use Mozilla Thunderbird as my email client on my laptop[5]—not just because I used to work at Mozilla, but because I think it is a great email application. It handles high volumes of email reliably, works well offline, and has a lot of useful features. One of my favorite features is its archive-by-year function. By pressing just one key, you can move a selected email to the appropriate archive folder based on the timestamp of the email. For example, if I select one or more emails sent to me this year and press the letter "A", Thunderbird moves the selected email(s) from my inbox to the Archive/2021 folder. At the start of each new year, Thunderbird automatically creates a new folder for the new year![6]

As soon as I finish reading an email—while still in preview mode —I either press the letter "A" to move it from my inbox to the archive folder for this year, or I press "Delete" to move it to trash folder. Either way, the email is out of my inbox quickly, with only one keystroke.

Thunderbird also supports customization through the use of software extensions and automated macros. I use an extension called "Send and Archive[7]," which gives me a "Send and Archive" button beside the usual "Send" button. When replying to an email, I click "Send and Archive" to send my reply and also move the email I was replying to from my inbox to the archive folder[8]. This reduces archiving to literally zero effort.

---

[5] An email client is software used for sending, receiving, and managing email. Examples include Mozilla Thunderbird, Microsoft Outlook and Apple Mail.

[6] Occasionally I receive an email with a timestamp of 1st Jan 1970, sent from a misconfigured email client. Depending on the time zone, these emails archive into folder Archive/1969 or Archive/1970. When this happens, I nudge the sender to fix their email client.

[7] This "Send and Archive" extension recently stopped working because of Thunderbird internal API changes. I keep mention of it here, while I keep watch for an updated version of the extension that works with the newer internal APIs. Meanwhile, I've recreated this functionality using Thunderbird automated filters.

[8] If you use Google's web-based gmail, there is a similar "send and archive" option in Labs, which is similar.

Every morning, I move all email from my Sent folder to the archive folder. It's quick (Select-All and then press "A" to move to the archive folder). This gives me a quick chance to remember who I sent emails to yesterday, on what topics. When finished, I see a clean empty Sent folder before I start my day—something I find oddly satisfying. This step ensures that all emails, including replies sent by me, can be found when later searching the archive folder[9].

This archiving process, with its arrangement of archive folders by year, makes it trivially simple for me to store and later search for past email. This is a vast improvement over my earlier search-multiple-custom-folders approach, and reduces my decision fatigue. Finally, when searching, I am much more confident that I have found all of the right emails. For very old topics, it also helps me recall what else was happening around that time.

Using the Preview Window, Threaded, Sorted by Date

When dealing with a high volume of emails in your inbox, I found opening each email one-at-a-time simply takes too long. Instead, it was faster to skim read through an inbox using preview mode. After some experiments, I found it fastest to use a three-panel layout in my email client:

- ◆ The preview panel covers the lower two-thirds of my email window, big enough to show the first few parts of the selected email, the subject, and all recipients.

- ◆ The inbox panel at the top right of my email window is big enough to see the sender and subject of the emails before and

---

[9] This habit also helps you avoid losing email if your physical phone or computer is damaged, due to technical details of how SMTP and IMAP email protocols work. Most email systems use IMAP for inbox and archive folders, replicating between your local physical device and your email provider's hosted cloud servers, so you automatically have immediate backups as each email arrives, is moved or deleted. However, outgoing email uses SMTP, which (depending on your settings) often means that the email in your local "sent" folder is the only copy you have. This puts you at risk of losing all emails from the "sent" folder if your device is damaged. Also, keeping years of emails in a local "sent" folder can hit operating system limits. To reduce these risks, I recommend a routine daily habit of moving all emails from "sent" to your per-year archive folder.

after the selected email. All replies on a thread are grouped together. Emails are sorted by date—the oldest email is at the top of the thread, the newest are at the bottom.

◆ The left sidebar contains a list of folders.

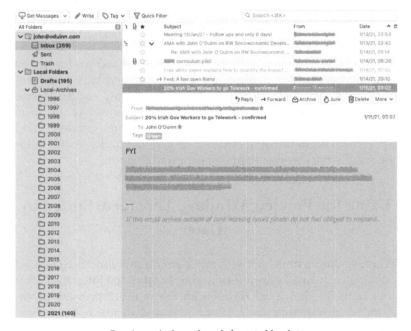

Preview window, threaded, sorted by date

Using this approach, I can quickly see any red, orange, or green emails. With one mouse click I can preview the first part of each email.

At the same time, I can see each email in the context of all other emails in my inbox. This helps me notice hot-and-heavy threads, such as 50 responses from VIPs in the last hour, or multiple concurrent threads about the same topic.

Email "threading" keeps a series of related emails together. This helps me quickly navigate a thread of red, orange, or green emails. It's easy to preview the first and last emails in a thread and quickly decide if I need to read the entire thread. If the first and last email aren't interesting and all of the other emails in the thread are black (not red, orange, or green), I archive or delete the entire discussion thread. This by itself is a massive timesaver. When replying to a discussion thread, I move the entire thread to archive with one quick and satisfying click on "Send and Archive."

As soon as I delete or archive the selected email, my email client displays a preview of the next email.

Asking Humans to Send You Email

As a manager, a large part of my role was removing obstacles to help others get their work done.

When someone asked me to help them—in a one-on-one meeting, a group meeting, or an impromptu corridor conversation or video call—I used to say: "Yes, I'm happy to help you. Let me check and get back to you." Soon afterwards, I would start to write an email, but stop when I realized the request for approval also needed important context. Context I did not have summarized.

In my attempt to be helpful, I had just volunteered myself into writing a summary of someone else's project and their problem at hand. This was time-consuming and usually got interrupted, so this email would linger in my drafts folder. On my constant email treadmill, if an email scrolled out of sight I never saw it again. It was literally out of sight, out of mind. Later, when they asked me for an update, I realized I had never sent the email—it was still sitting in my draft folder, half-written. Even worse, they remained blocked, waiting for me to do what I had agreed to do—simply send an email.

This was my own fault, and I set myself up for this. Over and over again. After several embarrassing situations, I fixed this by changing *how* I agreed to help others.

Now, when someone asks me to help, I say: "Yes, I'm happy to help unblock you. Can you do me a favor and send me an email summarizing this problem, the gotchas, and why you need this? Nothing long or detailed. Keep it short, one to three paragraphs max, so people will read it. Even just writing down everything you told me just now would be perfect. Oh, and check for typos, because when I get your email, know that I will immediately forward it, cc-ing you, along with my approval, up to ..." At the same time, I clarify that this is not a Dilbert-style "pointy haired boss" delaying tactic. I explain that this will make things faster, ensures that the email writeup is accurate (because it's written by the person who knows the area best), and eliminates the risk that I will forget an important detail. I don't need to put the item on my to-do list, except maybe to remind the person for email if I don't get it quickly—but this is rare, because they want it done!

This streamlined my work—and I quickly discovered that others preferred this too, for several reasons:

- ♦ They don't have to worry that I will remember all of their project details correctly.

- ♦ The person asking will do a good job explaining the problem *because they know it best*. (I do proofread the email before forwarding it, and I occasionally propose small changes to make it more readable to the intended audience.)

- ♦ It's a quick, efficient request for my time. All I'm doing is forwarding an email with a quick approval message, or context on the urgency, instead of spending most of my time writing the initial summary.

- ♦ It's an effective use of delegation. As a manager I now spend more of my time on work that *only* I can do, which helps everyone in the group be more productive. It also helps raise people's visibility across the organization.

- ♦ If I declare victory, saying we did what was asked, but the original person remains blocked, we can go back to the original email together and figure out the cause of the disconnect.

For me, this process is typically faster—not slower—than having a meeting about the same topic. When something is urgent I can talk or video-call with all parties immediately. I don't recall ever needing to call, though, because email is fast. I have fewer meetings, less confusion about agreed-upon decisions, and my coworkers get what they need quickly, regardless of their location.

Making the "To" and "Cc" Fields Accurate

When writing a new email—or replying to an existing email thread[10]—I quickly check the "To" and "Cc" fields as follows:

- ◆ I make sure that the people I need an answer from are listed in the "To" field. If they were in the "Cc" field, I move them to "To"; if they received the email because they were a member of a cc'd mailing list, I add their name to the "To" field. This helps others see the thread quickly, if they use inbox filters. In addition, in the body of the email, I explicitly address "To" recipients by name on the very first line of the email, so they know to read further. If an email is "To Chip, Mary" and the first line starts with "Hi Chip, Mary," everyone can see who is expected to respond.

- ◆ If I don't need a response from someone, but think they might want to be included, I move them from "To" to "Cc."

- ◆ If I think some people no longer need to be included, I move them to "Bcc." In addition, in the body of the email, I explicitly state on the first line that I've done this. For example, "(Moving Jean to bcc to spare him the noise.)" This will allow them to see my decision and ask to be re-added if interested.

On a long email thread I add a first line that directs recipients to specific parts of the thread; for example, "Hi Chip, see comments inline below. John." Now, when Chip opens the email, he immediately sees his name on the first line, and he knows to scroll down the long discussion to find my comments. He will also see adjacent discussion, for context. In contrast, if you reply-all to a long email discussion and, without warning, insert a comment four pages down saying, "Hi Chip, do you know the answer to this?" he might miss the question unless he scrolled through the entire email, in every email in the thread, looking for any mention of his name. It's not fair to the recipient; you wouldn't want someone to do this to you.

Effective use of "To," "Cc," and tailored opening lines makes it easier for others to prioritize your message and, if necessary,

---

[10] On a long, crowded email thread it's easy for the "To" and "Cc" fields to diverge from the two guidelines.

respond efficiently. Raising this as a culture in the team will encourage others to do that when emailing you—which helps you be more effective with your email.

Using "fyi" and "tl;dr"

Use "For Your Information" ("fyi") and "Too Long; Didn't Read" ("tl;dr")[11] for sharing email context and summarizing main points, while also clearly signaling that no immediate action is expected of the reader.

When I receive an email thread about a strategically important topic or potential political hot potato and my management chain is not already on the thread, I forward the email to them. I include a concise summary at the top; for example, "Nothing to do, just fyi. John." When they open the email they know that I do not expect any action, but they are now aware of the issue. They will not be blindsided by it later. Because I forward the most recent email on the discussion thread, if anyone wants more information they can simply read more of the discussion contained in the email.

When an email thread is complex, "fyi" isn't enough. Instead, I forward the thread and add a short summary at the top for context. Here is an example:

```
tl;dr: It looks like we're not going to make the December
release. If we make it, it will be two weeks late because
of the Christmas party. Investigating possible breach of
support contract depending on exact revised date. See
details below.
Nothing for you to do yet, just FYI.
John.
...
```

Almost every boss over my career has told me (without prompting) that they find these summary emails useful, especially the explicit "nothing to do" part[12]! While I mainly use this for communicating upward to my boss, I've found equal success using

---

[11] This used to be called an "Executive Summary."

[12] For more on this, see Angell, D. & Heslop, B. (1994). *Elements of E-mail Style.* Addison-Wesley.

"fyi" and "tl;dr" to share and summarize email discussions to my group, and across to managers of other groups elsewhere in the company.

Writing Like a Journalist

Journalists put a lot of attention into how they structure an article. They use a technique called the inverted pyramid, based on the idea that most people only read the first paragraph or two in an article before deciding whether to continue reading or move on to another article:

+ The first paragraph gives the reader overall context—the essentials, in the shortest possible number of words. This lets readers decide if they care enough to continue reading.

+ Additional paragraphs supply details for readers who want more information.

In a last-minute rush, if the newspaper editor needs to trim a few column inches from a story, they typically trim the last few paragraphs.

You can do something similar when writing an email, but instead of thinking about newspaper columns, think in terms of people reading your email on their phone. You want them to see the context of your email quickly, so they can decide if they care to read further, or not.

If your email is a long, detailed explanation of why a project is important, and the project needs speedy approval for funds, consider starting your email with something like the following:

```
tl;dr: We need Project Snoopy to compete in the mobile
marketplace. It'll cost x, and best case will ship in 6
months. If we start next week, we might be ready for the
big conference. I think we should do this, even though we
will need to reassign people and delay other projects,
like Project Aurora.
For the curious, see details below.
John.

Background: ...
```

For some readers, the one-line summary will be enough to grant approval and stop reading. For readers who want to dig further, they quickly have context. They can then decide if they are curious enough to read the multi-page detailed description of business, market, and technical issues of the project.

> *"Being a good writer is an essential part of being a good remote worker."*
>
> *Jason Fried & David Heinemeier Hansson, co-founders of Basecamp/ 37signals*

Making the "Subject" Match Reality

When an email discussion goes back and forth and the topic drifts, adjust the email "Subject" line to match reality. This sounds obvious, but it is rarely done in reality—and sometimes this oversight can cause operational problems.

Anytime I see an email thread discussion morph, I change the subject to match. I do so carefully, retaining the original subject. For example, changing "Subject: old topic" to "Subject: new topic [was "old topic"]."

I first discovered the importance of this in a long email thread where lots of people were talking about holiday party logistics, possible venue locations, and dates. At some point, somebody asked, "Hey, will that date disrupt the December software release?" Someone else replied, "Yes." Suddenly, 15 emails into the Christmas party planning thread, we had a very serious operational discussion about schedule impact to a publicly committed release. I expected several people—who cared about this release and were on the email thread—to respond, but they didn't. (I found out later that they simply stopped reading the never-ending "Christmas party planning" email thread.) I changed the subject from "Christmas party planning" to "Impact to December release schedule [was "Christmas party planning"]," wrote "tweaking subject to match reality" on the first line of the email and hit Send.

Everyone on the thread instantly knew that the discussion had shifted. The people who cared about the December release started reading the thread again. By modifying—but not completely replacing—the subject, people could also quickly find the original discussion, simply by remembering that it was something to do with the Christmas party.

Organizing Mailing Lists

Organizations often have numerous mailing lists, which make it easy to broadcast email to groups of humans based on organizational structure or topics of interest. Your organization's mailing lists should be crisply arranged and continuously maintained.

This quiet maintenance work helps others know who should subscribe to each mailing list. It can take time to do this, but it saves significantly more time by preventing confusion caused when some (but not all) of the needed people are on an email list. Clarity about who needs to subscribe to each mailing list is good for organizational efficiency. It also helps new hires succeed, because they won't miss important emails.

Set up one mailing list for your organizational team. When someone in your group wants to join another mailing list, ask them to add your group's mailing list (not their individual name) so that everyone in the group receives those emails. This has two important benefits. Firstly, everyone in the group has context if someone on an important project is unexpectedly out sick. Secondly, as a hiring manager you only need to add new employees to one mailing list—your own team list.

Periodically review which email lists you are on:

- For each list, ask yourself: "Do I really need to be on this list?" If your job has changed over time, maybe a list you used to be very active on is no longer relevant.

- If you are on a mailing list where you almost always delete incoming emails without reading them, consider unsubscribing. If unsubscribing feels uncomfortable to you, create a filter that moves all emails from that list into a temporary to-be-deleted folder. Review that folder after a month. If you can delete every email in your to-be-deleted folder, then unsubscribe.

Depending on organizational culture, sometimes unsubscribe quietly. Other times I announce that I'm leaving the list due to changes in my workload, and I ask people to cc me if something related to my work comes up in the future. Interestingly, when I started doing, this several others followed my lead—they unsubscribed from lists that were no longer useful to them. This started a wider discussion about deleting obsolete lists—a healthy sign.

If you find yourself getting a lot of irrelevant email from a specific list, and you have already confirmed that you should be on the list, it's possible that the messages are being sent to the wrong mailing list. Is there is a different list that would be better suited for them? If so, then reply-all, add the new mailing list, and move the incorrect mailing list to the "Bcc" field (so they'll see themselves being dropped, but they'll be spared from future reply-all emails). Include a one-line comment like the following:

```
This looks off topic for mailing list #1, so I'm moving
mailing list #1 to bcc, and adding mailing list #2.
If I've missed something, please undo with details.
John.
```

Managing Automated Emails

Organization-wide monitoring, ticketing[13], and customer support systems generate a range of alerts and notification messages. This is a mixed blessing. When configured correctly, these systems send messages to a single location (your inbox), and they only send messages when something serious needs attention. When the systems are configured incorrectly, they become highly efficient spam generators, flooding your inbox.

No matter how much I've tried, I've never managed to get these systems to generate zero spam. I have come to accept that there will always be some noise, but it's still worthwhile to spend some time on improving the signal-to-noise ratio. Here are several suggestions:

---

[13] By "ticketing systems" I mean systems that track issues, bugs (for engineering organizations), customer relationships (for sales organizations), and so on. All of these systems generate email notifications automatically.

◆ As with mailing lists, notice when you find yourself continually deleting emails as not-useful. When that happens, consider changing your ticketing system preferences to reduce the number of areas that you are notified about. While it's nice to think that you can watch all updates in all areas all of the time, it is simply not practical. More bluntly, it distracts you from keeping your own areas under control. If someone in another area needs your help they can mention you by name, which means you will get a "green" email in your inbox. This generates a much better signal-to-noise ratio.

◆ Send automated alerts to an email list, not an individual. That way, if the main recipient is on vacation or it is the middle of the night in their time zone, others will see it and react. While it can be tempting to create a separate list for alerts, you would need to maintain two mailing lists, and it is too easy to forget to add new hires to the second list.

◆ Continuously evolve your filters. When an alert comes in for something that *is* an emergency, deal with the emergency—then adjust your color-coding filters to highlight that alert (and any future alerts like it) as "red." Similarly, if an alert came in as "red" but should be highlighted orange or green, adjust the filter.

◆ Set up your ticketing system so that if anyone in your group notices a discussion or issue of interest to the group, they can quickly add the email list for the entire team as a "watcher" of a ticket. The entire group will start receiving updates to this ticket and, so everyone is automatically kept informed. This works much better than trying to add individual team members—it's less error-prone, it's faster, and I found it quickly helped improve our cross-group awareness.

Lastly, if you are getting updates about an issue you don't care about, find out why. Sometimes, the issue was filed incorrectly. This means people who don't care are getting updates, and more importantly, people who *do* care are *not* getting updates. If that's the case, I move the ticket to the correct area while adding a comment like "Moving to correct component, so the relevant people are notified."

Group Chat Etiquette

Takeaways

- Have everyone use the same group chat system.

- Arrange chat channels carefully. Too many, or too few, channels are counterproductive.

- Use public channels by default, private team channels when appropriate, and private one-to-one direct messages when needed.

- Moderate all channels. Some idle chatter is healthy, but too much is disruptive.

- Set explicit expectations on response times, so others can plan their work accordingly.

- Treat all chat as transient. Copy any important discussions to Single Source of Truth.

Group chat applications allow everyone in an organization to send text messages to each other, quickly and easily through real-time text messages. Group chat is very useful for simple questions and rapidly paced text-based conversations.

To help organize how humans communicate, chat applications arrange these conversations into groups, often called *channels* or *rooms*.

These channels can be *public* (entire organization or wider internet can join), *private* (only selected individuals are invited to join) or *direct message* (one-to-one private communications, also called "DM"). In addition to arranging channels by group or by organizational function, organizations can create channels for use as backchannel in video calls. You can also directly message ("DM") one or more coworkers, by creating dedicated channels between specific individuals.

Group chat is less intrusive than impromptu office chatter and daily standup meetings, because you can catch up on what others are doing at a time of *your choosing*, instead of being interrupted at a time of *the other person's choosing*! This is especially important for distributed teams.

There are various competing chat tools available—as standalone apps, as features in audio-video tools, and as part of some enterprise collaboration software packages. The specific tool isn't important; I've seen IRC, Slack, Microsoft Teams[1], Signal, WhatsApp and others used well and used poorly. Well-organized group chat, with good social etiquette, will speed up discussions, reduce long email threads, and eliminate some meetings. However, poorly organized group chat will become yet another endless stream of messages that people need to try to keep up with.

Use One System

The goal of group chat is to reduce barriers to cross-organizational communication, allowing people across different groups to communicate with each other quickly and easily. This is useful in general, and it is especially important to have a chat system in place before an unexpected emergency forces humans who don't typically work together to coordinate with each other quickly.

When an organization implements group chat, it might be tempting to allow different groups to choose which program to use—the experience of individual choice might feel good. However, this approach creates barriers to cross-group communication. Before you can send a cross-group chat message, you need to confirm that all intended recipients are running the same chat program. If your intended recipients use a range of chat programs, your attempts to chat will become exercises in frustration—haggling over which group chat application to use instead of focusing on work to be done. Over time, this will cause cross-group chats to degenerate into multiple separate one-on-one chats, each using different group chat products instead of one shared group chat channel.

---

[1] and Microsoft Lync, Skype for Business and Skype.

In some organizations where I've worked, this issue was so entrenched that I resorted to installing multiple apps. The process of relaying communications between incompatible islands of group chat users was error-prone and time-consuming. Left unchecked, this situation encourages people to ignore group chat and instead send an email or schedule a meeting.

Using different chat applications requires you to install and maintain current availability status across multiple apps. This makes it difficult to consistently signal your availability and expected response times to other humans in different teams, causing organizational friction. For more on availability signaling, see "Setting Response Time Expectations."

One reason email is globally ubiquitous is because application developers use common standards to make sure your messages can be exchanged with other email applications. An email sent using Apple Mail on a Mac can be read by a recipient using Outlook on a Windows PC or Emacs on a Linux system. This level of interoperability is not yet available for group chat applications. Until these interoperability issues are solved, find a chat program that most people across your organization like, and declare it the official standard for your entire organization.

Use a group chat tool that provides full-text searchable history of all messages in all channels[2]. This permanent scrollback feature is important and I am still surprised when new commercial products do not offer this.

Full-text scrollback, along with active channel moderation (see "Active Moderation"), allows people to quickly catch up on what happened while they were away overnight or while on vacation, and it helps new hires understand out what others are working on.

---

[2] Different group chat systems provide different search capabilities. My personal favorite is how IRC logs all messages into plain text files. This makes it quick and easy to grep search through all public channels at one time, in a consistent, vendor-neutral format. Searching private/protected channels is more complicated, but doable.

Carefully Arrange Channels

Create a carefully organized minimal viable set of channels.

When a group chat system has too many channels, it is hard to figure out which channel to use for a given topic. People become frustrated because they can't talk about a topic until they figure out which channel to use. Sometimes they give up and use any channel that is close enough. It is also hard to figure out which channels are important to monitor closely. You'll know you have this problem if you hear frequent complaints, such as: "There are too many channels to keep track of," or "I missed that discussion—what channel was that in?"

Too many channels scatter human interaction, which makes community-building harder—each channel feels like an abandoned, unpopulated wilderness with very little traffic, which makes it harder to foster trust and community.

At the opposite extreme, when a group chat system has too few channels, each channel has so much overlapping, unrelated traffic that it feels like it is drowning in noise. All of the cross-chatter makes it hard to tell what's going on.

The following arrangement of channels has worked well for me in several companies of different sizes:

- ◆ Create a public group channel for each organizational team of humans. Post the name of the public channel on a wiki page and distribute it widely within your organization, so that coworkers across the organization can quickly and reliably chat with everyone on the team.

- ◆ Create a private group channel for each organizational team of humans. Restrict membership to employees who report to a specific manager. This private channel is used by everyone in the group to keep track of what their teammates are doing, and to talk about personal items that would be typically reserved for private casual chat with teammates at a typical office—children, pets, movies, and other social activities intermingled with collaboration on work projects. This helps give everyone in the group a reasonable idea of what their teammates are working on, and indicates their availability as the day progresses—regardless of their location.

◆ Require everyone in the team to scroll back through the private group channel first thing in the morning, every morning, and to keep an eye on it throughout the day. This is a quick, information-dense way to find out what everyone else has been doing (or plans to do) since they were last at their computers. Typically, it only took me one cup of coffee each morning to find out what everyone else was working on and how everyone's day was going. Doing this *at a time of your choosing* is faster and less disruptive than having the entire team attend a daily status meeting. Especially when the humans are in different time zones. You know this private group channel is working well if the team does not have daily status meetings, yet everyone knows what everyone else is doing and you start hearing "We are the Borg!" jokes.

◆ Create a public event channel for each recurring cross-group event such as a weekly cross-group meeting. Include the name of this predefined dedicated channel in the recurring calendar invite, so that others can easily use the channel for background chatter during the meeting and debug any audio or video problems during the meeting.

◆ Create a public event channel for unpredictable, high-priority cross-group events that require rapid cross-group communication, such as a customer-visible interruption in production systems. Even if there is no production outage *right now*, pre-creating and advertising these channels within the organization will help people know where to go when an emergency does arise.

Don't worry about creating a perfect and exhaustive set of channels from the outset. Instead, create an initial set of channels for recurring events you've dealt with recently that you believe will happen again. As business needs change over time, simply create, morph, or delete role-specific channels organically, and continue to moderate them carefully.

Be as Open as Possible

By default, use public event channels and public group channels. For more sensitive conversations within your team, use your private group channel where appropriate. Use private one-on-one channels only when needed.

If it is not clear which channel to use, pause for a moment to determine which audience (and hence which channel) is most appropriate. Consider the topic, your audience, and the first few possible paths the discussion might take. If it is still unclear, err on the side of caution: start the discussion in a private one-on-one channel. If it turns out later that the discussion can be shared more widely, post a quick summary of the private channel discussion into the group channel, and continue the discussion in the group channel. If the discussion reaches conclusions that others need to know about, post a summary in the official Single Source of Truth. For more on this, see "Single Source of Truth."

When you use the group channel by default, you foster group cohesion because coworkers can read and participate in discussions with each other. It is also helpful when decisions are being made. Even if most group members don't have anything to contribute to a decision, simply having them *see* the decision-making process (and tradeoffs) helps them understand the eventual decision. It also helps them feel included. Later, if needed, they will be able answer questions on what factors were and weren't considered for this decision. This prevents the misperception that "decisions are made behind closed doors," which is important in any organization—and especially important in distributed organizations.

Using the group channel by default also eliminates overhead and repetition errors due to multiple separate one-to-one IM chats[3]. There are cases where direct one-to-one private chat is appropriate —for example, when dealing with personnel issues—but these are relatively rare.

---

[3] Here is an example: You have a private one-to-one IM chat with your coworker Alex about an upcoming project. Later, you repeat the entire discussion with a mutual coworker, Bernie. Then you repeat the discussion again with another coworker, Christine. This is suboptimal for several reasons. It takes time to repeat the information. If you make any errors in the re-telling, each coworker may have a subtly different understanding. If anyone raises an important issue that causes a change to the plan of record, you need to go back and update everyone one at a time about the evolving plans. During that re-telling, if someone discovers a problem with the proposed change, you might need to un-re-tell the plan of record. This is very confusing to everyone. All of these private one-on-one chats take much more time than a single group chat.

Different humans have different comfort levels for conversations in front of others—whether that is in a group chat channel, an open-plan office, a crowded meeting room, or a crowded elevator. Cultural sensitivity for these differences is important, and it requires constant attention.

Active Moderation

Some non-work social chatter is normal in any work environment —face-to-face, on group video calls, and in group chat channels. These important social interactions help us remember that we are all human. It helps foster a sense of community, and it can help defuse tensions in high-pressure situations.

Taken to an extreme, though, too much off-topic chatter hampers work being done in the channel. Left unchecked, humans who are doing focused work will move their discussions to a quieter channel. Be very alert for this. If off-topic chatter starts to get in the way of work being done, politely and firmly moderate the discussion. Ask those individuals to continue their discussion in a different channel, while noting the importance of the work that is correctly being done in this channel.

Another part of moderating is knowing when it is appropriate to expand an active group chat discussion. This is best done by explicitly mentioning additional participants by name. They will be notified, and will quickly be able to find discussions where they are needed. They can scroll back through the discussion to build context before participating in the discussion. However, please moderate how often you do this; think before you ping or *@mention* someone. Done well, you include people in discussions when it is most helpful. However, just like calling someone's cell phone, you are choosing to interrupt them without knowing the importance of what else you are interrupting.

It is important to moderate these channels actively. Consistent moderation raises everyone's overall awareness. Over time, more people will default to doing the right thing, reducing the need for future moderation. This will also help others feel empowered to moderate when you are not available.

Setting Response Time Expectations

Cultural group norms are part of how humans agree to work together, and they are important—whether they relate to email responsiveness, meeting attendance, meeting punctuality, or other work interactions. For group chat, it is important to agree on norms such as the expected response time for a chat request—and to be consistent. It is essential these expectations are clearly communicated and, when necessary, politely yet firmly enforced.

I recommend responding to a chat within a few seconds, so that your response in group chat is as fast as walking to a nearby coworker's desk, if both of you were in the same location. Unexpected lack of availability impacts the work of *others* in the group, similar to prolonged absences from the office in the middle of a workday.

This is not to say everyone must be super-responsive on email, group chat, and phone every minute of every day. Everyone has different response times throughout the day, depending on the ebb and flow of their work. To handle this, set an explicit default response time. Ask team members to let the group know if their response time will be outside the agreed-upon expectations, so others know what to expect. Clearly signaling availability helps others decide whether to wait, see if someone else can help, or escalate. It is frustrating to ping someone repeatedly on group chat —only to find out much later that they'd gone to bed hours ago, so they never saw any of your increasingly frantic messages. Similarly, it is frustrating to work uninterrupted at the keyboard for hours, only to return from a short break to find repeated pings from coworkers wondering if you are really there or not!

Most group chat applications have an Auto-Away feature: if you stop typing for a specified number of minutes, the application notifies others that you are not at your keyboard, and hence unlikely to respond immediately. This is better than nothing, but is not sufficient because Auto-Away does not communicate when you intend to *return*. In addition, because the "away" signal is based on a lack of typing, it cannot know that you are sitting at your desk reading complex documents or focused on a tense video call. To me, Auto-Away is like arriving at a neighborhood store only to find they a sign on the door, saying "Closed 10 minutes ago." It doesn't communicate the information I care about, which is the time the store will reopen! Similarly, a sign saying "Back in 10 minutes" is not helpful unless it is timestamped. I can't tell if the sign was posted one minute ago, 20 minutes ago, or accidentally left up days ago when the shopkeeper went on a multi-week vacation.

If I ping a coworker who claims to be at their keyboard, yet I get no response within the agreed-upon response time, how long should I wait before giving up? When I give up, should I phone them? Ask others instead? Escalate to their manager, looking for an alternate contact? When this happens a few times with a specific coworker, I start to wonder if the person is really working. On the flip side, a person who thinks "I was only away for a few minutes" can quickly be frustrated by the perceived impatience of others.

In traditional offices, humans follow social cues. If you walk down an office corridor to get a quick answer from someone, only to find they are not at their desk, you do some instinctive deductions to figure out if they will be back soon. If their jacket, bag, and computer are still there, they haven't gone far. If their jacket and computer are gone but the bag is still there, maybe they went to a meeting in a nearby building. If the jacket, computer, and bag are not there, maybe they have gone home for the day.

Similarly, to signal your availability to others in group chat, you need to use one shared group chat product across your entire organization. Unclear response-time expectations in group chat cause frustration and friction. Anticipate and avoid these mismatched expectations by explicitly stating response times and communicating your availability to others as your availability changes throughout the day. It is your responsibility to let others know your availability.

When walking away from the computer, state your estimated return time in the private group channel. Start and end each day by saying hello and goodbye to your team in the private group channel—just like you would to humans if you were at an office. This helps others know if and when you are available, and it helps others in your group answer questions like "Hey, is John still around today?"

Here are several settings that worked well for me to show others my expected response times:

- **joduinn**: I'm at my computer, working and available if needed. Response time: seconds.

- **joduinn-coffee, joduinn-brb**: "Be right back." I've stepped away from my computer for a few minutes. Response time: 5 to 15 minutes.

- **joduinn-lunch, joduinn-food**: I'm not at my computer, but I am still working today. If there is something urgent that can't wait until after I finish eating, you can text or call my cell phone. Response time: 45 to 60 minutes.

- **joduinn-commute**: I'm traveling to or from the office or a client site. Phone calls are probably ok, but there will be background noise. Email or SMS might work if I'm on public transit, but not if I'm driving. Response time: 1 to 2 hours, depending on traffic and weather.

- **joduinn-dnd**: "Do not disturb." I'm busy working on a complex topic that requires uninterrupted focus time. Please do not ping. If something is urgent, you can decide whether to interrupt me, knowing that I am nearby. Each time I go "-dnd" the situation is different, so when possible I post a time estimate in the private group channel, saying when I'll next resurface and check back in.

- **joduinn-mtg**: I'm in a meeting, with my laptop. Response time: from 1 to 30 minutes, depending on the meeting.

- **joduinn-afk, joduinn-zzz**: I'm away from my computer for the rest of the day and night. Response time: multiple hours. See who else can help, but if it is urgent and no one else is around, call my cell phone.

- **joduinn-pto**: I'm on vacation. Response time: days to weeks. Depending on my travels, I might be completely unresponsive. Contact others in the public group channel.

It is important to use a group chat system that timestamps all messages, including username changes like the above examples. When others can easily see that I changed by status to "-lunch" or "-brb" five minutes ago, they know that my status is accurate. This reduces stress for anyone seeking to make contact.

People expect others to be busy during the day, so they will understand if you cannot always talk with someone *immediately*. It is important, though, to clearly and truthfully communicate when you *will* be able to respond to them, so that they can plan accordingly and move forward with their work.

Ping in a Useful Way

When starting a chat with someone, don't just ping or @*mention* them by name. Let them know *why* you are looking for them and what the urgency is. This helps them build mental context before responding, so they are better prepared to answer your questions.

When I need to contact someone, I ping them even if I know they are unavailable. They can reply to me when they are back online and they see my ping. When someone responds hours later, sometimes I've forgotten why I originally pinged them! To solve this problem, I include the reason for my ping in my ping—for example, "Hey, I've got a quick question about xxx." When they respond a few hours later, they ask, "What did you need to know about xxx?" This also reminds me why I pinged them.

Another benefit of an early ping is that if the original recipient is not the right person, they can redirect you to the right person—helping all of you work more effectively.

In the past if I was busy when someone pinged me, I used to say, "I'm in the middle of something, can you give me five minutes?" They'd politely say "yes" and then wait... and wait. All too frequently, my five-minute estimate was inaccurate. When they re-pinged me 30 minutes later, I'd feel bad. After this happened several times, I changed my response. Now I say, "I'm in the middle of something, and you are third in line. Is this urgent, or can it wait?" If it is urgent, I drop what I am doing and phone or video-call them immediately. If it isn't urgent, they'll know they're third in line, and they'll know that I will ping them as soon as I'm free. Because I have some context of why they want to meet, I can prepare—or if I'm not the best person to help with the issue, I can immediately redirect them to the right person.

Treating Group Chat as Transient

As group chat become a standard organizational tool, some discussions will naturally turn into impromptu decision-making processes—these back-and-forth decisions happen, for example, when coworkers discover and address issues with their official plan of record. Reaching decisions in group chat is fine. Done well, this can be *much* faster than calling a meeting.

However, it is impossible to expect all humans to read all group chat channels all of the time. That would become a full-time job in itself. Instead, treat all group chat as transient.

Any decisions reached in group chat that are worth sharing with others must be cross-posted to the official Single Source of Truth for that project. A simple copy-and-paste of the discussion is usually fastest and easiest, although sometimes a short summary of a long discussion is better. Regardless, the responsibility for sharing the decision is not fulfilled until those humans update the Single Source of Truth. This ensures that everyone working on the project is aware of the new decision. This requirement is also true for decisions made in unrelated video calls or in-person coffee shop discussions. For more on this, see "Single Source of Truth."

Allow impromptu discussions and decision making where they feel best—in group chat, email, unrelated video calls, and (when it happens) in-person meetings. It's all fine, so long as anything worth sharing is then posted to the Single Source of Truth.

Humans and Culture

Recruiting and Interviewing

Takeaways

◆ Do you *need* to hire? One quick way to make your existing group of humans more productive is to reduce or remove busywork.

◆ The ability to hire better candidates and hire faster is a recurring competitive advantage of distributed teams.

◆ Do you want to hire the best person for the job, or the best person for the job who lives nearby?

◆ Conduct initial interviews on video, and treat any logistical issues (such as scheduling across time zones, setting up video, or internet connectivity) as a red flag.

Recruiting, interviewing, and hiring have become daily operational needs for every organization.

As detailed in "Distributed Teams Are Not New," the social change toward no more job for life has an important side effect. People change jobs more frequently, so companies need to hire continuously, simply to backfill for the constant flow of people who leave. Companies with 95% retention rates are constantly hiring to replace the 5% who left. If your organization is growing, you need to hire even more!

If your organization is remote friendly—with well-functioning distributed teams—you will be able to choose from a *significantly* larger pool of candidates, leading to better, faster hires and a more diverse group of humans.

Making your ongoing hiring process more efficient is a recurring competitive advantage.

Hiring Remote--Or Not!

Before you post a job vacancy on your company website, if you have an office (or offices), ask yourself: "Do I want to hire the best person for the job, regardless of where they live, or do I want to hire the best person for the job who lives nearby or is willing to relocate?"

This is a decision you need to be honest with yourself about, from the outset. Your answer will guide where you post your job description, how you screen applications, which candidates you choose to interview, how you conduct interviews, and what skill sets you interview for. Being fully honest about this also helps you avoid spending time interviewing candidates who have no intention of relocating but *thought* they were applying for a remote position, only to find themselves being pressured during the final offer to relocate near your physical office[1].

If you secretly think, "I'll hire a remote person only if they are great, if I can't persuade them to relocate, and if I can't find someone just as good locally," then be honest with yourself: you want to hire locally.

Be aware, that *requiring* people to work from an office will limit your candidate pool. Many suitable applicants will not even apply for the job because of the barrier imposed by the commute to and from wherever you put your physical office. For more on this, see "The Real Cost of an Office."

---

[1] It is of course possible that the hiring manager is such a great negotiator, the company is so great to work for, and the position so appealing that a candidate might change their mind and decide to relocate despite their earlier objections. This is very rare. More likely, the candidate will resent this "bait and switch" tactic, decline the job offer, and then start warning their peers about the lack of honesty. This will damage the company reputation, making future recruiting by the company even harder.

Conversely, if the candidate is a better negotiator, the company might reluctantly agree to hire them to work remote while the rest of the company is together in one office. The candidate did not "win" the negotiations; the candidate is now the "canary in the coal mine," a situation that is unlikely to end well. For more on this, see "Organizational Pitfalls to Avoid."

"Tech companies are dying for talent. The motivation to go find talent wherever it is, is unbelievably high."

Marc Andreessen

Recruiting Diversity

This is an important enough topic that I encourage re-reading "Diversity." Don't worry, it's short and very relevant to recruiting new employees.

Writing Job Postings

If you decide to hire the best person for the job regardless of their location, make it easy for remote candidates to find your job posting.

Even if your company website says "all jobs are remote-welcome" in the banner text, it is still important to explicitly state "Remote Welcome" in the job description, in case the job description is cross-posted to an external job board[2].

If your organization has an office, is remote-friendly but with operational restrictions (such as HIPAA, national security, data privacy legal issues, and so on), write "Remote within US," or "Remote within New England," or "Remote within EU," or "Remote within the following time zones: ..." as appropriate.

Don't exclude local candidates who apply, just be location-agnostic. After all, the best person for the job might already live within an easy commute distance of your office.

If your organization has offices and your website design requires all job postings to list an office location chosen from a menu of office locations, add a new office location to the menu: "Remote or Work From Home."

---

[2] For recommended sites that specialize in remote jobs, see "Further Reading."

Active and Passive Recruiting

When seeking job candidates, consider both active and passive recruiting.

For active recruiting, you publish the job posting on your website, and cross-post it to other job boards and social networks like LinkedIn, Twitter, and Facebook. You ask coworkers to contact or post to their social networks. If your company doesn't already have a referral bonus plan in place for active recruiting, set one up immediately and make sure your coworkers know about it. Some companies, such as LinkedIn, also have an alumni program where former employees help find candidates for new vacancies.

Passive recruiting involves candidates who are not currently looking for a job, or when your organization does not have any current job openings. Passive recruiting requires ongoing communication and connection with potential candidates over a prolonged period of time. This approach is far more valuable for recruiting top-performing candidates, and it is especially important for distributed teams. It's hard to find passive candidates with the right skills and relevant job experience when they are not looking for a new job. If you wait until you have a pressing need, you risk making poor hiring decisions under time-pressure.

Instead, help potential candidates find *you* even when you are not actively recruiting.

Use conferences and blog posts to publicly describe how smart humans in your team are solving complex important problems. Ask others in the group to also talk about their work publicly. These steps are good for your group morale, help grow the reputation of the team, as well as the individual humans. These also attract the attention of other smart like-minded people—after all, most smart people want to work with other smart people.

If you don't have any job vacancies when you are first approached, tell them immediately, and meet them for an informational interview anyway. If the person seems like they could be a valuable addition to the team, save their contact information and keep in touch.

Later, when you do start hiring, post a job description *and* contact your pre-vetted list of passive candidates. I've seen hard-to-fill positions be filled in days by outstanding candidates using this approach.

Observing Interview Logistics

Use video calls for all interviews. Do this from the outset, and be consistent. Video calls are faster and less expensive than flying each candidate out for in-person interviews. For a distributed team, video calls are also more realistic. If you hire the candidate, or if (as a candidate) you accept the job, you'll be on frequent video calls with each other.

Pay careful attention to the smallest mechanical problems, and treat recurring problems as a red flag.

The candidate, all interviewers, and the hiring manager should be able to run productive video calls consistently, regardless of travel schedules and time zones. How efficient is everyone at scheduling meetings and calendar haggling, especially across time zones? Does everyone join calls consistently on time or early[3]? Is everyone comfortable with their video-conferencing software and physical setup? Are the camera and microphone positioned properly and working well, so the call starts immediately with no awkward delays caused by basic setup problems? Does the candidate's internet connection have enough bandwidth for reliable video calls? Is the lighting good? Does the visible background help or hinder the call[4]? Are meetings missed or cancelled on short notice because of time-zone math errors? Are meetings cancelled because someone is traveling for work, working from home, unable to start video calls outside of the office, or simply forgot?

If you are a job candidate, watch for issues such as audio-only interviews, starting meetings late without warning[5],

---

[3] For more on this, see "Own Your Calendar."

[4] For more on this, see "Phones, Cameras and Microphones" and "How Do Others See You?"

[5] One co-founder was more than 20 minutes late to a video call to interview me. When he did finally join, he claimed he had been on time in the physical office

miscalculating time zones for interview calls, cancelling interviews on short (or no) notice because someone wasn't in the office, or having no other remote coworkers to interview with.

During an interview, both sides make an effort to give the best possible impression. Any problems at this stage risk becoming *worse* after an offer has been accepted.

Important Topics During Interviews

Every human has different behavioral and cultural norms. This means that each human hired into a group helps shape the group's culture. Interviewing potential new hires is an important way to help shape group culture.

As a hiring manager, be efficient with time. Don't take so much time with the interview process that a desirable candidate gives up and finds another job. Don't spend time interviewing someone who you know will not be a good fit; don't waste their time with pointless interviews.

Discuss the interview process with your candidates:

◆ Make sure they know that they will have a series of interviews. Give explicit timelines for the next interview or two, and give them contact information for a logistics person for the entire series.

◆ Describe who they will meet, and why.

◆ Ask candidates to let you know if there are any scheduling delays: "If you haven't heard by Friday, please email me."

---

meeting room waiting for me, and eventually contacted the recruiter to discover the interview was scheduled as a video call. Then he discovered that he had never used the video software agreed upon by the recruiter, so he had to install it. This told me all I needed to know about how this potential new boss would value me and my work, if I joined as a remote employee with strategic responsibilities. I also found it interesting how he blamed all this on the recruiter, even though he had been actively involved in the email thread scheduling the video call and was on the calendar invite that included the video call details. This reinforced my earlier concerns with the company's recruiters only doing audio-only calls for this remote position. Because of these red flags, I declined further interviews with this potential employer.

This way you can quickly debug any internal process problems and be respectful of their time. This also helps set expectations about timelines.

- Ask if they have any deadlines, such as competing offers that you need to be aware of.

- Point out that they will meet many different future coworkers, including other remote people, throughout the interview process. This is carefully and intentionally done to help the hiring manager, the rest of the group, *and the candidate* make an informed decision on whether this would be a good fit (or not)[6].

Consider who will interview each candidate, and in what sequence. I am the first interviewer for anyone who will report directly to me, and I am always somewhere in the interview schedule for candidates elsewhere in my team. My interviews focus on identifying technical and culture mismatches; verifying that the candidate can work effectively from a remote location; and selling the job, the group and the company—so they know enough to be excited about the job and they want to be hired. Toward the end of the interview I discuss logistics and next steps in the interview process.

Include others on your team. Each interviewer brings a different perspective, which reduces the chance of a poor hiring decision. Best-case, all team members are comfortable interviewing candidates, they understand the process, and they cross-calibrate feedback to reduce individual bias and interviewer blind spots. This will also help the team continue to interview and hire effectively if you decide to leave the organization—important for business continuity.

If you are mentoring someone who is new to interviewing, schedule them later in the interview schedule. Make sure they know this schedule placement is intentional, as you are helping

---

[6] I explicitly state this during interviews after one candidate misunderstood our series of interviews to mean, "We are not sure if we want to hire you." The candidate accepted a competing offer, simply because the other organization had fewer interviews and "seemed more eager." That candidate later confided that their new job-in-reality was not the same as the job-as-advertised; they were now looking to move again.

them safely grow their interviewing skills, while at the same time reducing the risk of botching a candidate hiring decision. If it helps the new interviewer learn, arrange practice interviews where they interview *you*. This helps you review their planned questions, coach them on how to handle tricky half-answered questions and how to summarize feedback for later debriefs. These are skills needed in order to grow the skills of humans in your team who can share the interview workload and help scale team recruiting in a consistent manner.

When a candidate first interviews with a company, they are evaluating the interview, the interviewer, and the company. By the time the candidate meets the last interviewer, the candidate has already made up their mind about the company and most of the interviewers who are potential future coworkers. An anomaly near the end is less damaging to a potential hire. Each new candidate is a real human, looking for a real job. Each new interviewer is trying to do something new—with someone else's career in their hands. Create a process to be respectful to all involved!

It is valid and appropriate for a remote candidate to ask what remote work life is like at your company. As a hiring manager, if a remote candidate does *not* ask about this, gently raise the topic and explore their remote experiences much more carefully. Here are a few ways I've gently started this discussion:

- "I've worked remotely for a few companies now. Some companies handled remote work well, and some did not. How do you make sure that remote people don't feel like second class citizens?"

- "How many other people in the team are remote, and can I interview with some of them?"

- "How tightly knit is the team, including the remote people? How was this group cohesion created?"

- "How do you know if a remote person is doing their job well? How does a remote person know if their manager is doing their job well?"

- "Can you give me an example of last time a remote person was promoted, and why?"

As a candidate, watch for corporate-speak answers like "We treat everyone equally. Trust us, it will be fine." Unless the interviewer adds more information about *how* everyone is treated equally, this type of response should signal a red flag.

In contrast, consider the following response: "Ah, good question, glad you asked. We have 18 people in 14 cities in four non-adjacent time zones. We have the highest retention rate in the company for six years and counting. People like what they're doing, they're solving important problems, and they're using cool technology to do so. Several of them have been promoted, including two first-time managers who are remote from me and remote from the people they manage. Everyone is encouraged to talk publicly about their work at conferences. But don't take my word for it—you're scheduled to chat with some other remoties in later interviews, so make sure to ask them what they think." This answer provides concrete information, addresses root (even unstated) concerns, and demonstrates that remote people are routinely well cared for[7]. Every time I responded like this, it resolved the candidate's doubts about the team's distributed culture and improved the tone of the remaining interviews, further improving my ability to hire.

What retention and promotion statistics could you share with candidates, to show how they would be valued if they joined? If you don't have, like, or know of such statistics in your organization, start measuring that data. These metrics will also help you track and improve your remote hiring efforts.

---

[7] Always follow up with new hires on their first day, and again a few weeks after joining, to explicitly reconfirm that they feel accepted and valued. After that, make sure this is a quiet part of regular one-on-ones. For more on this, see "Hiring and On-Boarding."

Hiring and On-Boarding

Takeaways

- The quality of hires in a team helps build (or erode) the team's trust in leadership.

- "You never get a second chance to make a good first impression."

- Even if others are responsible for part of the on-boarding process, the hiring manager is ultimately responsible for ensuring that the person they spent time recruiting has a great first-day experience. Pay attention to all of the details.

- Create a "Day One" page that everyone can see and update. Show this to each new hire, and ask them to update the page as they progress, until the next new hire joins.

When deciding whether to hire someone, consider hiring *and* not hiring them. Will the person will be a great addition to the team? Do you have any doubts?

When it's time for a new hire to start, advance preparation makes the on-boarding process easier and smoother for them. It is also less error-prone and stressful for the hiring manager, and it helps group succession planning by making it easier for future team leaders to onboard new hires into the team—following the same reproducible tried-and-tested process.

To Hire or Not to Hire?

Changing jobs is a big milestone in a person's career, financial life, and social life. For almost every company I've worked at, I can clearly remember exactly where I was—and how excited I felt—when I heard I'd been hired.

As a hiring manager, you have a moral responsibility to your job candidates. When you hire someone, you are most likely taking them from an existing job into this new job. If you decide this was a bad hire[1] and quickly fire them, they are now actively worse off. They might not have been happy at their previous job, but at least they *had* a job, with income to pay their bills. Now, unexpectedly, they need to start looking for another job—on short notice, with no income. They are also in a weaker position to negotiate salary—it's hard to avoid an awkward silence when an interviewer inevitably asks, "Why did you leave your last job so quickly?"

When deciding whether to hire a candidate or not, only hire if you are *certain* that the person will be a great addition to the team, that they can help with the current ongoing projects, and—in case of last-minute project changes—they are flexible enough to be able to help with future not-yet-defined projects.

Keep in mind that when your new hire starts, your team will be net *negative* one half-person for the first few months, because an existing team member needs to spend time helping the new hire get up to speed. The exact amount of time needed depends on several factors, but allocating 50% of one person's time for the first three months has been a good rule of thumb for me. I prefer to assign one mentor in advance[2], which means reassigning some of the mentor's current projects to others in the group. The sooner the new hire is productive, the sooner the mentor can go back to their own work, and the sooner your group will reach net positive productivity.

---

[1] Many people describe this as "a bad hire" or "a hire that didn't work out," implying that the candidate was solely responsible for not being able to do the work. Instead, consider describing it as a "bad hiring decision." This implies that others, including the hiring manager, has some responsibility for faulty interviewing or a poor hiring decision. This is an important shift in responsibility and accountability. Mistakes happen, but learning from each mistake is important. Debrief every hiring and firing. As hiring manager, you are responsible for figuring out what can you do better next time.

[2] Some companies share mentoring across multiple group members. However, this rarely worked out well. More usually, the everyone-is-responsible intention risks becoming no-one-is-responsible, leaving the new hire to learn the ropes alone, without consistent mentoring. This hampers on-boarding.

Never hire people who *might* work out, thinking "No problem, we can always fire them later if they don't work out." I've worked with hiring managers and in-house recruiters who thought like this and tried their best to persuade me to do the same[3]. If you have doubts about a candidate, treat the mere existence of doubt as a red flag and do not hire. I've ignored my doubts a few times—and regretted it each time.

> *"Whenever there is any doubt, there is no doubt."*
>
> Robert De Niro as "Sam" in the movie "Ronin"

If you hire the wrong person, not only will you be net negative a half-person during the ramp-up period, but you will also need to clean up the unfinished work left behind when the new hire leaves. Who will take over the work that had been assigned to the new person? Is it easier to fix substandard work or start over from scratch? Meanwhile, you still don't have the extra help you needed when you started the interview process.

If you repeatedly hire the wrong person, your team will lose confidence in *your* ability to attract and hire good people. Existing employees will notice that you hire and fire without appearing to care about the consequences. At some point, they will start to wonder when you might eventually fire them.

Do this often enough, and your team will start to assume that *all* candidates you hire will be disposable under-performers. Even if you do eventually hire a good person, the new hire will have an uphill struggle proving themselves because your team will expect another under-performer! All of this is really bad for morale, group cohesion, and trust.

A pattern of bad hiring decisions will cause existing employees to wonder if they, or the entire team, are viewed as under-performers by others. Smart people enjoy working with other smart people,

---

[3] I usually saw this in organizations that evaluated hiring managers on their hiring rate, not their retention rate. I also saw hiring managers who viewed each new hire as a disposable interchangeable resource instead of a real live human. Many of these same managers complained about how the competitive job market was causing good people to quit—taking better offers elsewhere with no loyalty to their employer!

and they are the most hirable. They will start leaving, making your hiring needs even more pressing.

> *"Steve Jobs has a saying that A players hire A players; B players hire C players; and C players hire D players...This trickle-down effect causes bozo explosions in companies."*
>
> *Guy Kawasaki, Apple's first evangelist*

To resolve the hire-or-not question as clearly as possible, choose interviewers with complementary perspectives on the candidate and the role. Obtain brutally honest feedback from every interviewer. Listen carefully to all of their feedback, and ask firm, direct, questions. Ultimately, the hiring manager is responsible for making the decision to hire or not. You don't need to hire a candidate just because all of the interviewers were unanimously in favor of hiring. You don't need to reject a candidate when some interviewers are in favor, some not. But you always need a good reason for your decision. If you find yourself thinking about what you'd be willing to sacrifice to get this candidate into the team, go ahead and hire this candidate as fast as you can. I sometimes describe this mindset as "building a highly effective SEAL team, not building an empire."

A respectful, preplanned hiring mindset might lead to hiring fewer people. You risk not hiring someone who might have turned out to be great. However, you also reduce time spent cleaning up the disruption, legal aspects, and organizational headaches after a bad hiring decision. Importantly, each hire has a much lower failure ("bounce") rate and a higher retention rate. These successes, over time, help build lean, tightly knit, cohesive teams.

Making a Job Offer

As a hiring manager, extending a job offer is important enough that you should do it yourself as much as possible, even if you can delegate this work. Like anything else, practice until you are consistently good at it. Why spend time screening and interviewing multiple candidates, only to have your ideal candidate decline the job because the mechanics of the job offer itself went poorly?

I've given, and received, job offers in many different ways. Over time I developed a script that works for me. You can find it in "Script for Making a Job Offer." Feel free to use this as a starting point; change it as feels best to you.

Preparing for Day One

A bad "Day One" experience is the fastest way to disillusion an excited, eager new hire.

As the hiring manager, you are responsible for successfully on-boarding your new hire. You spent the most time and effort recruiting them, and you have the most to lose if the new hire does not stay.

The on-boarding process involves detailed work *preparing for* Day One and *on* Day One.

Here are some steps to do before Day One, for every new hire who directly reports to you:

♦ About a week in advance, make sure that the new hire's computer preferences and email aliases are working. Even if someone else unboxes their computer, configures it, and sets up their email account, you should still take a few minutes to verify that these are set up correctly.

♦ Send an email to the new hire's email address. Use the new hire's computer to read that email. Send a reply, and make sure you can see that reply in your own inbox. This quick test should work the first time, but I've been surprised enough times that I now always verify it myself. Lastly, triple-check the spelling of their name—typos are embarrassing, and they're much easier to fix *before* the new hire starts.

♦ Add the new hire's email address to your group mailing list. If you organized your mailing lists as described in "Email Etiquette," this one step ensures that the new hire will automatically receive email from *all* company mailing lists that anyone in the group thought important, as well as any random individual emails to the group.

♦ If the new hire will need to use VPN software, verify that it works and make sure they have a valid password. If you are verifying VPN in an office, use your cell phone as a hotspot to verify it works when *not* connected to the company network. Debugging VPN issues can be tricky, annoying, and time-consuming. It is particularly tricky when the new hire starts on Day One from a remote location, needing VPN to complete even the most basic on-boarding steps. Debugging VPN setup is *significantly* easier when you have another working computer nearby to help you debug it, and (unlike the new hire) you already know what systems you're supposed to be able to access once VPN is working correctly.

♦ Schedule a meeting with the new hire for the morning of Day One. Schedule a second meeting toward the end of the last day of their first week. Verify that you see both of these meetings in their calendar.

♦ When email, calendar, and VPN are verified, pack up the computer. If the new hire will be working from the same location as you, keep everything near your desk, ready to hand to them in person on Day One. If the new hire will be working from a remote location, ship the computer to them, timed to arrive before Day One. Send them the tracking number. Include a welcome kit with business cards and swag items such as t-shirts, notebooks and pens. If the new hire will start work during a group event, bring the new hire's equipment with you.

Don't share passwords for these systems until all formal paperwork is signed and the new hire is officially an employee.

Even with advance preparation, a new hire will need to do some things on their own during their first day. To help make it easier, create and share a Day One page on a group-editable system such as an internal wiki server. Add what you remember doing on your first few days, and ask others in the group to add anything they wished they knew when they first joined. Use this page to collect all Day One activities as people think of them.

Lastly, find a short, relatively simple project for the new hire to work on. Ensure that the details are in your ticketing system. Before the new hire starts, ask someone on the team to mentor them on this first project.

Completing these steps before Day One helps the new hire have a good Day One experience. Their inbox has email in it, which reassures them that their email is working. They don't need to do anything with those emails, but in idle gaps during their first few days they can sift through the messages, build context about what people are talking about, see who is working on what, and start asking questions.

All of these preparations help new hires get up to speed quickly.

Day One

If your new hire will work in your office, prearrange what time they should arrive. Be explicit about dress code. Nothing demoralizes an eager new hire like waiting outside their new office at 08:50 on the first day, in business formal suit, until their manager eventually drifts into the office around 10:00, in ragged jeans and a t-shirt.

If your new hire will work at another office, ask someone there to act as your trusted surrogate—and remind them about it the day before.

If the new hire will permanently work from home, try to schedule their Day One so that it happens during a group gathering (see "Bringing Humans Together"). If that is not possible, prearrange a time (and time zone) for them to start work. Send their verified equipment to them early, so they have time to unpack and set up their new machine in advance.

At the start of their Day One, use the scheduled in-person or video meeting to confirm that all paperwork is signed, they have all necessary passwords, their email is working, and they see a complete, correct series of meetings on their calendar. Ask your new hire if they have any questions so far, and wait patiently for their answer. Some people are reluctant to ask silly questions of their new boss on the first day, so you might need to nudge them a few times before they understand that you are looking for ways to help them succeed.

Remind them that you have a meeting scheduled with them at the end of their first week to find out how they are settling in, see if anything is blocking them, and answer any questions. Verify they can find the event in their new calendar and understand the video link details.

Introduce the new hire to the most recent previous new hire, who can also help with any on-boarding questions.

Show the new hire the Day One page, and ask them to follow all of the instructions on the page. Ask them to maintain the Day One page until the next new hire joins. New hires are perfect testers of this page—they will approach it with fresh eyes, and they are fully motivated to become productive at their new job. Systems and internal group processes change continuously, so it is hard for "old-timers" to remember what it was like as a new hire on Day One. Rotating the ownership of this page to each new hire is an easy-to-describe tactic for sharing the burden of keeping the Day One page fresh and accurate.

One-on-Ones and Reviews

Takeaways

♦ Schedule one-on-one meetings every week with each direct report and with your boss—even if you both think you don't need to meet.

♦ Each one-on-one should be 30 minutes long.

♦ Always use video. It helps everyone stay focused, it is more humane, and it makes meetings go faster.

♦ The less-senior human (the "manag-ee") is responsible for sending an agenda in advance—ideally the night before the one-on-one—so that the manager has time to prepare.

♦ Have 360 reviews every six months. Create a process for doing these efficiently. These 360 reviews help remind people they are working *with others*, not just working *for the boss*.

♦ There should never be a surprise in a review.

Organized correctly, weekly one-on-ones keep everyone on the same page about their work, *reduce* the number of meetings in a given week, build trust, and simplify the process of holding regular 360 reviews.

Scheduling One-on-Ones

Schedule weekly one-on-ones with your direct reports and your manager, even if neither of you think you need to meet. Regular one-on-ones are important if you all work in one location, and they are particularly important if one person is physically remote from the other—it might be the only "live" contact that person has with their boss all week.

It can be tempting to cancel a one-on-one when you're both busy and everything seems to be going fine as far as you can tell—but do not cancel one-on-ones. Often, once you meet and start talking, something important will come up, especially when people are in different physical locations. If not—if you find that everything has been covered after a few minutes—you can always end the meeting early after some brief social contact.

Holding a one-on-one meeting only after something has gone wrong sends a bad cultural message that there needs to be a problem before you will get any time with the boss and that high-performing individuals are ignored and unappreciated. Well-run one-on-ones help you identify and resolve issues *before* they become major problems.

Think like a chef working in a kitchen: good chefs do not only pay attention only when a pot boils over; they check all of the pots on the stove, all of the time, while keeping a watchful eye on incoming work orders.

Cadence

A cadence of shorter, more frequent meetings is important for building trust. Find a day and time that works for both of you, and stick to it! A predictable weekly meeting time helps both of you plan the rest of your week. It eliminates needless calendar haggling every week—frustrating for all involved—and helps avoid the slippery slope of "let's skip this week."

For me, the "let's meet when we both have free time" approach rarely works, and frequently leads to not meeting at all that week. Instead, holding 30-minute meetings with *every* direct report, *every* week, *reduces* the total amount of time I spend in meetings. If an issue comes up between one-on-ones, people can judge for themselves whether they need a one-off escalation meeting, or if the issue can wait until our next one-on-one—secure in the knowledge that the scheduled one-on-one will happen.

By contrast, when one-on-ones are unpredictable or when they're scheduled every two weeks, people are more likely to escalate instead of waiting. At one point I tried hour-long one-on-ones every two weeks, instead of every week. This had an interesting side effect: people scheduled more short-notice emergency meetings, claiming that their request couldn't wait until their next one-on-one. These extra meetings consume more time. They force a mental context switch, interrupting work in progress.

If someone chooses *not* to escalate—because they believe this will avoid causing trouble between one-on-ones—the one-week cadence guarantees that you will hear about possible issues within a few days. If the issue is serious enough to merit escalation you can address it and start cleanup sooner.

Shifting to a weekly cadence of shorter, more focused, crisply organized meetings reduced the number of surprise emergency meetings, and gave everyone consistent, frequent contact that was far more valuable.

Duration

A 30-minute one-on-one meeting every week is better than an hour-long meeting every two weeks, even though the total time spent is the same.

Bring the agenda (see "Structuring One-on-Ones") and stick to it. This keeps meetings efficient, within the time limit, while still allowing time for all-important personal chit-chat.

Informal "meet for an hour to chat" one-on-ones are fairly common yet unproductive, rambling along until the entire hour is filled. This worked well enough when I managed small teams, so I kept doing it. However, this approach did not scale. Larger teams with multiple levels of managers need structured, efficient one-on-ones. Smaller teams benefit from these too.

If you need more than 30 minutes because of one specific topic, introduce the topic in the one-on-one, then schedule a separate 30-minute meeting for that specific topic.

Structuring One-on-Ones

Develop a basic agenda format that works for you, your manager and everyone you manage. Ask your manag-ees to send you the agenda before each one-on-one meeting. Establish a speaking etiquette for one-on-ones, and always use video.

Develop an Agenda

Design a simple but consistent agenda format, to help keep one-on-ones short and productive while leaving time to talk about other things. Ask your manag-ee to send it to you before the meeting, ideally the night before, so that you have enough time to read and react to the agenda before the meeting starts.

If you do not receive the agenda beforehand, join the meeting anyway. Ask your manag-ee to write the agenda and email it to you, and quietly do other work until you receive the agenda. After you receive and quickly read the agenda, both of you will be informed and ready to start a focused, productive meeting in the remaining time. Being consistent about this minimalist agenda helps people focus and take these meetings seriously.

After some trial and error, here is a simple agenda format that worked well for me:

```
Subject: 1x1 dd-mmm-yyyy


Top of mind:
* Why did xxx leave company?
* Why was Project Snoopy delayed by 3months after we
worked late nights last week?


Done last week / Accomplishments:
* Interviewed candidates—Mary, Adam
* QA team asked for code review of new automation work,
see bug#1234433
* Bug#2222222: get answers to Marketing Dept about signing
keys certificate
* Scoped out and started bug#1234567 after production
outage post-mortem.


Blocked on:
* Need root access to production machine to debug outage
* Need budget sign-off to buy license code-scanning
service


ToDo / Plan for this week:
* Bug#1234567: refactor alerting code to fix intermittent
production issue
```

```
** after code review, will plan exact time for landing in
production
* Blog post about last week's outage
* Buy plane tickets for next group gathering
*  Bug#2468246: dropped  to  work  on  urgent  bug#1234567.
Restarting this week.
```

"Done" and "ToDo" items are not meant to contain long status updates. Instead, these sections should contain a list of one-line descriptions, each linking to the Single Source of Truth for details.

As the manager, when you receive the agenda, first read the "Blocked On" section. If the manag-ee is blocked waiting for you to approve something or escalate an issue with another manager, start dealing with it immediately. It's possible that one or more blocking items can be unblocked—or at least progress started— before your one-on-one meeting. Speed-read the other sections, to confirm that their accomplishments and plans match what you expect. Hopefully, everything you care about is already here. If not, you are now prepared to follow-up with specific questions during your meeting.

The "Done" and "ToDo" sections are also a good way to keep both manag-er and manag-ee honest. If someone says they will do something next week, but doesn't, you'll be able to notice that across status updates. If someone keeps being interrupted from planned work by last-minute urgent work pushed on their plate by others, you'll see it here. Surprises do happen every now and then, but a pattern of recurring surprises is a cause for concern for both humans.

When your manag-ee routinely and objectively writes down this information and you review it weekly, you both prevent confusion and mismatched expectations.

Establish Etiquette

In every one-on-one, ask the manag-ee to go first. They should do most of the talking.

The manag-er can append items to the agenda, but is not allowed to drive the meeting. Instead, the manag-ee owns and drives the meeting, making sure to cover everything on their agenda. All too often, I have experienced the frustration of going into a meeting with my boss, with items of big concern on my list, only to discover that my boss just finished an unrelated meeting that went badly. My entire one-on-one is consumed by my boss reacting to the previous meeting. I don't get to address issues I care about—and then my one-on-one is over. Not good. To prevent that, the manag-ee sets the agenda and goes first.

During the meeting, most of the time should be spent on "Top Of Mind" and "Blocked On," discussing context around a project or brainstorming on a specific blocking issue.

Spend some time on the "Done" and "ToDo" sections too, acknowledging work done and confirming future plans. You might find that the "Done" section quietly contains a series of complex tasks, all completed early by a soft-spoken human who is uncomfortable bragging, yet hoping you will recognize those accomplishments.

Here are several other guidelines:

♦ Make sure that your manag-ee feels comfortable speaking about what's important to them—after all, this is their big "meet with the boss" meeting.

♦ Listen for disconnects between what the manag-ee is working on and what their manag-er expects them to be working on. This type of problem is worth explicitly noting and quickly fixing.

♦ Only after the manag-ee covers all of the topics in their agenda, should the manag-er raise any topics that were missing.

♦ If any agenda items were added, make sure both humans have them for the next one-on-one: a tactic that worked for me was, at the end of the meeting, to reply to the agenda email with any additional items.

♦ Make sure your manag-ee hears about complaints *quickly*—in their next scheduled one-on-one or sooner. If they screw up, they should be told about it while it is still in recent memory and before it can happen again. Be constructive, but be truthful, honest, and timely. These teachable moments are invaluable for growth, mentoring, and building trust. Do not wait for the next formal review before telling someone that they messed up months ago[1]. Surprising someone months later is a great way to erode trust.

◆ Make sure your manag-ee hears about compliments *quickly*—in their next scheduled one-on-one or sooner. When someone does something amazing, don't assume that they and others already know it was amazing, so they don't need to be told. On the other hand, don't go over the top, congratulating people for simply doing baseline work. That devalues later compliments for outstanding great work that genuinely takes your breath away. Make a point of complimenting them on great work[2]. As a human, it's also very nice thing to hear explicitly said about you; it's what you'd like your boss to do with you. Treat others the way you would like to be treated.

◆ Compliment publicly, criticize privately.

Using this structure, you might be surprised to find that you can cover everything within 30 minutes—leaving time to chat about equally important, more personal things: "Hey, I saw there was a nearby earthquake, is everything ok?" or "Why did Fred transfer to another department?" or "Why did Adam leave the company?" or "Why was Project Snoopy cancelled?"

Remote people are just as curious about these things as local people, so remember to include them in these informal discussions. When asked, I tell people everything I heard, even if various rumors contradict each other: "Here are all the rumors I've heard so far. I heard Adam left because he got fired, because he was head-hunted into a great role in a cool new startup, because he wasn't promoted, and because he *was* promoted but didn't like his new job." I relay all of the contradictory data, without adding editorial changes or filtering them in any way. This is tricky to do but important in order to avoid starting rumors myself! I end with, "Yes, I know they do contradict each other. Now you've heard

---

[1] Don't chicken out—conflict avoidance makes things worse, not better. People can't learn to change if they don't know what the problem is. If someone messes up and doesn't know it was their fault, and you don't tell them, you cannot be surprised if they make that same mistake again.

[2] If possible, and if appropriate for the person, compliment publicly. It helps remind others how great the person's work was.

everything I've heard, so you can choose what you want to believe." This reminds everyone—local and remote—that rumors are messy and inaccurate, and that each human has different theories about what happened. For hybrid organizations, this helps humans not-in-the-office feel as equally included and equally in flux as humans in-the-office. Occasionally, I am asked about new rumors that I can quickly dispel with facts. Then, with idle curiosity abated, we move on—no longer interested in the rumors and now able to focus on work again.

Use Video

Always use video for one-on-ones with remote coworkers. Make the video window as large as possible on your screen, while still leaving the agenda visible. Hide other windows, including your email inbox. As with all other meetings, audio-video one-on-ones go faster than audio-only—for more on this, see "Hidden Tax of Audio-Only Meetings." You might be able to get away without video in some calls, but if a moment comes up where nonverbal video feedback is helpful, it is too late to ask, "Hey, would you please turn on your camera?" Because of this, always use video for all one-on-ones from the outset.

Sadly, I originally didn't do this. I thought, "Most of this verbal status isn't important; I know it already. I can listen while I check my inbox for email." I started skimming through emails while nodding and making encouraging sounds like "Uh-huh...ok. Uh-hum, oh really? Uh-hum." Most times, I don't think my coworkers noticed—or at least they didn't say anything. So I kept doing it.

My wakeup call came one day when someone asked for my advice. They were thinking about changing jobs and weren't sure what to do. Happy to be trusted on this important topic, I listened while they explained their situation... until an urgent mail came in. I started replying to the email, thinking to myself, "I'm smart, I can type and listen at the same time." Except it turns out that I cannot. The email was more complex than I thought. As I typed away, I suddenly realized that the other person had stopped talking, and had been silent for a few seconds. I froze, stopped typing mid-word and frantically replayed the last few words I could remember hearing. The last thing I could remember was, "...so, what do you think?"

I had no idea what they said before that. They trusted me enough to want to talk with me about this important life issue; they were pouring out their heart and soul to me, looking for help—and I was not even listening. That was rude of me, and it was something I would never do if the person were physically in the same room as me. Why would I do that when they're not in the room?

Ever since then, I minimize my inbox and silence all group chat notifications. I fill the screen with the agenda and video window. I make sure we can hear and see each other clearly, without distractions.

Then we start.

Holding Skip-Levels and Other One-on-Ones

When managing managers, it can be helpful to have "skip-level" one-on-ones, where you meet with people who report to managers who report to you.

Some people find talking to two bosses confusing, and do not want skip-level one-on-ones. Others appreciate this type of access, as it gives them visibility to the boss's boss, who can answer questions, give them additional context about higher-level strategies, and help debug any disconnects they have with their direct manager. In groups that have grown rapidly, where peers have been promoted to managers, holding skip-level meetings can help ease the transition for humans who now report to a former peer.

To avoid any signs of favoritism, I find it best to offer skip-level meetings to everyone during a shared group meeting or event, and eagerly encourage anyone who privately takes me up on it.

For anyone who does take me up on this, the skip-level one-on-one has the usual 30-minute duration but the cadence is much lower—maybe every three to four weeks[3]. After working in companies

---

[3] Caution: In skip-level one-on-ones, be careful not to undermine or surprise managers in the middle. I make sure everyone knows that skip-level meetings are happening, and during these meetings I avoid saying or making decisions about anything that might undermine the manager in the middle. If someone mentions a concern, I coach them on how to ask their manager additional clarifying questions. When appropriate, I follow up with the manager directly. This is particularly

that do and don't encourage skip-levels, I've found it helpful to do skip-level one-on-ones *upward*, too—with my boss's boss, and with peers of my boss's boss.

Have regular meetings with your peers, too—leaders of teams in other parts of the organization—as well as your internal and external customers. Even when these meetings are not called one-on-ones, I personally think of them in the same category, so recommend having them every three to four weeks.

Etsy was the first company I saw which took this one step further; they encourage people to meet random people across the organization every two weeks, recreating the "I met a random person in the corridor" experience for people who are physically remote from each other[4].

Doing Reviews

Reviews give everyone in your team a concise, written summary describing how they are doing in their job. If your one-on-ones are consistently going well, there should never be a surprise in a review. Holding written reviews at a predictable cadence is an important way for each human to cross-check for any possible miscommunications.

To further reduce surprises, always do reviews in a predictable format. Each review should include things that are going well; anything that needs improvement; and pointers to help them learn, improve, and grow; all phrased in a constructive way.

helpful when managing people who previously reported to me directly and now report to a manager who reports to me.

[4] Etsy wrote a tool to randomly pair coworkers and then create calendar events at times both are free. To encourage others to use it, Etsy open-sourced the code here: github.com/etsy/mixer. There are now also some commercial alternatives.

After trying traditional top-down reviews, 360 reviews[5], and continuous feedback[6] in various organizations, I'm a strong fan of 360 reviews. I find that 360 reviews are faster and higher-quality than traditional reviews. When you merge feedback from several people, you reduce personal biases and accommodate different communication styles—including your own. This helps make sure that no particular strength or weakness is overlooked. This in turn helps ensure that the overall review is fair and unbiased, which is important. Reviews need to be written carefully—you are a human dealing with another human's job and career!

I've worked in some organizations that didn't schedule formal reviews because managers were supposed to provide continuous feedback during ad hoc one-on-ones. While this sounds reasonable in theory, there was no cross-check to verify that those feedback conversations consistently happened. An uncomfortable, tricky conversation can trigger a conflict avoidance pattern as people convinced themselves that they were too busy to talk about the topic this week—and beyond. Despite best intentions, feedback gradually became patchy or nonexistent. Because of the hypothetical continuous feedback, formal reviews and one-on-ones were simply never scheduled, so there was no way for organizational leadership to detect these miscommunications. In one organization, I discovered some coworkers hadn't had a review—or even a semi-serious one-on-one conversation—in *years*.

Without any neutral evaluations of how they were doing, substantial differences emerged between humans' perceptions of their own work and how their work was perceived by others. Some under-performers convinced themselves they were Rockstars. Some high-performers, frustrated by lack of recognition and doing-more-of-the-same work, were convinced they were failures or sidelined—and were on the verge of leaving a company they liked, simply so they could seek recognition, promotion, and career growth elsewhere.

---

[5] A process where an individual is reviewed using feedback from peers, coworkers, direct reports and their manager. Also called 360-degree reviews, 360-degree feedback, or multi-source feedback.

[6] Where the manager is supposed to provide feedback continuously throughout the year as the opportunity arises, without formal review events on the calendar.

Organizational lapses like these are bad when everyone is in one office—and worse in a distributed team.

Even when incremental reviews happen in weekly one-on-ones, it is still important to summarize and discuss progress over a longer period of time. Requiring reviews on a fixed cadence, and reminding everyone that "there should never be a surprise in a review," are gentle ways to ensure that productive one-on-ones continue to happen regularly. Think of formal reviews as a safety check—a way to verify that all of the good (and sometimes hard) conversations in one-on-ones do actually happen.

I've tried three different cadences for reviews:

- Once a year seemed too infrequent. Accomplishments from a year ago felt disconnected from work-of-today, reviving old issues felt petty, and planning that far forward felt unrealistic in our rapidly changing work environments.

- Once every three months was too frequent to notice major growth in personal behaviors.

- Once every six months seemed just right—frequent enough that everything still felt relevant, yet infrequent enough to notice major growth in personal behaviors.

Good reviews are essential for growth. Doing reviews well, and doing them consistently, is part of your role as a leader. For me, I found 360 reviews held every six months worked best. Experiment to find what works best for you and your team—and be able to explain your reasoning to others.

Preparing for a Review

Create a process that makes reviews as easy as possible, so you are not tempted to "skip just this one time." Here's the process that works for me:

Four to Six Weeks in Advance

Seek feedback from different perspectives. By email, ask each of your direct reports to nominate five to seven people who can give feedback for their upcoming review[7]. Ask for nominees they've worked with on different projects and, if possible, in different roles across different groups. As part of this email, I explicitly note that I will privately add or remove nominees from their list as I see fit.

Three to Four Weeks in Advance

Review and adjust the list of nominees. Not surprisingly, some people only nominate those who will say good things[8]. Compliments and positive feedback are great, but this is about getting a *balanced* review, so make sure to include people who have been less happy.

Send a short email to each individual nominee, asking for private feedback. Keep your request very, very, short. You are asking others to do work, so the shorter and easier the questions, the higher the response rate. Here's the format I use:

```
Subject: Review feedback for Fred Flintstone
Hi;
Fred will be doing 360 reviews soon, and I know you've
been working with him recently, so I was hoping you could
help Fred by answering these short questions:
* What has Fred done recently to impress you?
* Is there anything Fred can do to improve?
* Anything else you think Fred would find helpful to hear
in growing their career?
* Anything else I should have asked?
Thanks
John.
```

---

[7] At first I created the list myself, based on what projects I remembered over the last few months, but then I noticed I almost missed a few important perspectives. Starting with a list of nominees helped.

[8] Interestingly, one engineer *only* nominated people who would give very critical, negative, feedback, so I had the opposite problem with him: I needed to adjust his list to include people I knew really appreciated working with him. When I eventually noticed this pattern and asked him about it, his response was perfectly logical: "I know I do good work. You know I do good work. When I ask people informally what I can do better, they tell me I'm already great! I want to keep learning and improving, but no one will tell me how. I hope these people will tell you what I can do better, and then you'll tell me. Then I can get even better."

Avoid using language that sounds even vaguely like formal HR-speak, because this makes nominees feel they need to write a formal response. This takes more time for nominees to write, and hence I get fewer responses.

Two Weeks in Advance

Some nominees might respond on the day that you request feedback; others need repeated reminders. Send reminders to nominees who have not yet responded.

Schedule an hour for each review meeting. It might not take that long, but it's good to have the time just in case. In your own schedule, reserve a 30-minute meeting beforehand to focus on last-minute prep. During the 30-minute preparation meeting, shift your mental focus away from the rest of your day and do one last speaking-out-loud rehearsal of the written review. Reserve 30 minutes afterwards for a mental break, coffee, or fresh air[9].

One Week in Advance

Send another reminder to nominees who have not yet responded. Nudge them verbally in meetings and in corridors, whenever you interact with them about anything. If people complain that they don't have time to give feedback, offer to meet them in person to get their verbal feedback—this also helps with delicate feedback that people don't want to put in writing.

Sometimes you will need to give up on a nominee. Despite making it as easy as possible, I consider five out of seven responses good enough. Sometimes I get all seven in a day or two; other times it feels like pulling teeth to get five out of seven. This can be very unpredictable between one review cycle and the next, even with the same nominee.

After you have enough responses, schedule a few hours of uninterrupted focus time to read all of the responses at one time, your collection of one-on-one agenda emails for the last six months, the person's previous review, and any miscellaneous

---

[9] I find that I am unable to do back-to-back reviews, so I scatter reviews over the week, a couple per day, to do a proper job with each one and still have headspace to deal with the rest of my day job!

notes you might have. With all of this in hand, write a draft of the review[10]. I keep the review short, ideally one page, but occasionally I continue onto a second page. I think the longest review I've written was one and a half pages.

Include direct quotes—both good and bad—all unattributed. (I anonymize quotes as much as possible, but some humans can deduce the author from writing style. That's ok!) These quotes create a visible indication that this feedback was collated from several people. This is the clearest way I know of, to emphasize that reviews are about how well a person works with others. It is not just about pleasing the boss.

Here is a very simple review format that works well for me:

```
Fred Flintstone's review, dd-mmm-yyyy
What they liked
    . . .
Quotes
    . . .
What you can improve
    . . .
```

The Night Before

If any last-minute feedback arrives the night before the review, decide if you want to adjust the written review for this.

Reread the review to fix English grammar and typos. Pay particular attention to sentences that could be misinterpreted. Read the entire written review out loud from start to finish, just like you will during the review, to make sure it sounds right when spoken aloud. Tweak words, and repeat, until you can read it aloud smoothly from start to finish.

If the review will be held on a video call, print one copy to read during the meeting and have a PDF ready to send during the review. If the review will be held in person, print two copies—one

---

[10] Sometimes I can write a review in one uninterrupted sitting; other times it takes several iterations over a sequence of days. This is similar to how I write blog posts and, for that matter, this book—so maybe this is just about me. All require dedicated focus.

for you to keep and one for you to hand over at the end of the review.

Conducting the Review

Start the review by reminding the review-ee that there should never be a surprise in a review—and if there is, it's my fault, not theirs[11]. Everything they hear should have already been covered in one-on-ones during the last six months; they should consider this a condensed summary of all of our one-on-ones.

I tell them that they will get the written review at the end, but I'd like to read through it with them first so they don't skip ahead and focus on specific items without keeping track of the overall context[12].

Ask if there is anything they want to ask before we start—and I only start when they say they are ready.

I literally read every word on the page, including headings. I take my time. I've rehearsed the material and could read through it faster, but this is their first time hearing it, so I pace it accordingly.

Allow time for the words to sink in. Encourage interrupts, and if needed, take time to discuss items with extra details. At the end of each section and before starting the next, check to see how they're doing. When ready, switch to the next context by reading the next heading out loud. When you've finished answering questions about the final section in the review, give them a paper copy of the review (if remote, send them an email with the PDF file attached). Sit patiently with them for a few more minutes while they read what you've given them. Sometimes questions will pop up that they didn't think of earlier—that's fine, it is exactly what this

---

[11] I started saying this after one person who moved into my group as part of a company reorganization, and one person whom I hired, were very nervous in these reviews. One had a series of previous managers who had routinely surprised her with bad reviews, so she was nervously expecting more of the same. The other was starting his first job, so he never had a manager or reviews before—but he had heard bad things about reviews from his friends, so he was expecting the same. It takes time to reset broken expectations and build trust about reviews.

[12] This is also why I do not send people a copy of their review in advance.

meeting is for. Take the time to answer any questions that come up.

When all their questions are answered, end by asking if anything in the review was a surprise. Don't rush it—remained seated and wait patiently while they think that over. Their answer to this question is very important feedback for you, a useful self-check to see if you have done a good job since the last review.

If anything was a surprise, apologize. Investigate quickly how it happened and how to prevent it from happening again. Make sure to let them know what you are now doing differently to avoid another surprise in future reviews. Hopefully, they will say, "No surprises, as usual," which is perfect.

Even though it can feel a bit formal, I make a point of shaking hands, saying "thank you," and ending with, "...and of course, I'm always happy to talk again in our next one-on-one if anything else comes to mind later."

Mentoring for Career Growth

Part of your job as a leader is to mentor humans, helping them grow their skills. This makes them more valuable to the team and to the organization. Beyond this, though, you are also doing the right thing for humans—what most of us would like others to do for us.

The hard question is: How to figure out how to help?

When I started as a manager, I routinely asked, "What do you see yourself doing in five years?" This was what my boss had asked me. My intent to care for people and their career path was genuine, but the question felt artificial. It is also such a cliché that many people prepare a canned answer in advance that they think will sound good—typically something that shows ambition, a strong work ethic, and company loyalty.

I did this with my own boss. I consider myself smart, career-focused, and motivated, yet I didn't know what I wanted to do in five years. I have core principles that have remained fairly constant throughout my career, but I had no idea about future job titles, job roles, names of future employers, and so on. As detailed in "Changes in Social Contract," the average tenure in several leading technology companies is now 1.2 to 2.0 years. It was hard to imagine my work five years in the future when several companies I've worked at were not even five years old! Even looking back at the jobs I'd held in the past five years, it was hard to predict how one job would lead to the next.

In that context, asking someone what they'll be doing in five years feels useless. Even if you ask this question on the first day someone joins your company, in five years the person will have probably left your company—and at least one or two other companies. Some of those companies don't even exist yet. Why should I expect them to know what they'll be doing in five years?

When I thought about it more, I realized that the question was all wrong—and if you are unlikely to get a useful answer, don't even bother asking. Instead, make it safe for people to talk freely about their personal long-term dreams.

Here's how I usually start the conversation:

> *Imagine it is 20 years in the future. As you know, there is no such thing as a job-for-life anymore, so people change jobs more and more frequently. Last I heard, the average tenure at a job in the software industry was 18 to 24 months. I'm not saying this to encourage you to leave—I want you to stay. However, it is realistic to think that you probably won't still be working here in 20 years' time. In fact, statistically it's unlikely that this company will still exist. If it does, I am unlikely to still be here.*

> *Either way, you are 20 years down the road in your career. Maybe you've bought a house and are married with kids in the same neighborhood that you live in now. Maybe you've packed up your belongings and are living the single expatriate lifestyle as a global nomad. Maybe you've changed careers and become a travel photographer. Whatever.*

> *So, there you are... 20 years down the road, several job changes later... talking to friends (or family) about the different twists and turns of life. At some point you say, "You know, the big turning point for my career was 20 years ago, when I worked for this company that doesn't exist*

anymore, with this crazy boss who first let me try working on 'X'. I was curious about 'X' but I didn't know the first thing about it, and my boss found a way to let me try it as a safe experiment while still doing my paid day job. I loved it! From that point onwards, I knew what I loved doing, and the rest was history. If it wasn't for that crazy boss letting me try that experiment, I would have never discovered that I love doing 'X', and I'd be still doing ..."

What is that crazy thing that you'd like to try doing?

Some people are uncomfortable with questions like this from their boss. Based on past experience, some fear the conversation will end with, "Well, that's nice, but we don't currently need that skill. Maybe you should start looking for a job someplace else." Because of this, it might be helpful to give two quick disclaimers:

- ◆ First, you are not criticizing their work in their current job. This conversation is not meant to encourage them to leave the company. You are fishing for what gets them excited. It helps you to know their preferences when assigning new projects in the coming months.

- ◆ Second, given the realities of work, it might not be possible to find a way for them to try exactly what they want to try—but if you know what they care about, maybe you can find a way to get close. Some of their ideas might not be directly related to what your group currently does, and it's important to find a way to do these experiments safely, but maybe you will see something close enough[13] that fits in with what other people in the team are doing, and what the company needs.

After I give these disclaimers I sit very still and listen quietly. If asked, I happily talk about my own ideas and experiments.

---

[13] One person who worked for me was doing well in his current role, but was considering quitting to become a university professor. As we chatted about this possible career switch, it turned out he'd never done any teaching or public speaking before. I pushed some conference speaking events and intern mentorship roles his way, and encouraged him to find and speak with some of his former professors to see what their job was like before he quit his well-paid job. At our next six-month review, he confided to me that he would have hated full time teaching, loved his new roles and was glad that he hadn't quit.

Typically, once people trust you enough to comfortably talk about what they are passionate about, it's hard to get them to stop!

The idea here is to find a way to tailor their job to be a job they love doing. This makes it easy for people to be self-motivated and develop their professional skills, while eagerly thinking about new things they'd like to work on. When humans have a chance learn and grow without needing to leave the company to do so, it is good for them. The self-motivated part makes life easier for the manager, and the improved employee retention is good for the company. A win-win-win situation.

> *"Your company should act as a springboard for ambitious employees, not a set of shackles."*
>
> Sir Richard Branson

Firings, Layoffs, and Other Departures

Takeaways

♦ Never lie to avoid a hard conversation. You will be found out eventually, and you will instantly destroy your credibility—forever.

♦ Over-communicate. A lot. This helps reduce rumors and FUD[1].

♦ Treat humans with respect—just like you'd want to be treated.

♦ If the person leaving is a manager, hold three-way reviews with each of your direct reports and their new manager. This prevents surprises and misunderstood communications, which destroy trust and cause attrition.

Company reorganizations, mergers, acquisitions, layoffs and strategic company pivots are all situations where you could find yourself inheriting a team of people you did not hire, or losing a team you worked hard to grow. You can also find yourself working for a boss you don't know, or working on new projects with new coworkers. Treasured projects can be killed, while new work lands on your team's to-do list—all with little notice.

Changes like these are tricky when people are in one physical location—and trickier when the team is geographically distributed. It takes special attention to avoid a "run on the bank," where good employees start leaving because of rumors and uncertainty.

---

[1] Fear, Uncertainty and Doubt

Communicating Organizational Changes

Reorganizations, mergers, acquisitions, layoffs and strategic company pivots are disruptive to yourself, the humans on your current team, and any other team(s) that are affected. They are also very disruptive to the work being done by all of these humans. While it is tempting to "circle the wagons" and downplay the disruption with claims of "nothing to worry about, it is all fine, just carry on," the reality is that life will be changing in significant ways for each of these humans.

As a leader in the organization, before you say or do anything, cross-check what you've heard with your own boss and other trusted C-level executives. This is one of the rare times that warrants the interrupt of a cell phone call to wake people up or get people out of meetings. Ask what's going on, listen for unspoken gaps, cross-check what you've heard, and quietly take note of any discrepancies.

After you've heard similar news from a few trusted sources, take decisive action. Get ready to lead your group through this change. Focus on your people and their emotional reactions. This is when you discover the value of the trust you've built up thus far. Clear your calendar for the next few days—you are about to have a lot of one-on-ones and group meetings.

Ideally, if possible, schedule a group event just before the news breaks publicly. Failing that, start meeting people within an hour or two after you hear about the upcoming changes. Speed is of the essence. Company grapevines are *spectacularly* fast, and they thrive on the absence of trusted information. Part of your job is to limit the damage that false rumors can cause to the company and to the humans on your team.

First, meet with each person individually for a very, very, quick meeting—no more than five to ten minutes each. Tell them you have information that you need them to keep confidential for another few hours, explaining that you want them to hear it first from you. And you would like everyone else on the team to also first hear it from you. Calmly cover the few details you know you can safely share. Be explicit about what is fact and what is opinion. Remind people that this is a rapidly changing situation, so it might change with new updates over the coming hours or days. Promise you'll quickly share any updates as soon as you have it. Most likely their response will be shock, but be prepared for everything from rage to tears to denial to stunned silence. Give people enough time to recover. If they have any immediate questions, give honest, very brief, answers—and ask that they re-ask that same question at an all-group meeting later the same day. If they are uncomfortable asking the question in front of others, ask if you can paraphrase it as an anonymous question in the group meeting. End the meeting by again asking them to respect the confidence you entrusted to them; you'd like others to also hear the news first from you.

Repeat this very brief meeting with every person who reports to you. If anyone is on vacation, contact them if possible. Work very quickly; time is not your friend.

Next, gather everyone together at one time. Time is of the essence. If the change is due to be announced during a regularly scheduled group gathering, then have everyone meet in person. If all meeting rooms are busy, squeeze everyone into your office or into the nearest available meeting room. If the team is geographically dispersed at that moment, have everyone meet on a video call with their own head-and-shoulders cameras, as you normally do for any other group video call. This is yet another situation where it is important that everyone is routinely comfortable doing video calls on short notice, and where everyone visually appears equal, including yourself as the boss.

Don't have a knee-jerk reaction and tell everyone to fly to one location to meet immediately. That will delay the meeting, spark rumors, and make the situation sound even worse than it is, causing disruption and panic.

In tense situations like this, I've found brief handwritten notes important for making sure I don't accidentally forget something. When the meeting starts, begin by saying that you've already talked with everyone privately. You know that this news is a surprise, and it is easy to get caught up in the drama. Tell them that you are meeting with everyone again, all at one time, for the following important reasons:

◆ You want to share what you know, because you think this will help short-circuit misinformation and rumors.

◆ You want anyone who might have mentally blanked out in shock to hear it all again, so they catch details they missed the first time.

- You might have new information since your individual meetings with everyone a couple of hours ago. Ask them to listen carefully, as new developments might cause minor differences since the earlier meetings.

- You want everyone to know that everyone heard the same story. This is important to help prevent paranoia, and to limit rumors. It also lets people know that they can now talk openly with each other and you about this—an important way of processing this stressful event with coworkers they trust.

- You want everyone to see, hear, and feel how other trusted coworkers are just as anxious about the exact same concerns. This helps people realize that they are not being irrational.

Next, let them know how you will handle upcoming communications:

- Be explicit that you will only tell them what you know to be true, because you know if you lie it will destroy their trust in you—trust that took a long time to build, and trust that will remain destroyed long after this emergency-du-jour becomes dim history. Then, only say what you know 100% to be true. If something is uncertain, say that. Use phrases like, "I've heard that ...," and "I think that ...," and "I know for a fact that ..." Resist the temptation to say something you think is comforting—for example, "Don't worry, we'll all keep our jobs..." until you know for sure that it is true. Resist the temptation to give reassuring "It'll be all fine, don't worry, trust me" speeches. These will only make things worse and erode your reputation. Respond in ways that show you're being honest and taking care to make sure everything and everyone fits together, like "I'm working on it, there are lots of different things to juggle here. I don't know yet how all the pieces will fit together."

- Tell them the information you believe to be true, based on discussions with multiple sources.

- Tell them the information that is less clear—you've heard different versions from different people. Don't editorialize; that just adds to the mix of rumors. Instead, accurately repeat the various stories, even when they are contradictory. Others will draw their own conclusions.

◆ Remind them that things are changing rapidly, so even as you try to validate information, some of this could quickly change.

◆ Ask for questions. Repeat that you will not lie; if you are asked a question that you are legally prevented from answering, you'll say, "As a manager, I can't talk about that yet, so I will not answer that right now. I promise to tell you everything I know when I'm allowed to talk about it." If people latch onto this and start asking multiple yes-or-no questions, politely and firmly short-circuit it with, "Feel free to ask me about this again in our next meeting. I'm not going to get into a guessing game on this item right now. Next question?"

◆ Ask if there are questions they'd like you to find answers to. Encourage people who asked questions earlier to ask them again in the group meeting. Some questions will be hard; be mentally prepared for that. Some questions will be different than you expect—they might be questions you can answer immediately, or can quickly get answers to. If someone is unwilling to ask their question in front of others, write it down in advance with them, then read it out as an anonymous question. If someone asks a question and you simply do not know the answer, say, "I don't know, but I will get you an answer."

◆ If people are reluctant to ask the first question, start by repeating and answering some of the questions you were asked earlier. Each question and answer shared is another rumor successfully nipped in the bud.

◆ Remind everyone that you are intentionally over-communicating to help reduce rumors. Explicitly note you are concerned that at times of change like this, some humans (who you want to stay) may decide that no news is *bad* news, and find another job elsewhere. Working through company reorganizations is tricky enough—without also having valued employees leave during the turnaround transition work.

◆ Invite them to be involved in the solution, with comments like, "Dunno what I can do yet, but it would help me to hear what you *like* working on." This will give them a way to contribute, instead of sitting in the background, feeling helpless and wondering what fate may deal them next.

- ◆ Warn them that external headhunters and the press are particularly tuned to disruptive events like this, so they should expect unsolicited calls. Some headhunters will fuel rumors, with the vested interest of hiring candidates away to one of their client companies. I've even heard of people calling who claimed to be headhunters, but were actually from competing companies, fishing for corporate intel. The press might find your number, looking for information not filtered by the public relations teams. There is no way to prevent these calls, but ask your group to please not engage.

- ◆ Let them know that you will meet with them all again tomorrow, with any updates and to answer any new questions they might have. Or sooner, if needed. Promise to be available to meet with everyone again in the coming days, and quickly clear your calendar for this. In one extreme situation, I started meeting the team first thing every morning for a couple of weeks until the situation calmed down. This gave people a reliable cadence of factual, trusted updates, and a trusted, predictable forum for asking questions as well as confirming, denying, or investigating rumors. Interestingly, it also reinforced the culture of trust between everyone on the team. After a few days, these meetings became shorter and less stressful. Soon, people spent less time concerned by rumors, and they instead started to refocus on working together on projects again.

While it is easy to assume everyone will have the same reaction to the changes, reactions are likely to be mixed. Some might be unhappy about being forcibly removed from a role they enjoyed in their former group, or concerned that they might not have the skills needed by their new group and be unable to find a new role elsewhere. Some might eagerly look forward to a new role after feeling trapped in an unhappy role in their former group. Some might be unsettled by the change, but cautiously watch to see how it all plays out: Will I like the new boss? The new people? The new work projects? All of these are serious and legitimate concerns.

When an organizational change adds new members to a group, there is usually not much trust built up with the newcomers. Existing team members wonder how the newcomers will disrupt their work, and what the change means for their current-known-state world. New team members want to know where they fit it, and usually have concerns about whether this move will be followed by them being laid off. All of this further complicates the situation.

I've lived through layoffs, firings, and reorganizations, all of which were emotionally disruptive at the time. How humans are treated during these stressful times goes a long way towards how they recover afterwards. Trust, and respect in each other, continue long after the emergency-du-jour—and sometimes the company—has ended.

Being Told You Have to Leave

There are many possible reasons you might be asked to leave your job.

Not doing your work is one reason. Breaking HR rules is another. If these happen you might not like it, but it should not be a surprise.

There are also times when you are doing all the right things, but the organization changes around you, and your role disappears "when the music stops"—in a corporate version of musical chairs. Common terms for this include layoffs, downsizing, reduction in force (RIF), "remix" (Yahoo-speak for layoff), "resource action" (IBM-speak for layoff), "de-frag" (Google-speak for layoff if you don't relocate), or any other term that describes a change in an organization's priorities.

Regardless of the fairness of the situation, behave professionally. Don't participate in public rant flame emails that end with "I quit." Regardless of what your work was like during your time at the company, those left behind will feel disrespected by your flaming "I quit" emails, and they will remember the disrespect and anger long after any good work you did is forgotten.

Work with your boss to find new owners for projects you've been working on. If it is possible to complete projects before you go, do so—but also find owners who will be up to speed for the inevitable follow-up questions after you leave. Have the new project owners start working on the projects immediately, while you are still at the company. This helps coworkers find out who will become the contact person, and they will feel more comfortable with the transition. This also helps the new owner get involved and quickly up to speed while you are still there to help. If there are no new owners and your projects are being cancelled, document what you have in case it might be useful for similar projects in future.

If you maintained your Single Source of Truth consistently and well, there shouldn't be much need for people to call you after your last day on the job. However, let them know that you will happily answer any phone calls about questions that might arise even long after your last day on the job. When the inevitable call comes months later, out of the blue, answer gracefully and do what you can to help your former coworkers. Just like you would want them to do for you.

When to Tell Someone to Leave

As a leader, if someone who reports to you is not working out, it is your job to let them know. Quickly and humanely. And then help figure out why. Maybe the person started helping out with something they were not qualified to do, and they were doing it well enough that the organization never filled the role as promised —leaving them unable to switch back to their actual job that they *are* qualified to do. Maybe this is the first time they heard that their work is not meeting expectations. A good mantra here is: "A stitch in time saves nine."

You are not doing anyone a favor by avoiding a crucial conversation with them, letting them continue to do their job badly for years—and then firing them out of the blue when an external event triggers layoffs. This is not humane. This is you avoiding doing part of your job which you find unpleasant. If you delay the conversation, you cause more hurt to the other human and more work for yourself when you do finally choose to act:

- ◆ First, they can genuinely claim that it has been ok to do this same work (poor or well, depending on different perspectives) for years. Why fire them now, after all of these years?

- ◆ Second, the longer they have been stagnant in the same role, doing poorly and not progressing in their career, the harder it will be for them to find a new job.

- ◆ Third, as people age—especially in the computer industry— older employees have a harder time getting new jobs.

Delaying until people are older actually makes the next steps even harder for the soon-to-be-former-employee.

Weekly one-on-ones and regular 360 reviews provide essential structures for sharing good and bad news quickly—from each side. These structures help remind each human to do their part. For more on this, see "One-on-Ones and Reviews."

Leaving When You Are a Leader

If you are leaving a group where you have a leadership role, you have unique obligations to the humans you are leaving behind. Especially when the team is distributed and you need to ensure that the transitions go smoothly. There are, of course, all of the usual steps for transitioning projects you've been working on. Beyond that, there are important human projects that are easy to fumble in this transition, such as visa paperwork-in-progress, promotion paperwork-in-progress, pay and stock negotiations-in-progress, and career transitions-in-progress. All of these need to be transitioned smoothly to new managers, with intentions and expectations clearly discussed in explicit detail.

These human projects are important regardless of your title, your reasons for leaving, or your next role—in another part of the same organization or in a different organization. It is your highest priority to ensure that the transition goes smoothly for the humans left behind.

The best way I've found to handle these obligations is to hold reviews for everyone in my team before I leave. Even if this is off-cycle for the usual cadence of reviews, these interim reviews help smooth the transition and prevent surprises on both sides later—during their first regular review held after you leave. Holding three-way reviews for each direct report will take time. However, your meetings and other projects should be transitioning to new owners, freeing up more and more of your time as you get closer to your last day.

For these interim reviews I use the usual format (see "One-on-Ones and Reviews"), this time with the new manager present. As usual, everyone is equal—all in the same physical room or all joining the video call on their own head-and-shoulders camera. Forewarn your group that these three-way reviews might feel awkward, but they are the best way to make sure nothing is missed—they are important for all. The new manager will be listening, but the work to set up the entire review is your responsibility, like usual.

Even if a three-way review feels odd or personally intrusive, it is important. It gives continuity to the manag-ee and the new manag-er. At the end of each three-way review, ask the other two to remain for a few minutes after you leave, so they can talk through anything on their mind without you present—and to schedule their next one-on-one meeting. This will help make *future* one-on-ones and reviews feel more natural.

This work helps smooth the transition. When you make sure that all parties have a clear, consistent understanding of their last review before you leave, you help prevent problems later. Surprises in reviews after transitions are not just minor administrivia, they impact the careers of employees and managers. Surprises like these destroy trust, cause human attrition, and are 100% avoidable. Ideally, the next regularly scheduled six-month review should hold no surprises or misunderstood communications. Remember: there should never be a surprise in a review. Leadership transitions are just one example where your responsibility in a review continues after your departure.

Culture, Conflict, and Trust

Takeaways

◆ Organizational culture happens whether you want it or not. The question is: do you work shape the culture as it grows, or work to change it later after the culture is established.

◆ Globally distributed teams deal with different social and cultural norms every day.

◆ Conflict occurs differently in distributed teams. Watch carefully for any conflict avoidance.

◆ Trust requires consistent behavior over time to develop, but takes only one careless interaction to destroy.

Culture develops through unwritten rules and day-to-day norms of behavior that guide how humans behave.

As a leader it's important to shape culture, foster trust, and manage conflict effectively.

Team Culture

Culture is not just touchy-feely stuff written in on-boarding documents for new hires to read on their first day and then ignore. For those with offices, culture is not about free ping-pong tables in the office or free catered lunches. Culture is about unwritten rules and day-to-day norms of behavior that guide how humans behave —especially when no one is watching. Culture is what makes a loose collection of humans into a tightly knit team.

As a leader in an organization, people watch everything you say and do—looking for differences between the two. This is not just about you. Humans have evolved to be good at recognizing threats, unfair behaviors, and inconsistencies. Communications explicitly said, explicitly unsaid, and implied-between-the-lines become cultural cues for a team. Careful attention to your cues will help you shape your organization's culture over time. When leading distributed teams, you need to be even more careful about cues you transmit in the exact wording and between-the-lines tone of your written communications.

To avoid misunderstandings with humans who have different sociocultural backgrounds and native languages, use short sentences with carefully chosen, short, non-technical words. To help reduce confusion, use separate paragraphs or separate emails to describe different concepts. For additional suggestions, see "Email Etiquette" and "Group Chat Etiquette."

To become aware of team culture, you need to continuously observe how humans behave, even when you are not physically nearby. Frequent one-on-ones can help; for more on this, see "One-on-Ones and Reviews."

Read all email, group chat and live meeting discussions at two levels: the business topic, and how people treat each other while they work. If you are happy with what you see, great. If you notice problems, intentionally lead by example. For more on this, see "Meeting Moderator."

Start focus on team culture early—even when you don't think you need to. This extra attentiveness takes effort. However, it is less effort—and less organizational risk—than ignoring culture until after a serious problem surfaces. Changing established culture is hard. Depending on the severity of the situation, if there are lawsuits, investigations, forced reorganizations, or senior staff departures, a culture that has become toxic may not be fixable quickly enough to save the team, or the organization's reputation in the marketplace.

"Today, job security and long-term tenure are rare. This means that leadership, influence and organizational culture are the reasons people come back to work tomorrow."

Eric McNulty, Harvard University

Global Culture

It takes even more intentional effort to develop a healthy culture in globally distributed teams.

An organization is composed of many humans, each one a unique individual with different hidden assumptions. When different humans are presented with the same situation, we perceive and react to different things. If you ask five humans a complex question, expect multiple different answers. If those five humans are from different generations, different races, different countries, and different religious backgrounds, you have visual cues that help you expect different answers. However, if you ask the same complex question to five as-identical-as-possible humans—all of them born at same time, 25 years old, 5'10" tall, white, blue eyed, blond, raised in Menlo Park, California, graduates of Stanford University—you again get multiple different answers to your question.

As a leader it is important to communicate and coordinate with other humans. An ability to read between the lines and ask others for their perceptions is an invaluable skill when communicating, and when debugging miscommunications.

Things become more complicated very quickly when you consider that human social norms and communication styles are different in different parts of the world. Behaviors that seem normal in your hometown might make absolutely no sense in the context of someone else's culture. Similarly, what is natural to locals might make no sense to you as a visiting outsider, unaware of the unwritten cultural cues. The definition of "normal" is very different in Berlin, Dublin, Doha, Jakarta, New York, San Francisco, and Tokyo. Be aware of these cultural differences when working with humans of different cultural backgrounds on a globally distributed team.

Here is a simple example: What happens if you ask your team, "Will the project be ready on Friday?" Ask the individuals separately first, then later ask the entire team together. Compare both sets of answers. Groupthink is one concern. Another is trust—is a junior employee with more detailed information comfortable contradicting a more senior employee? This question is interpreted differently by humans from Germany, Ireland, the United States, Japan, and India. The German person might think in terms of a

17:00 local time deadline, and say "yes" if they are confident in their ability to finish their project work by that time. The Irish might plan to finish before midnight, and work late that night if needed. The American might think, "We're working hard, doing our best," and hope to finish the project before 09:00 Monday morning. The Japanese and Indian persons might say something like, "Oh yes," and continue working hard, even when they believe the deadline is simply not realistic[1]. They are not being deceitful; the human would be genuinely offended at such a suggestion. It's because their cultures consider it poor social etiquette to give bad news to your boss, especially in front of others. In some cultures, it is considered poor social etiquette for a leader to even *ask* questions that require someone to answer with bad news—leaders are expected to know better than to ask questions like that publicly in the first place. In general, keep in mind that in addition to different individual perspectives, there are also different cultural norms.

It is important to note that these cultural differences are generalizations, and there are plenty of counterexamples for each of these. They have nothing to do with the nature of the work or the fact that a team is physically distributed. Cultural differences can arise even when humans are standing outside an office building, trying to decide where to go for lunch.

Be precise and consistent about how you communicate times, dates, and schedules, especially for distributed teams. Avoid imprecise times like "end of day," "end of the week," "lunchtime," or "soon." "End of day" could mean 17:00 your local time, 23:59 your local time, or 23:59 my local time. "End of the week" could mean 16:59 Friday or 08:59 Monday. Similarly, avoid phrases like "midnight Monday," which could be interpreted as Sunday night/ early Monday or Monday night/early Tuesday. By contrast, the phrase "Monday 23:59 PT" is crystal clear and requires less typing. Be precise; don't set your team up for unexpected last-minute emergencies.

---

[1] This can be further complicated by gender or power imbalances—for example a female employee being asked by a male supervisor.

When asking questions, intentionally ask open-ended questions[2], carefully phrased in a way that makes it hard for others to tell what answer you hope to hear. For example, instead of asking, "Do you think we'll ship on Friday?" ask, "I know what the schedule says, but I'm curious—when do *you* think we'll ship?"

Feedback styles also vary widely across cultures. In the US, criticism is often softened with a compliment before and after[3]. In Germany, criticism tends to be more direct. In India, criticism is usually only given when it is socially safe to do so. In Japan, criticism is usually unstated, even after repeated asks. It will eventually be communicated discretely in a carefully thought out, constructive message in a carefully chosen setting.

One way to raise your awareness of these different cultural norms is to travel—not just to a holiday resort surrounded by other humans like yourself, but to locations and cultures where there are no others like you. Personally, I love living and working in a different culture for at least a month at a time. It forces me off the tourist path, negotiating through public transit, markets and other day-to-day situations which helps me gain insight into the work culture of the humans there[4]. Travel can also help you foster a diverse set of social friends while traveling and after you return "home." For more on this, see "Diversity" and "Becoming A Nomad."

> *"If you want to build a company and not just a product, then you need to put as much thought into your culture as you put into your company."*
>
> Pascal Finette, Singularity University

---

[2] Open-ended questions can't be answered with a "yes" or "no" response; they cause a person to reflect on the question and reply in a way that works for them. In contrast, closed-ended questions can be answered with a quick "yes" or "no."

[3] This tactic is sometimes called "The Sh*t Sandwich."

[4] The "CultureShock!" series and "The Culture Map" books are a great introduction to the different social norms and etiquette you will encounter in globally distributed teams. Reading these books about your own culture will help you see your "normal" life through the eyes of humans from different cultural backgrounds. For more on this, see "Further Reading."

Conflict

As a leader, be aware that there are several types of conflict that can damage trust and collaboration.

Situational conflict is caused by the physical situation humans are in; it has nothing to do with their work. This type of conflict can be caused by trying to arrange physical office space in a way that pleases all humans, all of the time. In open-plan offices, examples include phone conversations and impromptu meetings that repeatedly disrupt people trying to do focused work, thermostat temperatures set too warm or too cold[5], and whether dogs are allowed in the office or not. These are just a few examples of how office arrangements can cause friction between coworkers. These conflicts disappear when each person works from their own home office, customized just the way they like it.

Professional conflict happens when humans are passionate about their work; they each bring different perspectives, backgrounds and personal values; and they stumble into different expectations of what should be done. Don't be confused by the term "conflict" here—I used to think that all conflict was bad. Some conflict can be healthy, a sign that humans care enough about their work to stand up for their opinions. If they didn't care about the work, you would notice careless apathy and a lack of professional conflict, whether the team is distributed or works in one location.

Sometimes the communication medium (such as email or chat) is a factor in a disagreement. One early morning as I entered my office, I walked past Alex. He was already at his desk, upset and typing furiously. My casual, "Good morning, how are you?" was met

---

[5] Most offices calibrate their thermostats to an industry standard "ASHRAE Standard 55," which was created in 1966 based on the resting metabolic rate of a 40-year-old male doing light office tasks, weighing 70kg (154 pounds), and wearing a suit. Anyone else is either too warm or too cold. Since then, workplace dress code has changed and more women are now in the workplace. Research published in the journal *Nature Climate Change* found that men and women tend to have different metabolic rates, causing them to be comfortable at different temperatures. Source: Kingma, B. & van Marken Lichtenbelt, W. (2015). Energy consumption in buildings and female thermal demand. *Nature Climate Change, 5,* 1054-1056. For a BBC summary of this research, see "Air-conditioning: Why might women feel temperature differently from men?"

with a frustrated response: "Oh, I'm having a terrible day, blah, blah, blah, I can't believe Fred [a coworker in another office] wants to ..." Neither Alex nor Fred worked for me, but I knew both of them and thought they worked well together. I put down my bag and listened carefully. It turned out that Alex and Fred had been emailing back and forth, arguing about a particular topic for more than three hours. Long multiscreen emails, each reply more combative and taking even longer to write. When I asked, "Have you tried talking to him?" his immediate response was to dismiss the idea, "Don't have time for a meeting—I'm too busy." Alex was too busy writing long multiscreen diatribes to Fred, and Fred was doing the same back to Alex. After letting Alex vent his frustrations for a few more minutes, I muttered something noncommittal, stepped into a nearby meeting room, closed the door, and started a video call with Fred. Fred was equally upset and angry at Alex. Once Fred calmed down enough I opened the door, leaned out and asked Alex to come in. I gently closed the door and asked them both, "Hey, I know you both like and respect each other. So I'm surprised to find that you are both upset with each other right now. I'd like both of you to tell me what's going on. Who wants to go first?" There was a long moment of angry silence, followed by sheepish silence, before anyone started to talk. That multi-hour email flame-war was caused by a simple misunderstanding that was untangled in a five-minute video call.

The longer a conflict goes on, the more it damages people's trust in each other. By the time I intervened, Alex and Fred were three hours into a toxic flame-war, destroying trust and respect built up over months of working together. Left unchecked, it could have impacted their work on future projects—all over an initially small misunderstanding.

The preceding example illustrates the limitations of the chosen communication channel used, and conflict avoidance by humans. If you're on your third message back and forth about a particular topic and haven't reached an agreement, step back and pause for a minute. This is no longer about fine-tuning your words or finding more data to support your point of view in your next response. This is about the communication channel not working. Upgrade the channel quickly—before the disagreement starts to damage trust. If the discussion started in group chat messages, upgrade to email. After the third email, upgrade to video.

In situations like this, it is also important to watch carefully that agreements after conflict are true agreements. One human giving up an argument is not the same as two humans reaching agreement.

"If you say something in a given medium three times and it still isn't working, then find a better communication medium."

John Lilly, Venture Capitalist at Greylock and former CEO at Mozilla

Conflict in distributed teams is sometimes harder to deal with than in all-in-one-location teams. Sometimes it's easier, and it's always different. People argue based on their personalities and cultural backgrounds, which means that in a globally distributed team, people tend to argue in very different ways. Differences in time and distance can help cooler heads prevail—or make conflict avoidance easier, allowing unresolved arguments to fester until they resurface angrily much later.

Nonverbal cues are important. When conflicts happen during face-to-face conversations, humans receive nonverbal cues through body language—posture, gestures, eye contact—and facial expressions. However, when conflicts happen on an audio-only phone call, or a video-call where people don't turn on their cameras, humans suddenly lack these essential nonverbal cues.

Don't wait until a conflict arises to ask someone to turn on their video camera—that will only make the situation worse. Similarly, don't use audio-video solely for calls that you expect to be tricky; people will notice the pattern. Instead, use audio-video calls for all meetings, so that everyone is comfortable using the software, and everyone's head and shoulders are routinely visible. This helps the team learn each other's nonverbal facial cues during routine interactions, which helps later if tense situations arise. For more on this, see "Video Etiquette."

Conflict between humans who speak different first languages is even more complex. It might be tempting to try to win an argument using a native language advantage, but this is not about winning the argument by suppressing the other human. It's about seeking and reaching agreement with a coworker. If you're part of the discussion, listen carefully to what everyone is saying. Through modeling this careful listening, encourage everyone else to do it too. Imagine how you would fare if a verbal argument was being held in someone else's native language. Be patient when it takes time for someone to find the right words. Paraphrase and repeat back what was said, to make sure that what you heard is what they meant—this quickly surfaces any translation errors, and reassures the other person that they translated correctly, you are actively listening and you understood them. This process takes care, patience, and respect.

While it might sound like it takes too much time, I've found it actually speeds up discussions by reducing time spent arguing over misunderstandings caused by rushed mistranslations.

Trust

"Everything you do as a leader has to focus on building trust in a team."

Colin Powell

It's easy to dismiss trust as a touchy-feely thing that doesn't matter in tough, real-world business environments. Personally, though, I believe trust is an important factor in developing humane work environments.

If you only value trust from the perspective of cold hard cash, consider that building trust measurably reduces the amount of time and money spent on recruiting and on-boarding people, and the amount of valuable knowledge lost when a human leaves the organization. Retention is important too; it affects an organization's reputation. If candidates notice high turnover they will be concerned about their own career paths, and they will hesitate to accept your job offer. Minority candidates will wonder if they will be able to succeed. The ability to hire faster, hire better, increase diversity, and improve retain of humans all create a valuable competitive advantage.

Trust starts during initial hiring interviews, builds during the on-boarding process, and continues long after you no longer work together.

One startup founder I worked for, Ted, was completely trusting and honest with me. He shared funding updates, letting me know when clients did not pay and when new funding came through. Ted treated me—and every other human at the startup—with the same high level of integrity and honesty. Ted's consistent behavior helped build solid trust between us. Before one particular make-or-break project started, Ted warned me that he could pay me for some (but not all) of the hours this new project would require. The new project could help launch the company, but there weren't enough funds in the bank account to pay me for the whole project. He promised that if funds arrived later, he would honor his commitment to pay me in full. We both knew that I was planning to leave the company, and the country, in a few months, so there was no way I could realistically force him to pay me later. This was a matter of trusting his word. He had been consistently scrupulously honest with me and others, so I agreed to complete the new project even though he could only pay me for part of my work. Months later, the company's cash flow improved because of the success of that project. Long after I left the company (and the country!), he started sending me a series of partial payments and over time, I was paid in full. Trust was crucial to my willingness to work late nights on that project, dealing with late-breaking requirements—all for limited pay. That same trust was why I was willing to work for him again, when he called years later to offer me a new job at a different company.

This was in stark contrast to two other startups I worked in, where the founders repeatedly made up excuses about paychecks that bounced and expenses they decided to not reimburse. It took me a while to discover that this was happening to everyone, not just me. Over time, this changed the company's culture for the worse. As each payday approached, everyone stopped focusing on their work, concerned about their paychecks. My trust in those company founders was repeatedly broken, so like everyone else, I quickly stopped believing what they said and would cross-check everything with coworkers I did trust. Once I noticed this recurring pattern, I started looking for a new job. After I left I was not interested in working for those founders again.

Another situation that can erode trust is a lack of clear agreement about a project success shared across groups. As a leader, put careful thought into how you define success, and how everyone involved can independently measure progress toward that shared success. If you are not careful, you might unintentionally cause well-intentioned humans to behave in ways that are great for their own metrics, but counterproductive to the goals of the rest of the organization.

When the exact definition of success is not communicated clearly, it will not be understood in the same way by everyone. People assume they're all solving the same problem, but each of them is solving slightly different problems, each with slightly different definitions of success and slightly different assumptions about tradeoffs. In complex projects, tradeoffs that seem reasonable to one human can cause unexpected problems for other humans, who are working with different assumptions towards a different definition of success.

Examples include: sales teams that push hard to meet quarterly quotas, while customer support costs grow due to shipping low-quality code; engineering teams that focus only on shipping new features, in a culture that rewards new features and doesn't value high-quality code; and development teams merging code fixes and close problem tickets quickly, relying on someone else in their testing group to find problems and reopen problem tickets later if needed[6]—or waiting for customer support to file tickets as problems are reported by users.

All of these humans work for the same organization, but they are measuring and optimizing for very different goals. The sales

---

[6] This is not unique to software companies. Detroit's "big three" car manufacturers used to measure productivity by the number of cars coming off the assembly line every day. The hidden assumption behind this metric was that all of the cars were good enough to sell and problems could be easily fixed later without upsetting the proud new owner. Because of this hidden assumption, there were very strong incentives to keep the production line moving, even if someone on the line noticed a serious recurring problem with the cars. As a result, if there was a process problem with a car assembly, thousands of cars were built, shipped and sold with a known flaw. Proud new car owners were upset getting known flaws fixed.

In contrast, Toyota tried a very different "Toyota Quality Manufacturing" approach: if anyone noticed a problem, they were encouraged to halt the production line so that the process could be fixed immediately. They wanted to ship high-quality cars. This TQM, combined with their Kaizen attitude for relentless improvements, meant that over time, Toyota consistently created quality cars even as they kept improving the rate of building cars. In 2016, Toyota again produced the most cars of all car companies globally, creating over 19 new vehicles *per second* according to the World Motor Vehicle Production OICA correspondents survey.

people are measuring by sales quota, developers by number of problem tickets closed, and the testing group by time to verify or by the number of problems found. These differing metrics place humans at cross-purposes. In the software world, no wonder so many meetings include tense debates about whether something is a problem or not—each team is arguing for their definition of success. Left unchecked, trust quickly erodes.

The longer people work on different understandings of the same project, the more bad decisions and human conflicts arise. This in turn erodes trust among coworkers. As trust erodes, humans start writing more CYA reports and calling more status meetings. Over time, success becomes defined by looking good in status meetings, not by delivering a high-quality product to customers. At this point it is tempting for leadership to start micromanaging: holding multiple status calls per day and telling people every exact step they need to do as part of their job; micro-management in extreme. This reduces productivity, it is exhausting for the leader, and it's frustrating for everyone else. Instead, focus on making sure everyone—literally everyone, from the CEO to the newest intern— has the *same exact objective* in mind, and the exact same way of measuring success. This is harder than it sounds. It requires clear leadership, consistent communication—and trust.

When new projects are proposed or troubled projects start surfacing problems, I now start by asking three questions:

"What *exactly* is the problem you are trying to solve?"

"How *exactly* do we independently and objectively measure success?"

"What could *possibly* go wrong?"

I intentionally use open-ended questions with small, simple words that sound nonthreatening and are easy to understand by non-native English speakers. If the replies gloss over potentially serious miscommunications, I probe for more details. This line of questioning quickly uncovers hidden assumptions and differing ideas of what "success" looks like. It also lets me know if the team all agrees on the same clear way for everyone to objectively determine when the work is completed[7].

One person I worked for this did particularly well. Mark started every high-tension meeting by writing two headings on a board: *Fact* and *Opinion*. If there was no board, he would read out loud from written notes in his paper notebook. Under *Fact* he listed all of the indisputable facts of the situation as he saw them, carefully phrased as neutrally as possible. If anyone questioned a fact, he immediately moved it from the *Fact* list to the *Opinion* list. Then, under *Opinion*, he listed all of the opinions, suggestions, and ideas that he'd heard so far. Everyone in the meeting added items they noticed were missing from those lists, calling out whether they thought each item was a fact or an opinion. This continued until everyone agreed there was nothing else to add to either list. This process was quick—usually under five minutes. I found this to be a brilliant, fast way to uncover misunderstandings and hidden assumptions that could cause conflicts later in the meeting. It also helped highlight any "facts" that were actually assumptions that could be changed. Every time Mark did this, there were surprises about hidden assumptions, as well as misunderstandings about what was fact and what was opinion. Untangling these misunderstandings at the outset was a brilliant way to short-circuit potential arguments. This tactic quickly brought everyone onto the same page, with the same understanding of the objective and constraints. Only then would Mark let the team start actively working on a solution.

Trusting other humans is hard to do well, and it's hard to do consistently, but it's worth the effort. Trust helps things go more smoothly when all is going well, and it is *vital* whenever there is a problem. When a crisis is in progress, you can't stop to take time to build trust. By then it is too late.

As a leader, how do you know if people truly trust you?

If someone who reports to you says, "I'm thinking about changing jobs and I want to ask your advice," they trust you. They've exposed the fact that they might leave the

---

[7] You can tell this crucial step was missed at the start of a project, if you find people stuck mid-project debating (for hours) about "what does done mean?"

company. They trust you to not damage their career with a petty response, like "You can't quit, I'm firing you," or "I was planning to promote you, but now I'm going to promote someone else instead," or "I was going to give you a bonus for that great work, but now I'll give the bonus to someone who is staying."

When someone starts a conversation based on trust, quickly make time to meet with them. Gently start asking open-ended questions like, "Why do you want to leave?" or "Are you unhappy working on X; is there a project you're more interested in?" or "Maybe you're bored because you've been doing the same thing for a couple of years. Maybe we can find something you'd be more interested in, somewhere else in the company." Have a healthy, respectful conversation, aiming for an outcome that benefits both of you. Even if they decide to leave, the transition will be smoother. Others in the team will respect how the departing human was treated, and you will have gained helpful information about how to improve retention.

If that human had not trusted you, then instead of asking your advice they would have confided in others when making their decision. You would only hear the consequences of their decision later, when they tell you "I quit, I've accepted a job somewhere else."

"Trust is built up over lots of small positive interactions."

Laura Thomson, Author and VP of Engineering at Fastly

Feed Your Soul

Takeaways

◆ Intentionally structure your day. If you work from home, use an alarm clock and "commute" to a nearby coffee shop at normal work hours.

◆ Are you a morning person? A night owl? Learn the natural rhythm of interrupts and quiet times at your location. Schedule your focused work time accordingly.

◆ Humans are a social species—we treat solitary confinement as a form of punishment. Cabin fever and social isolation are real problems. Intentionally plan lunch, coffee, or social meetings with others nearby.

◆ Staying mentally, physically, and emotionally healthy is important for us and for our ability to do good work. Structure recurring casual exercise throughout your day.

When you work at an office, your daily commute to and from the physical office creates the structure for your day. Unspoken social pressures encourage you to go to the office in the 8am to 10am range, and go home in the 5pm to 7pm range—despite rush-hour traffic caused by everyone else following the same social pressure. The idea of arriving at 12 noon, leaving at 3pm, or eating lunch at 4pm, would be considered unusual. These external pressures impose a routine structure on your day. Within that structure, you then schedule meetings, focused time to get work done and plan your social life outside of work.

Whenever you change office jobs, and start commuting to a new location, you adjust your life to fit the new daily structure created by your new job and your new commute patterns.

By contrast, when you work from home all (or most) of the time, you no longer have that structure imposed on you.

If you usually worked with others in an office and were recently forced by COVID-19 to work by yourself at home, you may not notice this lack of imposed daily structure at first. If you do notice, it may feel liberating. It is easy to miss the importance of this daily structure in helping you avoid burnout.

To successfully work outside of an office, long term, you need to explicitly and intentionally plan the structure of your day.

If you started working from home because of COVID-19, it is worth explicitly noting that "working from home" is not the same as "working from home during a global pandemic, an economic crisis, and political turmoil." Even for those already comfortable working from anywhere in distributed teams, these are stressful times[1].

Structuring Your Day

When you first start working from home full-time, it is easy to stay up late working on something. Why not? There is no commute, you are already home and you can get more done by staying "in the flow." Going to bed late, you decide to not set your alarm clock for the following morning. After a few days of this, you have successfully time-shifted yourself into a different time zone.

Importantly, you have time-shifted away from nearby friends and family. This reduces your ability to socialize with others. With fewer social interactions, dress code and personal hygiene standards can gradually feel less important and personal comfort

---

[1] My dentist described how he would usually see one or two clients a week with broken or chipped teeth. Since COVID-19 hit San Francisco, he's treating multiple cases per day and confirmed his peers are seeing the same "epidemic of broken teeth" with their clients. They attribute this to "bruxing" (grinding teeth) because of stress. Some early research is now emerging, see here: "Awake Bruxism Intensified During COVID-19 Pandemic by Cumulative Stress – An Overview" by Hassan KA, Khier SE, Journal of Clinical Research, 2020 and "Temporomandibular Disorders and Bruxism Outbreak as a Possible Factor of Orofacial Pain Worsening during the COVID-19 Pandemic—Concomitant Research in Two Countries" by Emodi-Perlman et al, Journal of Clinical Research, 2020.

in social settings can start to erode. The transition is so gradual, you may not notice the trend. But others will. Over time, this is a serious mental, emotional, physical, and social problem. I know. This happened to me when I first tried working from home as a self-employed computer programmer, eventually causing me to change jobs simply so I could work at an office with other humans.

Avoid this trap by intentionally planning a structure to your day and then keeping to it. Use an alarm clock to get up in the morning at a "normal" (according to business hours) time. Shower and dress as if you were going to commute to an office. Encourage yourself to stop work at a normal time. Exercise at times of the day you would traditionally commute. Explicitly plan non-work events to create reasons for you to interact with others—in person or on video calls. Put intentional effort into planning social interactions.

Before COVID-19, a pattern that worked for me was to get up at a normal commute time and leave the house in the morning, as if I'm commuting. My "commute" to the second-nearest coffee shop was a pleasant 15-minute walk each way. I didn't make phone calls, read the news, or listen to podcasts—I enjoyed the few minutes mental break of the quiet walk. I enjoyed brief (and socially distant!) human contact at the coffee shop, organized my plans for the day, and then walked back home with a good coffee. Of interest, walking from the coffee shop back home now felt like walking to work! By the time I arrived at my front door, I felt enthusiastic to start work—just like I felt when I arrived at the offices of previous employers. My contrived commute was far more enjoyable than a typical stuck-in-traffic commute. It gave me the same mental structure, which helped me focus. Sometimes I commuted back to another coffee shop at the end of the day—a pleasant commute to end my workday and a scheduled transition to home life.

When COVID-19 hit, I expected disruption to my personal life, but as I already routinely worked from home, I was surprised by how much my work life was also disrupted. The "shelter in place" lockdowns here in California closed the coffee shops along with most other businesses. Most car and foot traffic disappeared from my vibrant neighborhood, literally overnight. Walking around the boarded-up neighborhood while masked and staying socially distanced became stressful, not relaxing. In addition to COVID-19, for some months in California, there were also significant smoke issues from nearby wildfires making the outside air unhealthy to breath. It took a few months to figure out new daily structures that worked for me within all those new, ever-changing, real-world constraints.

Here are some other examples of structure-creating habits that I found interesting. Ethan puts his shoes on at the beginning of his workday, and takes them off at the end of his workday—even though he never leaves his home. Mary drives 15 minutes away from her house, turns the car around and drives 15 minutes back home again—recreating her 30-minute drive to/from her now-closed office. Adam takes his dog for a walk in the morning before starting work, in the evening when finishing work and mid-day when taking lunch. Jeff structures his workday around having breakfast and lunch with his child and promising to take his child to a nearby playground "after work". Teaching his child how to tell time helped the child wait without disturbing his work—and also know exactly when it was officially ok to tell Daddy to stop work and go to the playground as promised.

To help people create structure in their day, and avoid burnout, I've heard of leaders trying to impose rules like "no email after 6pm," "no work on the weekend," etc. While the intent is good, this approach can backfire.

Working parents, at home with small children, are typically busy from late-afternoon "after school" until the children are asleep in bed. Requiring parents to also complete their work in the middle of this busy time can increase—not decrease—their stress. Instead, ask if it would help them to stop work late-afternoon, deal with family logistics, and then finish off the rest of their work after their children are asleep. COVID-19 school closures complicate workdays with new childcare and home-schooling support needs. Caring for elderly parents is complicated by restricted visiting, lockdowns and quarantine rules. Even routine shopping to buy milk have become time-consuming, preplanned expeditions, with socially distant lines waiting outside stores with restricted opening hours.

Each individual is coping with their own unique life schedules, as well as rapidly changing COVID-19 lockdown/re-opening rules. Imposing clock-time restrictions that fit *your* daily life structure onto others is unlikely to help.

Instead of setting the same fixed times for everyone, encourage others to structure their day and avoid burnout. Clearly and repeatedly communicate the importance of structuring your workday to remain productive over time and avoid burnout. As a leader, model this behavior. Find what works for you and lead by example.

Make sure that your calendar and group chat programs accurately display your working hours, so others know your typical working hours before scheduling meetings or messaging you. These also act as gentle daily reminders to yourself about when to start/stop your workday.

In group chat, explicitly let others know when you start—and stop —work each day. For more on this, see "Group Chat Etiquette."

When sending emails at unusual hours, be explicit on what is urgent vs. can wait until their next working day. For more on this, see "Email Etiquette."

In one-on-ones, remind others how seriously you take burnout by explicitly talking about non-work things you did—and asking about non-work things they did. Watch for early-warning signs of burnout and quickly intervene when needed. For more on this, see "One-on-Ones and Reviews."

Creating Transition Times

When working in an office, you automatically have transition times imposed on your day.

You transition from home-life to work-life by physically commuting to the office. In the office, you transition to a meeting by walking from your desk down corridor(s) to a meeting room and then sitting in the room waiting as stragglers trickle in. You transition out from a meeting by talking with other attendees as you all walk back down the corridor(s). After work, you transition from work-life to home-life by physically commuting home.

When you change employers, you change commute patterns, change the cadence of your workdays and change your personal and social life to fit around these new transition times.

These transition times[2] are important for helping you mentally tidy up any remaining loose threads from one event and resettle emotionally—before you switch focus to the next event. It's easy to not notice them until they are missing.

When you start or end your workday instantly, by opening/closing your laptop, you lose this transition time. When you join or leave a meeting instantly, by pressing a "join/leave" button in your video call software, you lose this transition time. The rapid context switching can be jarring. Worse, the lack of transitions cause your mental and emotional load to accumulate, especially if you create a daily schedule of back-to-back video calls. Over time, this lack of transition time can lead to mental fatigue and burnout.

When your work no longer forces these transition times on you, it's up to you to intentionally find ways to re-create these transition times for yourself.

Structure your day to create an "artificial commute" that marks the start and end of your workday, using the tips and suggestions in this chapter.

Within your workday, structure your calendar to create brief gaps between meetings. For more on this, see "Own Your Calendar."

Within meetings, structure brief time at the start and end of each meeting for people to mentally switch context to the meeting and wrap up loose ends before leaving. For more on this, see "Meetings."

All of these are small, easy to overlook tactics that you have full control over. Find what works for you. While each of these may sound trivial, I've found over years of trial-and-error that each of these are essential for avoiding burnout.

Creating Time With No Screens

Office workers naturally mix spending time with humans and with computers: working on computers, attending in-person meetings, meeting someone for lunch or coffee break—and of course in-person commuting. This mix of in-person and screen time is

---

[2] Also called "liminal times."

important. If you suddenly started "working from home" because of COVID-19, it is easy to not notice the importance of this at first, and spend all day at your computer screen. At first, there is no problem, because you are focused on your work. This pattern of working longer hours can also mislead coworkers and supervisors that people are being more productive at home—not aware of the impending burnout this is causing. However, over time, this lack of human interaction can become a problem—and you will typically be the last person to notice the mental isolation, emotional issues and burnout developing.

To prevent this, here are some habits I've developed over the years, which have been helpful for me and others. Obviously, a lot depends on your personal home and life situation, so if these specific examples are not helpful, find your own ways to recreate how these habits help you mentally and emotionally.

First thing in the morning, don't look at social media or news. This can be a hard habit to break if you are used to scrolling social media and news while on your commute to an office—the trap here is that you are accustomed to a forced stop once you reach the office. If you start your day doing this at home, you'll quickly lose the momentum you had by getting up early, and can find yourself doom scrolling until you are about to join your first call of the day. This can make you feel unprepared and demotivated—over time, this will reduce your motivation to get out of bed in the morning. Instead, I recommend you avoid looking at social media or news *at all* until after you have sent your first wave of emails or done something useful from your todo list. This helps you mentally start working with a fresh brain, and feel motivated that you accomplished something. Only look at social media and news later in the morning, when taking a mid-morning coffee break. By this time, you are already mentally in the swing of work, so you'll be inclined to keep this distraction brief and then get back to work.

When you stop working for the day, and step away from the computer, it is important to do exactly that—step away from the computer. Avoid spending the evening on activities that involve yet more screen time, like watching movies or playing computer games. Instead, spend time reading a physical paper book, playing old-fashioned board games with other humans, doing gardening, exercising or taking walks outside with nearby friends or neighbors. Socially interactive online events like live group dance classes, class reunions, affinity groups, are fine, so long as the emphasis is on the human contact, not the video screen.

If you are living with others, intentionally plan at least some meals together, and avoid cancelling these. Literally sit together, break bread and talk with others about anything *except* work. This is healthy human contact. It is also important to intentionally plan solo time away from everyone, and away from a screen—just quietly by yourself. For me, reading a book in a quiet corner, doing solo exercises, sweeping the street outside or just quietly sitting looking out the window for a few minutes can be the best mental break.

The point here is not to follow all these ideas exactly as described. These are some things that have worked for me, and others I've interviewed for this book. The idea here is to be aware of what time structure and social contact you used to have imposed on you in your office-based life before COVID-19. Then find ways to recreate the aspects that are important to you. While each of these may sound trivial, I've found them all essential to avoid burnout.

Morning Person or Night Owl?

For most of my career, I was convinced I was a night owl. Whether I worked in an office or from home, I did my best work between 10pm and 2am—and I enjoyed it!

I recently worked for a distributed company that required me to be up very early every morning because of the commute to an office. To avoid heavy traffic I had to be out of bed at 5:15am, driving away from the nearest coffee shop at 6:00am, to reach the office by 7:30am[3]. Because of these super early starts, I was no longer able to work late at night. Trying to do focused work during the day amid lots of interrupts was an exercise in frustration. Sitting at my desk in an open-plan office, looking up whenever someone walked near my desk, was an ongoing distraction—even if no one actually stopped and asked me something. By contrast, being in the office early in the morning, long before anyone else arrived, guaranteed no interrupts. I could focus. I slowly realized that I was doing my

---

[3] This was best case, with no rain and no accidents causing delays. If anything went wrong, travel time could easily double.

best work between 7:30am and 9:30am—the quiet time before others started arriving at the office. Somehow, I had become a morning person?!

Later, when I started my own company and started working from home again, I realized that I was no longer able to get focused work done early in the morning or late at night. This was because of other activities and distractions at home. Instead, I was now most productive between 10am and 5pm.

It turns out I can be a night owl, a morning person, or a normal-office-hours person. How could I unintentionally change my work habits so significantly—yet again?

What I crave is time in each workday without *any possibility* of interrupts, so I can focus on complex work. For me, simply knowing that there is no way I can be interrupted for a few hours is essential for deep-dive focus work ("in the zone") on complex projects. It's not just me—one survey found that only 7% of respondents were productive in an office during regular office hours[4]. This cannot-be-interrupted focus time was what I craved when I was a night owl, when I was a morning person, and (now that I am working from home again) during "normal" office hours.

Now that I am aware of this, I plan my day accordingly. I choose to do administrivia (answering emails, scheduling meetings, doing finances, and so on) during times when I risk being interrupted. I reserve deeply focused work for times when there is no possibility of interrupt—in an empty room with the door closed and my cell phone, email and group chat turned off. Now, my focus will not be interrupted until I next choose to take a break and check all these interruptive devices.

Learn the natural rhythm of interrupts at your location, and plan your focused work accordingly.

---

[4] Flexjobs, "2017 Annual Survey Finds Workers Are More Productive at Home, And More."

Networking and Social Events

My first work-from-home experience was in the early 1990s, when I worked as a self-employed consultant. Working at home, I wrote code for clients during the day, and wrote code for my research Masters in Computer Science at night. After more than a year of feeling isolated, I had to change something, so I found myself a new job at an office; I missed the social interactions with other humans.

When you work in a traditional office, you can network and socialize simply by standing in line at the nearby lunch counter with coworkers, and humans from nearby companies.

By contrast, if you always work from home, you can unintentionally slip into a routine where you do not see or speak with another person all day. At first this might seem like a nonissue—after all, you got more work done that day, and you see your friends on the weekends. The short-term avoidance of all social interactions helped you focus on a specific project deadline, and that might feel ok at first.

However, if continued over an extended period of time, this isolation becomes a serious problem[5]. While every human is different, keep in mind that humans are a social species. We use solitary confinement as a form of punishment, and cabin fever is a real concern in isolated rural locations. Be aware of this isolation risk from the outset, and create a plan to explicitly deal with it.

Schedule recurring social video calls with coworkers, mentors and friends, regardless of where they live. For more on this see "Organizing In-Person Gatherings."

Attend industry conferences and keep in contact with people you enjoyed meeting. Websites like linkedin.com, meetup.com, upwork.com, and flexjobs.com enable people to have distributed careers, recreating the personal recommendations and trusted friend-of-a-coworker network of loose connections that grow organically at offices, conferences, cross-company projects, and

---

[5] *Social isolation and loneliness as risk factors for myocardial infarction, stroke and mortality: UK Biobank cohort study of 479 054 men and women by* Christian Hakulinen et al.

volunteering events. There are also ad hoc groups formed on slack.com and on Facebook. Find a place to be active on these websites. Let yourself be found by your peers.

While you might be the only person from your company within easy driving distance, there might be peers in other organizations living nearby. Find recurring breakfast, lunch, coffee, or happy hour events with others who live nearby. If there are none, start one. Be a constant gardener of your professional network.

> *"When I switched from working in an office to working from home, my social life changed drastically. At first, it was disruptive and to be honest, quite lonely. Now I think it's for the better. When I was at the office, I had lots of trivial, short, superficial interactions throughout the day: "Did you see that game?" "What did you think of latest episode of [insert-TV-show-here]?" "How was your commute this morning in the rain?" All friendly, yet very superficial small talk. When I switched to working fully remotely, those superficial conversations all stopped instantly. At first I missed them. In hindsight, I realize I had very few genuine conversations with the people I had shared an office with. As you [John] suggested, I arranged recurring long lunch meetings with old friends, former coworkers and video calls with other not-so-near techies, making sure to allow time to talk shop and for real discussions about real life and real work. Now I have fewer interactions, but each one is much longer and really personally meaningful. This took premeditated effort to schedule, yet is much more meaningful and exciting. I'll never go back."*

CTO, 20+ years' experience (interviewed by the author and asked to remain anonymous)

Physical Exercise

When I worked in a large company office, I used to get casual exercise simply by choosing to walk (quickly!) between meetings throughout the day. When meetings were on other floors of the office building I ran up and down the stairs instead of taking elevators. (If the meeting was two floors up or four floors down, I found the stairs were also faster than the elevator.) For meetings in nearby buildings, I would walk fast instead of joining a conference call. I did not own a step counter, but I did a lot of walking throughout the day, every day.

By contrast, when working at home it is easy to unintentionally become very, very, sedentary. You leave a meeting by disconnecting from the video call, continue sitting in the same chair and continue working. Walking to the bathroom or the coffee machine in the kitchen become the only walks of the day. At first, you won't notice the gradual physical change—and on rainy, snowy, cold days it feels great to stay cozy and warm inside. Over time, however, this continuously sedentary life is a serious health risk.

One medical study asked volunteers to reduce their walking to around 1300 steps per day. This caused a 7% decline in their ability to absorb breathed oxygen into the bloodstream ("VO2 max," a metric for respiratory and cardiovascular health), a 17% reduction in glucose absorption (marker for diabetes), and a measurable loss of muscle mass[6]. Other researchers have found similarly chilling results. This deterioration took just two weeks.

"It is amazing that only two weeks of reduced stepping can induce numerous metabolic abnormalities."

Dr. Rikke Krogh-Madsen

In my home, I'd need to walk from my computer to the bathroom to the kitchen and back to my computer 17 times in one day, just to reach the minimum 1300 steps in that two-week medical experiment!

If you work from home, be aware of and vigilant to these medical risks. Repeated ongoing activity is essential. Explicitly plan some form of frequent, routine physical activity into your day. Invent reasons to go outside and walk around in breaks between meetings. Walk to a nearby mailbox and back just to mail one not-

---

[6] For more information, see the following two articles: Krogh-Madsen R., Thyfault J.P., Broholm C., Mortensen O.H., Olsen R.H., Mounier R., et al. (2010). A 2-wk reduction of ambulatory activity attenuates peripheral insulin sensitivity. Journal of Applied Physiology, 108(5), 1034–40. Breaks in sedentary time: Beneficial associations with metabolic risk. Diabetes Care, 31(4), 661–6.

so-urgent letter. Some people have a dog who forces them to take walks and get fresh air throughout the day. Some people jog or do yoga. I do Aikido warmup exercises. Depending on the weather, I "commute" walk to a nearby coffee shop, or sometimes, I use a broom to sweep the street outside.

This is not hard-core exercise by any definition, and it only takes a few minutes each time. The idea is to give you some basic physical movement and fresh air at frequent intervals throughout the day, each day, without disrupting your work—just like you would do if you were at an office. I also view these as transition times, just like commuting to a physical office or walking between campus buildings. I think about the meeting that just ended, mentally switch gears, and plan the rest of my day.

Even when the lack of a forced commute allows a lifestyle with dangerously reduced levels of activity, it is important to intentionally find ways to stay healthy so you can keep working like this for years.

It is also worth noting that *not* commuting reduces the risk of accidents, and eliminates a significant cause of stress in people's lives—which helps you stay healthy.

"You have to exercise or at some point you'll just break down."

President Barack Obama

Bringing Humans Together

Takeaways

- Have everyone meet in person every three months—even if you and your team think you don't need to.

- When possible, schedule 360 reviews (held every six months) so that they happen at these gatherings.

- Create a recurring budget specifically for in-person gatherings. A good rule of thumb is to use a percentage of the money saved by not paying for office desks. Keep track of exact expenses, so you can quickly address any perceptions that these gatherings are expensive, using data showing how you are saving money for the company by not using office space.

- Most travel costs are for flights and accommodations. To reduce costs, choose locations with major hub airports for less-expensive flights, lots of cheap hotels, and high-speed internet connections.

- During COVID-19 lockdowns, create a cadence of online gatherings until in-person gatherings are possible again.

If you usually communicate with coworkers via group chat, email, or audio-only calls, it becomes easy to forget that these coworkers are real humans, just like yourself. To detect this shift in your organization's culture, be vigilant for email flame-wars and chat-wars—where coworkers say things to each other in writing that they would never consider saying face-to-face.

To help maintain a personal connection in a distributed team, create recurring opportunities for coworkers to reconnect with each other. The best solution I've found is to use audio-video for all work meetings (see "Meetings," "Meeting Moderator," and "One-on-Ones and Reviews"), and gather your entire team together in person on a regular cadence. Obviously, COVID-19 has complicated some of this, with travel restrictions and social distancing restrictions making in-person gatherings nigh impossible.

This chapter summarizes what did (and didn't!) work well for my team gatherings held before as well as during COVID-19.

Organizing Weekly Social Events

Friday afternoon social events are common in Silicon Valley— almost traditional[1]. These socials typically take the form of a 16:00 Friday afternoon beer, wine, and food event in the office. Sometimes announcements are made and awards are handed out. Coworkers play video games, foosball, table tennis, pool, or board games. Sometimes they go to a nearby bar or restaurant, joining employees from other companies for happy hour events. These events are an important way to decompress after a busy week, while socializing and getting to know people in other parts of the organization and networking with friends of coworkers.

Anyone not physically in the office can easily feel left out of these social events. I've seen a few attempts to include remote people by bringing laptops and sharing the video stream. This simply didn't work—and despite the best of intentions, they were often counterproductive. The remote person was reminded of how excluded they are simply by being remote, and they were unable to participate in any meaningful way because of background noise.

Instead, schedule a video meeting called "Friday afternoon social" and invite the entire group—not just the remotes. If Friday afternoon doesn't work due to time zones, pick a recurring day and time that works for everyone[2]. When the calendar reminder goes off, grab water, tea, coffee, beer, or a glass of wine and join

---

[1] One friend of mine worked in a large, publicly traded software company that frowned on such events, so he quietly organized a very popular "standards meeting" held every Friday at 16:00 in the nearest Irish bar!

[2] Weekly calendar haggling is a time-consuming hassle; holding these socials at a fixed predictable time makes them easier to organize and helps everyone plan their work week.

the video call. Use your own head-and-shoulders camera, just like you would join a normal video-call meeting.

My team at Mozilla had "Friday Skype beers" meetings[3] each week as a casual forum for people to chat about anything. Occasionally, these meetings also served as an AMA ("Ask Me Anything") where humans could ask questions about company-wide events that happened since the last team meeting[4]. FlexJobs organizes "pub quiz" events on video calls: the organizer and all teams start by joining the main call, each team goes to their own breakout video room to discuss answers, and then they all rejoin the main call for the next round of questions. Etsy has "mixer" events that are scheduled automatically[5]. GitLab has "Coffee Break" video calls[6]. CivicActions has weekly scheduled "pod calls" with eight to ten people intentionally selected from different teams across the organization[7], as well as a monthly "open mic" event where anyone in the company can put themselves in front of a friendly audience to read poetry, sing, play music or even read portions of a book they are writing (like this one!).

Similar to social events held at a physical office, these social meetings usually have no formal agenda. Talking about work is not encouraged, but in practice it's impossible to prevent work discussions from happening some of the time. That is ok, as long

---

[3] This nickname stuck even after we switched to other video technology! Alcoholic drinks were not required and because of time zones, it was not even Friday afternoon for many participants.

[4] If this happens, answer the question when asked. Then ask the questioner to repeat their same question in the next group meeting, so you can re-answer the same question in front of the entire group. This helps reduce rumors and coming-to-meeting-just-in-case-itis. For more on this, see "Meeting Hijacking and Coming-To-Meeting-Just-In-Case-Itis."

[5] Their open-source software for this is available at github.com/etsy/mixer.

[6] See work.qz.com, "'Virtual coffee breaks' encourage remote workers to interact like they would in an office."

[7] The calls have a moderator; the role rotates through the group. Each week the moderator chooses a different discussion topic, knowing full well that topics can morph during the call. Every nine to twelve months these "pod" groups are reshuffled so that everyone gets to know a different eight to ten people from across the company.

as work doesn't become the main focus of the event. It's always great to hear an unexpected compliment from peers about a tricky work problem solved that week, but social events should be mostly about the humans, not the work. This is the time when it is ok to relax a little and learn more about each other. Take the time to find out that someone is a photography nut, with big plans for an upcoming eclipse. Or taking a martial arts test. Or was approved to adopt a child. Or recently got engaged to be married. Or is going to run a marathon. Or plays in a band and recently finalized an upcoming concert date. Or has a hobby of making homemade ice cream with unusual combinations of flavors[8]. These are all true examples—and they all added color and depth to my perceptions of each human on our team.

If some coworkers happen to live near each other, create ad hoc gatherings. Encourage them to meet every week for lunch or for a Friday social, and explicitly note that you will approve these (modest) expenses. These low-cost lunches and socials are a great way to get to know each other. Frequently, they also become informal recruiting interviews for potential job candidates.

Depending on your formal title or role in the organization, it might be tricky for you to participate without influencing how everyone else behaves. Be very careful. Don't let these social events turn into boring sessions where the boss pontificates about work goals again —or else people will find reasons to not attend future events. If in doubt, a good rule-of-thumb is "the boss talks the least."

Model the behavior you hope to see from others. Accept the calendar invite. Ask about non-work stuff. Be curious. Listen. Learn. Ask more. If asked about yourself, remember to be equally vulnerable and honest when responding.

Attend as many socials as you can, but if you end up missing one occasionally, ask everyone to meet without you. Find someone else in advance to host the meeting on the day you can't attend. Make sure to attend the following week, to show that these social gatherings are important to you.

---

[8] Some favorites were: a) rum apricot and b) blueberry vodka with blueberries. For other suggestions, see joythebaker.com.

These social events remind everyone that we are all humans, with different skills and interests outside of our work—which helps foster personal connection and trust.

Organizing In-Person Gatherings

Bring your entire team of humans together on a predictable cadence for group gatherings[9].

Maintaining the personal connection between humans is crucial for a healthy distributed team. When humans don't meet each other for a while, that human connection slowly erodes. The purpose of these gatherings is to continue getting work done, just like we usually do from our respective locations—*and* to introduce, socialize, and brainstorm large new complex projects; onboard new hires; and hold 360 reviews. These gatherings also remind everyone how much we like working with each other.

When possible, have new people join the team at (or just before) a group gathering. Joining a new company is always exciting. For a new hire joining a fully distributed team, meeting everyone in person is a great way to get to know their new coworkers, have a crash course on people's working styles and team culture, and quickly be guided around various systems. Because of random timing, I've had new hires join who didn't meet anyone in person for a month or two. It worked, but if you can simplify on-boarding of a new hire by aligning their start date with an upcoming group gathering, do so. For more on this, see "Hiring and On-Boarding."

Plan the dates of these gatherings well in advance, so everyone has time to arrange alternate help for care of kids, pets, or parents while they are away. Even if you are comfortable with last-minute travel, advance notice helps improve the ability for others to attend, which helps ensure that the gathering is successful. Advance planning also helps reduce airfare and lodging costs.

---

[9] In the past I have used (and have heard others use) terms like: "work weeks," "group offsite," "group onsite" (because these humans were offsite the rest of the time!), "group popups," "management retreats," "management offsites," and "strategy offsites."

*"The idea [of these group gatherings] is not to get work done—
although we do lots. The idea is that we meet so that people
will continue to work well together after they go back home."*

Mike "morgamic" Morgan

Organizing Online Gatherings

Since COVID-19, the immigration restrictions, quarantine
protocols, ever changing lockdown rules and genuine health
concerns make it unrealistic to gather humans in person. This is
true whether you are organizing a 10,000+ person conference, or a
50 person team gathering.

At first, these in-person group gatherings are not a priority. The
economic and health concerns from COVID-19 mean that the day-
to-day challenge of simply keeping your organization running,
your staff able to do their jobs despite new lockdown restrictions
and school closures while everyone stays healthy are all higher
priorities.

However, the need for human contact remains, and as of January
2021, these COVID-19 lockdowns continue. After the initial
disruptions calm down, and life starts to follow a "new normal"
pattern, the lack of human contact with coworkers becomes more
pressing. Left unaddressed, this will lead to isolation, burnout,
erosion of team culture and erosion of trust—erosion that gains
momentum and quickly leads to attrition and retention issues. To
prevent these problems, hold online gatherings until you are able
to resume in-person gatherings.

These online gatherings have some important differences—and
similarities—to in-person gatherings. Be explicit that these online
gatherings will be different to the usual in-person gatherings—no-
one should expect the online gathering to be identical to the usual
in-person gathering. Remind people that human contact and team
cohesion is the important part you are focused on. Ask people for
suggestions for events and for help with logistics[10].

---

[10] Be pleasantly surprised by people volunteering to help for the first time—
especially those never volunteered to help at in-person gatherings, because they
thought those events already had established people in established roles.

As with in-person gatherings, plan the dates well in advance, so everyone has time to arrange alternate help for care of kids, pets, or parents. This also allows people to schedule any work deadlines around this event, so all can focus on attending without work distractions. To help maintain the usual rhythm of company-wide and team-wide events, schedule these online group gatherings as close as possible to when you would typically hold in-person gatherings in the year. For example, if you usually have an in-person mid-summer company-wide gathering, and a mid-winter holiday party, use those same dates for online gatherings with a similar theme.

Obviously, there will be no travel or hotels, which saves money[11]. There will also be no group meals together in restaurants, so instead encourage people to buy and expense meals during the event—up to some pre-announced daily limit. Make this operationally easy for people to do, and operationally easy to be reimbursed for. If you typically hand out swag like t-shirts, physical awards and other mementoes at in-person gatherings, then figure out the logistics to mail these in advance to people's home addresses.

Post a schedule in advance, so people can start anticipating the upcoming event, and talking with each other about what sessions they do/don't plan to attend. Create early signup lists for each session—these let you see which topics are not gathering interest, so could be dropped to make time available for other topics that are popular and might need another session. Each session should be 30 to 60 mins short[12]. Intentionally schedule 10-15 minute gaps between sessions—this recreates gaps during in-person events where people can stretch, take a mental break for a coffee and

---

[11] Keep track of all expenses in a shared spreadsheet, like you would for an in-person gathering. Don't lose sight of the fact that while these gatherings cost money, they are significantly cheaper then renting office space. For more on this, "Logistics" and "Justifying Costs."

[12] If you have a topic that is usually a multi-hour in-person meeting, break it up into a sequence of shorter 30 to 60 minute video calls, with each call being on specific agenda topics and a short break in between. You are still covering all the same material. The important difference is that you now explicitly allow people to take mental breaks. This is similar to in-person marathon meetings, where people informally take mental breaks by checking email on their phones, stepping out of the room for a bathroom/coffee break or to answer an unrelated phone call.

casually chat with coworkers about the previous/next session before joining the next session.

Start each day with an all-hands meeting for leadership to welcome everyone to the day's proceedings, go through any logistical announcements, cover any organization-wide topics, like personnel changes/promotions/departures and major project kickoffs. Allow plenty of time at the end for a question and answer session—some may drift off once their specific question is answered, but others might stay riveted with interest to each question and it's answer. This is one of the rare times that leadership hears concerns directly from, and can speak directly to, everyone across the organization—so prioritize this valuable time. End each day with another (brief) all-hands meeting to answer any questions that might have come up during the day—but mostly to help everyone structure their day, hear announcements about the next day and then formally step away from their computer for the night. During the day, have a mix of all-hands meetings and smaller break-out sessions, depending on the topics of interest to your team or organization. Smaller break-out sessions allow for more focused discussions, coworking and brainstorming details on specific projects. Schedule a few break-out sessions concurrently to help cover more topics in the limited days available. Where possible, schedule unrelated topics concurrently, so people are not forced to choose between two topics they care about—and know that this is never 100% possible.

Unlike in-person group gatherings, explicitly do *not* hold 360 reviews during these online gatherings. Instead hold upcoming reviews beforehand, so any newly announced promotions can be publicly re-acknowledged during the gathering.

Unlike in-person group gatherings, it is important to explicitly schedule blocks of free, un-structured time. These "free times" help people avoid feeling like they are required to attend all-day-long video calls, which are draining. Instead, have a few short events close to each other at the start, middle and end of the day— and explicitly schedule "free time" in between. Some people will use this time to quietly read a paperback book in their backyard hammock, go for a bike ride, grab an impromptu video-coffee with a coworker or have a family meal with coworker's family. Others might form an impromptu session to work on a side project. The important part is to clearly communicate that everyone across the organization is free, at the same time, to do whatever *they* think is best for team cohesion.

Avoid events with complex technical needs—these can derail the session despite the best efforts of all involved, creating frustrating instead of bringing people together. Instead, focus on simple, low-tech, human-focused, interactive events, using the existing tools you use for everyday video calls, group chat and calendars.

Some examples that I've seen work well include: a cooking class preparing a unique dish—with everyone following along in their own kitchen; a neighborhood cafe style "open mic" event with impromptu signup sheet; a video call where each person is walking around their neighborhood, showing off highlights they most admire; parents-and-children face-painting[13]; multi-player games and even online versions of traditional card and board games.

The intent here is to maintain the healthy personal connections between humans in the distributed team, until in-person gatherings are possible again.

Cadence of Gatherings

Find a cadence for these recurring gatherings that feels comfortable and make them predictable, so people can plan around them well in advance. This cadence becomes an important "heartbeat" for maintaining team culture and cohesion.

Traveling too often causes people to quickly tire, it's intrusive to everyone's personal life, and it gets expensive. Traveling too infrequently erodes group trust and cohesion. Another important consideration is the operational work needed to setup and run these gatherings. Holding these too frequently can burn out people running logistics. Holding them too infrequently can cause people to forget the process that worked last time and have to do extra work re-inventing the wheel every time.

---

[13] This helps parents relate with other parents. This also helps the children of coworkers get to know children of other coworkers.

After some trial and error, I recommend a cadence of gathering every three months. This cadence has worked consistently in a few different companies[14], across multiple cultures. This cadence was frequent enough for humans to maintain personal connections between gatherings, yet infrequent enough to keep travel from becoming a financial burden on the organization or a logistical burden for everyone—including myself. In one team, we once found ourselves not meeting for six months. As we passed the usual three-month mark, I started noticing how much more time I was spending resolving personnel conflicts, and repairing fading trust, between humans on the team. These conflicts were noteworthy because they were between humans who I knew usually liked working together. These tensions almost always resolved themselves by the end of the first day of a group gathering—after we met up in person and the personal connections were reestablished over a meal together. After each gathering, everyone happily worked well together again for months. If you experiment with different cadences, watch carefully for these early warning signs.

In a few companies, I found specific individuals who would always complain loudly about the travel impact of each gathering —yet they were the most energized by midweek, the saddest on the last day during the goodbye hugs and the most vocal supporters of future gatherings in the immediate days after they returned home. I don't have a good explanation for this, but I have seen it enough to note it as a pattern to watch for. Before taking complaints about travel at face value, I recommend checking with all of the humans in the week before the gathering, and again in the week immediately after, to gauge opinions. Use that set of data points—and your own opinion—to judge whether the gathering was worthwhile.

If your company hosts a company-wide "all hands" event, you can use that as a substitute for one of the group gatherings. One cadence that worked well was having two group gatherings per year, six months apart, and two company-wide all-hands also six

---

[14] While interviewing others for this book, I found some publicly traded companies also decided on the same exact three-month-cadence. They did not wish to be named, but found this cadence by trial and error, then enforced this cadence by after-the-fact creating a policy of announcing quarterly financial results during group gatherings.

months apart, scheduled so that we always had one event each quarter. At another company, we did three group gatherings and one company-wide all-hands each year, again scheduled so we had one event each quarter.

When possible, plan the dates so that you can hold 360 reviews in person at these gatherings. It is possible to do 360 reviews by video call, and I've given (and received) many this way, but I prefer doing these in person if possible.

Duration of Gatherings

Be respectful and prudent when asking people to disrupt their lives with work travel.

Make sure the ratio of time-spent-traveling to time-spent-together makes sense. I've frequently been asked to attend one-day meetings that required two full travel days: one day to, and one day from the meeting. When 66% of the elapsed time is travel overhead, it feels excessive. Even three days of meetings with two travel days—40% travel overhead—feels like too much overhead. Most of the disruption to humans' personal lives, and most of the travel expense to the company, will be incurred even if the meeting is only a few hours long[15].

The incremental cost of an extra day (or two) is relatively small, and adding a Saturday night stay frequently *reduces* total costs because of significantly cheaper airfare.

---

[15] One company I worked for frequently asked employees to travel on short notice (under 24 hours) for meetings. Because the meeting was short, and flights were "under four hours" each way, employees were not permitted to stay overnight. Claims that this was a normal eight-hour workday ignored the realities of getting to and from airports before takeoff, dealing with security delays and time zones. The reality involved leaving home in the dark for a predawn flight from the nearest airport, and arriving back home from the airport very late that night. Several of us found ourselves resenting the personal disruption and the company's desire to not spend money on a hotel, but willingness to pay significantly more for the last-minute ticket purchase. The trust was further undermined every time we discovered the people we were traveling to meet knew about these meeting weeks in advance. Finally, I note the unpredictable personal life disruption of this policy quickly eliminated all caregivers from this team.

The best balance I found was to schedule group gatherings for an entire week—from 09:00 Monday morning to 17:00 Friday afternoon. This required everyone to fly in and be settled in their hotel by Sunday night, ready to work first thing Monday morning. It also reduced the risk of a flight delay disrupting planned meetings. People returned home late Friday night after work or on Saturday, depending on their time zones and flights[16]. This travel pattern had 29% overhead, which was low enough that everyone seemed happy. It also meant that everyone was focused on working together during the entire week, not distracted by travel logistics.

In globally distributed teams, remember to pay attention to jet lag. If someone's flight is longer than 12 hours, see if they can arrive a day or two before everyone else, to help them recover from jet lag before meetings start.

Extended time together enhances human group cohesion. Making the most of each group gathering reduces the need for travel to ad hoc meetings between regular group gatherings. In turn, this reduces disruption of personal life, and helps reduce attrition.

Disrupting Everyone Equally

If you hold enough group gatherings in enough different locations, at some point you will inevitably gather near a coworker's home. If this happens, the local person should stay in the same hotel with everyone else[17].

At first I thought this was a waste of money, because the local person could stay at home as usual, for free. Local team members also resisted the hotel idea at first, concerned about unnecessary disruption to their personal lives. After holding a few gatherings, though, a clear pattern emerged:

---

[16] A frequent concern about weekend flights is disruption of personal lives. Address this by letting everyone take two days off later, to compensate for work travel on non-work days. After all, when humans fly on a work day, the organization pays for those "work days" spent traveling. Depending on flights and hotels, flying on weekends may also save money.

[17] I use the term "hotel" for simplicity throughout. I know of several companies that prefer to rent large houses using Airbnb, VRBO, or other lodging services.

- Local humans left the rest of the group after usual business hours, to go home to their family. They missed out on all of the personal interactions with the rest of the group: over dinner, night social life, night-time hackathons and brainstorming sessions.

- Local humans needed to commute to the hotel in the morning, causing them to miss all of the personal interactions over breakfast.

This became frustrating to our local team members, who felt left out and excluded—simply because they were not staying at the hotel.

Meanwhile, visiting members of the group, who *had* disrupted their family life to better focus on the group during the trip, resented that the local person was not making the same effort, and they also resented not having a local guide help them explore an unfamiliar town.

Once I noticed this pattern, I made sure that *all* humans in the group stayed in the same hotel. Group dynamics improved immediately.

Similar dynamics can happen if the group stays in different hotels within the same city, so if at all possible have everyone stay at the same hotel. This might also get you a group rate for the rooms, which helps reduce costs.

Keep in mind why you are doing all of this: you are bringing all of the humans in the group together, to remember how they interact with each other as humans. Being together is important. Make sure no one is accidentally excluded, and disrupt everyone equally.

Logistics

Gatherings are so essential to group cohesion that I make an extra effort to ensure that the logistics work well for each gathering, while ensuring that they remain provably financially cost-effective even as the group grows.

It is, of course, possible to have gatherings be needlessly expensive: booking flights on short notice because of poor advance planning, flying business class to expensive airports, staying in fancy hotels in expensive cities, hiring rental cars that sit unused in hotel parking lots, spending more time traveling than actually meeting and dining out three times a day at expensive restaurants. Living a lavish, jet-set lifestyle without questioning the value of it, simply because someone else is paying for it. In my opinion, cultures that encourage that mindset are actively counterproductive[18].

When I first started arranging group gatherings, I simply did what others did—I asked everyone to travel to our headquarters. However, as the group grew, our visit was sometimes quite disruptive to others in the office. Yes, they would welcome the visitors, but the welcome quickly wore off when we occupied several meeting rooms for days on end, disrupting the normal work of humans based in that particular office. At one gathering I was asked to have people fly to a city where one of our offices was located—and then pay to use a conference room in the nearby hotel, instead of having the group come into the office. Even though other teams did this, it made no sense to me. This offered all of the downsides of expensive flights and hotels, with none of the upside: meeting humans in other parts of our organization.

After a lot of experimenting, here are several ways that I approach logistics for these gatherings[19].

Choosing Dates

Choose a few possible dates for the next group gathering, and ask people to rank-sort which dates work best for their personal lives. Choose dates well in advance, for people who have kids who are

---

[18] When humans start expecting to fly business class and work in fancy offices in prestigious neighborhoods with massage therapists, catered food, and other shiny perks; it is easy for humans to start thinking, "We've made it!" Drive and ambition can be replaced by complacency and entitlement. Left unchecked, this can quickly become a company-threatening problem.

By contrast, Ingvar Kamprad, the billionaire founder of IKEA, famously always flew coach class, took public transit, or drove a very old Volvo 240.

[19] "Behind the scenes: How we organize our twice-a-year full-company meetups" by Jason Fried shows how Basecamp handles logistics for their company gatherings.

trying to deal with spouses who are going to be taking care of the family while the other people are away.

As groups grow to 20 or more humans, it becomes hard to find a week that works for everyone. Explicitly state that concern upfront, and ask everyone to make all possible efforts to adjust personal life to fit. This is a special event, important for helping people continue to work well together, so it is important for everyone to attend if at all possible. The corporate perk of working at home—making it easier to help with family—might offset the impact of this one-week-per-quarter trip.

Transparency and a knowledge of others' personal lives are essential. When people see each other's availability, I've seen them adjust their own schedules, freeing up weeks that were "busy" to better align with coworkers who could not move a wedding or other family event.

Choosing a Location

Negotiating locations and dates is always tricky. Being over-transparent about all the constraints is helpful. I look for cities with a major hub airport, near plentiful cheap hotels with good internet connections. Major hub airports are important because airline competition helps reduce flight costs. Hub airports offer more flights with fewer connections, hence less risk of being stranded after a missed connection.

Rule out cities where the hotels are too expensive. For example, London and New York have major hub airports, but the hotels tend to be expensive all year long. By contrast, Chicago, Las Vegas, Frankfurt, Hong Kong, Honolulu, Miami, and Toronto have major hub airports with heavily discounted hotels at different times of the year. For example, Toronto tends to be less expensive in the wintertime, Las Vegas is less expensive between major conventions, and Honolulu is less expensive between major vacation breaks[20].

---

[20] After one group gathering in Honolulu, I was teased by other groups about my "group gathering as a vacation/junket" until I pointed out that as a bald, white, Irish person I spent the entire week in Honolulu without needing any sunblock—because we were inside working all the time the sun was in the sky!

Reserving Flights

Fly coach class, book tickets well in advance, and travel at low-peak times when flights are even less expensive.

Everyone is responsible for their own travel logistics, receipts, and expense reports. This autonomy allows people to choose flights that fit their personal preferences for airlines, flight times, connecting airports, and so on. Use a shared spreadsheet to show costs for each individual flight, and exert gentle peer pressure on everyone to be financially prudent.

Selecting Lodging and Restaurants

Stay in clean, safe, medium-rate hotels located near (but not at) tourist or business destinations. Ask for suggestions of possible hotels, and get group rate quotes from a few of these hotels for the week.

Alternately, I've heard good results from people who avoided hotels, and instead booked large vacation house rentals with Airbnb.com or VRBO.com.

Even if you stay at a hotel with conference facilities, use a nearby coworking space instead of the hotel's facilities. Coworking spaces are typically less expensive and more interesting. Those small business owners would be happy for the business, and there may be unexpected network benefits of your team meeting humans from other local businesses.

When staying at a hotel, dine at nearby, good (but not expensive!) locally owned restaurants. This can be a great change of scene, it helps support nearby businesses, and helps everyone experience the town after being cooped up indoors in meetings all day. Explorations like this become, in themselves, small bonding experiences—fondly retold later, many times over as part of group lore.

Tracking Costs

Mechanically and socially, it is very useful to have everyone in the team see and track all of their exact costs in one shared Google spreadsheet.

♦ Ask everyone to get their own quote for their potential airplane ticket and enter the price, date, and flight number in the shared spreadsheet. This avoids burdening one person with flight scheduling and cost details for the entire team.

♦ After formal approval, ask everyone to purchase the flight, and update the spreadsheet with final costs and booking confirmation numbers.

♦ Continue to use this spreadsheet to help coordinate logistics if any flights are delayed, or if people want to connect with others arriving or leaving around the same time.

♦ Throughout the week, if anyone pays for something, have them add it to the spreadsheet under "Additional Expenses" by the end of the week and expense it as soon as the gathering is over.

♦ Make sure the spreadsheet shows a grand total for travel, lodging, and additional expenses, so that you can show others exactly how much was spent in total.

♦ Schedule a brief post-mortem review a few days after everyone returns home to learn what went well, and what to change before the next group gathering. Add that information to the spreadsheet, so you can refer back to it as you prepare for the next gathering in a few months' time.

While people might have personal preferences for one location over another, or one flight over another, the visible objective reality of the total cost helps defuse arguments about choices (and costs) of flights, dates (especially around holiday periods), locations, venues, and even restaurants.

This shared spreadsheet also reminds everyone how much these events cost—a tangible reminder that the organization is willing to pay cold, hard cash to help keep this high functioning distributed team working well. Soon after we started sharing costs on a shared spreadsheet, I noticed people stopped thinking of these trips as fun junkets, social events, or a chore, and started seeing them as important work events. People started creating agendas beforehand, to make the team's time together even more productive. They also started focusing on relative costs between different times and locations, including noticing when flights on a Saturday would overall save money compared to the cost of an extra night in a hotel.

"It is not only for cost reasons that we avoid the luxury hotels. We don't need flashy cars, impressive titles, uniforms or other status symbols. We rely on our strength and our will!"

Ingvar Kamprad, Founder, IKEA

Justifying Costs

In advance of your first group gathering, meet with the CFO and other financial stakeholders. Work with them to calculate the recurring cost of office space if your entire group permanently worked in an office. Consider this the annual budget that you must stay within for your group's gatherings for the year.

Explain the distributed nature of your team—and if relevant, the nature of your team's work—then propose to hire people without requiring the company to pay for any office desks. Each time I've done this, all financial stakeholders are intrigued and listen carefully. I explain that I can hire, retain, and run a highly functional distributed team without the fixed costs of office desks. However, for group cohesion and retention, I will need to spend some of those significant savings on variable costs like periodic travel. I promise to never exceed the annual cost of office desks. Every single time I've explained this proposal, they are happy to immediately agree and approve, so long as I continue to provably show cost savings.

Some stakeholders genuinely care about the health of the group and would be willing to approve slightly increased costs if that ensured a healthy group—but the idea of a healthy cohesive group *and* reduction of office costs is an obvious win-win proposal.

Have this conversation once with your CFO ahead of time, with attention to all of the financial details—including estimates for costs of meals, taxis, and other incidentals. Explain how having to re-justify a group event for re-approval every time will be time-consuming and disruptive for everyone, so you are looking for approval to hold these sequence of group gatherings through the year, as long as you stay within the annual budget. Promise to track this accurately, and ask how best to report this data immediately after you return from your team's first planned group gathering. Show the shared spreadsheet you are planning to use with your team, and ask if they want to change anything about how data is gathered or organized.

Consistently track all costs for every group gathering, and make sure your annual total for all costs for all gatherings remains well below the cost of office desks.

After each gathering, bring the team's shared spreadsheet to the CFO. Review the entire actual expenses for the gathering, and use the shared spreadsheet to show how you are *saving* the company money, even with all costs included. Voluntarily providing accurate, detailed spreadsheets of data like this—before being asked for them—is a good way to build trust.

Over time, they may trust you enough to stop asking to review these spreadsheets after each gathering. Even if this happens, you should continue tracking the costs, and sharing the spreadsheets with them. Each time you do, they are proactively reminded, yet again, that you are consistently watching the finances. Sharing this data also provides your boss and the CFO with ongoing concrete data they can use to defend your group's cadence of gatherings, in case others across the organization raise concerns about costs. They might even use this data to encourage other office-based groups to become more distributed.

Even after doing all of this, you should still anticipate being asked to justify these costs to other stakeholders at various random intervals. Keep in mind that it is easy for office-based coworkers to consider an office as "free," forgetting about the hidden costs of an office. This causes them to view all gatherings as additional expenses, not cost savings. When this happens, avoid debates about being able to hire better humans because they are remote, or the improved disaster resilience for the organization, or the improved retention because of group gatherings. You can talk about these factors later, but from personal experience I've found it best to start by focusing these discussions on cold hard cash. Only after people are surprised to discover that this distributed team is provably *saving money*, will they be willing to start listening to the harder-to-measure benefits of distributed teams.

A good question to ask yourself and others is: "If this were *your* company, would you think this was a good use of your company's money?"

The Final Chapter

Takeaways

◆ Start small, in a low fuss, low drama way. Make baby step improvements. Start today.

◆ Keep your focus on the big picture. Relentless baby steps can fundamentally change cities, society, and (hopefully) save our planet.

This book contains a lot of ideas and approaches for working well with humans on distributed teams. Depending on your exact situation, it can feel dauntingly hard to decide where to start. Whether you are starting this culture change at a time of your own choosing, or find yourself suddenly thrust into this because of COVID-19 related office closures, I recommend you start with small, relentless baby steps, and keep your focus on the big picture!

Take Small Baby Steps

When starting or leading a team, you have two deliverables:

◆ Build the product or service that you provide to your customers.

◆ Grow the process by which you and your coworkers work with each other.

All-in-one-location organizations can sometimes be lucky with their improvised ad hoc processes—muddling along until they hit growing pains. In contrast, distributed organizations must be crisply organized from the start. Having this intentional focus at the start helps avoid potentially fatal growing pains later.

Distributed organizations also have the competitive advantage of being able to spend more of their finances on people and product while reducing (or eliminating) costs spent on physical offices. Distributed teams are also able to hire the best person for the job—not just the best person for the job who lives nearby or is willing to relocate.

Changing an existing all-in-one-location team into a distributed team is tricky. Whether you are doing this at a time of your own choosing, or are suddenly thrust into this because of COVID-19 office closures, large scale culture change is tricky. Avoid starting with big announcements that encourage unreasonable expectations—these can raise concerns about "yet another management fad," and quickly doom your initiative with cynicism. Instead, quietly start improving how day-to-day work is organized, in ways that are helpful to everyone—whether they are all-in-one-location or physically distributed.

Start by making sure that you and your immediate team are crisply organized, using audio-video calls, meeting agendas, shared meeting note-taking, and so on—each of the chapters in the "How" section of this book. These baby steps are low risk and low cost, and they improve day-to-day work life for everyone. Just as importantly, each improvement helps build trust that future changes will also improve work life for everyone.

As these initial improvements become a normal part of the team culture, start introducing higher level improvements from the "Humans and Culture" section of this book. Depending on your situation, the data and social trends in the "Why" section of this book may help shift endless "home vs office" (or "stay at home vs return to office after COVID-19") debates into a more useful focus on culture change, workforce diversity and operational efficiency. Keep relentless focus on making baby step improvements. Each step might not seem to be helping at first, but I have achieved everything I've described in this book in several different organizations through persistent, relentless baby steps.

If COVID-19 related office closures have forced you into this transition at short notice, follow the same sequence of baby steps, as quickly as you can. This should be your top priority—the survival of your organization depends on successfully making this transition as quickly as possible. Depending on the condition of your pre-existing office culture, this can feel more or less difficult, but it is doable. Just keep focused on relentless baby steps.

If your office is currently still open despite COVID-19, you have time to make this transition more gradually[1]. Focusing on this same pattern of baby steps, you (and the rest of your team) will be able to start working from home one midweek day each week, without disrupting each other or other teams across the organization. As more of your team becomes increasingly comfortable working from home multiple days per week, they'll start to view the office as optional. Eventually, your team culture will shift from all-in-one-office to office-optional. Ideally without even noticing the smooth gradual transition.

When your entire team views the office as optional, encourage them to quietly start encouraging other teams to take the same baby steps. Hearing a coworker say, "We work in the same company, and these exact same tools work great for us," is a great way for humans to realize that the existing tools work well, if used correctly.

When your entire organization views the office(s) as optional, it offers your organization an important new choice. Whether your organization endures through these challenging economic times depends in part on where and how you spend the scarce money you have. You could spend money on recurring lease payments for empty offices, while waiting for vaccine rollout, public transit and other logistics to be solved—then spend more money making these offices "covid safe" (for some definition of safe). And then layoff humans to save costs. Or you could reduce or close your offices—allowing you to focus your money on keeping humans on your payroll, working on the business of your organization. Decisions you make here clearly communicate your priorities to all humans across the organization. For more on this, see "The Real Cost of an Office."

The secret ingredient is consistent, thoughtful, humane, and crisply organized leadership.

> *"Sometimes your job is just to make stuff work."*
>
> *President Barack Obama*

---

[1] At time of writing, COVID-19 lockdowns and travel restrictions are changing almost daily, so do not take your current situation for granted.

Think Big

We are at an interesting inflection point in society, with multiple important tipping points happening at the same time.

Socioeconomic changes, like no more job-for-life and shorter employee retention in a job, reduce the value of relocating. After all, if people at high-paying organizations like Apple, Amazon, Facebook, Google, and Uber leave after 1.2 to 2.0 years[2], it means anyone entering the workforce today can expect to change companies at least 20 times in a 40-year career. This trend towards shorter retention is across most industries in society and is accelerating as gig work, free-agent work, and independent contract work become more commonplace. Moving house for your first few jobs might be fun as you explore the world, but the incentive to relocate for a job decreases if you expect to relocate again soon for yet another job. After a while, social inertia increases as most humans settle down with a partner, buy a home, grow a community of friends, raise a family, and take care of aging parents.

Another socioeconomic change—having both adults in a family working for income[3]—means that one wage earner relocating for a job forces the other wage earner to give up their job and search for a new job in the new location.

This combination of factors raises human inertia over time, and raises serious questions about the value of moving for a new job. The largest public dataset I found was for the US and clearly shows a trend of fewer people relocating[4].

---

[2] "Travis Kalanick lasted in his role for 6.5 years—five times longer than the average Uber employee."

[3] "7 facts about American dads." by *Pew Research Center*.

[4] "Americans Moving at Historically Low Rates, Census Bureau Reports, 2016; and CPS Historical Geographical Mobility/Migration Graphs, 1948-2019.

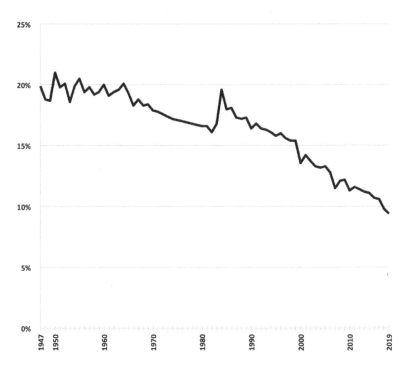

Percentage of people who move within the US each year (1947 to 2019). US Census Bureau

Technology changes like inexpensive high-speed internet and easy-to-use cloud-hosted services allow "information workers" to work from any location that has reliable high-speed internet.

These societal and technical changes are happening at the same time as an important generational change.

The largest segment of the workforce is now Millennials, with GenZ soon to be the second largest segment. Both of these generations grew up comfortably using high-speed internet, smart phones, and streaming video in everyday life. As they grow their careers into leadership positions, they will continue to question the status quo of how people lead—and it is important that they should. After all, previous inflection points allowed our predecessors to change the status quo of how they worked. The methods of working that were innovative in the 1980s, 1950s, or 1880s don't always make sense in today's society.

Leaders should continue to innovate as new technologies and social norms emerge.

These overlapping changes have a compounding effect, creating an inflection point for society. As we move from the Information Age to this new *Distributed Age*, changing how humans work together while physically apart is the "future of work."

This new Distributed Age will yet again change how we design and build our cities, as well as reshape our society[5]. While that might sound extreme, keep in mind that the idea of building suburbs to live in while commuting to an office in the city is "only" around 60 years old. It was only in the 1950s that humans started building suburbs around cities as the new "perfect" solution for people who wanted a meaningful career in an office in the city, while living far enough away to own homes in clean, safe neighborhoods with gardens for their children to play in.

Today, all of these basic desires still exist—after all, we are all human. The difference is that these recent technical and generational changes give us additional choices to communicate at work and lead meaningful careers. At the same time, recent changes in the social contract have accelerated this trend. Since the start of COVID-19 lockdowns, this trend has accelerated astronomically—as of January 2021, 42% of the entire US workforce now work from their homes instead of an employer's premises[6] and have been doing so for months. Commuting into a physical workplace is now widely acknowledged as optional for more roles across more industries.

The question is: How soon will we hit the tipping point where distributed teams are the norm, and commuting to an office is considered unusual? Have experiences gained during COVID-19 lockdowns already pushed us past this tipping point?

---

[5] The impact of this to urban planning is also detailed in Upwork's report, "Freelancing in America 2017."

[6] As of September 2020, 42% now work outside of their employer's facilities, 26% work at their employer facilities and 33% have lost their jobs completely. "How working from home is working out" Nicholas Bloom, Stanford Institute for Economic Policy Research, 2020.

Cities that will thrive in this new Distributed Age will likely be different than cities that thrived in the past. In the Information Age, businesses and cities clustered around early telecommunication and financial resources, with humans commuting in from suburbs and nearby commuter towns. Those cities were different from cities that thrived in the Industrial Age, built around large factories, ports, and railway hubs. Those were, in turn, different from cities that thrived in the Agricultural Age, built on hilltops for safety from land attacks, surrounded by good farming land and access to fresh water. Each of these transitions in human behavior led to new locations that thrived while previous locations withered[7].

As the needs of humans and society evolve, we change how we design and build the communities we live in, and change how we do business with each other. Our current transition to distributed teams is no different.

As more humans have meaningful career opportunities in distributed companies, housing demands in overpopulated, expensive and gentrified regions will change as people take advantage of their ability to live in more affordable, more appealing, mixed-use neighborhood communities with less traffic. Towns with walkable community neighborhoods and mixed-use buildings make sense again, bringing a welcome revival as communities grow and housing values gradually increase in a more stable, sustainable manner[8]. Attributes like good weather, clean air, high speed internet, stable government and public services like safe walkable neighborhoods, good roads, hospitals, schools, and cultural events will become essential for attracting new residents who can live anywhere—because they work in distributed organizations. Each of these new residents bring their own job with them, gently boosting the local economy by paying taxes and spending money at local businesses. They also show

---

[7] Property prices can help measure these transitions. For websites selling Medieval Castles across Europe for less than the price of a condo in San Francisco or New York or London, see "The Real Cost of an Office."

[8] Interesting to watch companies creating "co-living" spaces—where adults live in shared communal housing, usually renting coworking space in the same building. Some examples include Harbour Apartments (Shanghai), UrWork.cn, WeLive (part of WeWork), TheHubHaus.com, Roam.co and NoDeskProject.com.

existing residents how it is possible to stay in their community and find meaningful work online, alongside their new neighbor.

This trend to distributed has another interesting benefit. When most residents of a city work for one organization, the city is financially beholden to that one organization—not the other way around. When most residents of a city work for one employer, who has more power—the locally elected mayor or the CEO?

Locations with an "all eggs in one basket" economy suffer significant social and financial disruption when that one employer goes through boom-and-bust cycles or decides to relocate elsewhere. When all employees at a large employer lose their jobs, this quickly impacts the entire community—even those who never worked for the employer, but whose livelihoods depend on income from those employees. Communities that depend on multiple different employers in one industry have slightly more resilient economies, but are still vulnerable to boom-and-bust cycles in that specific industry. Communities with residents working across a diversified portfolio of employers across multiple different industries are the most financially resilient.

The traditional practice of giving incentives to large companies— so the company will move to your jurisdiction—makes less sense as the social contract around "a job for life" has changed. As the average job tenure continues to shrink, employers prefer to be in locations with large pools of pre-trained candidates, so convincing employers to move elsewhere is harder. At the same time, job seekers are reluctant to move to a location with only one employer —knowing they will have to relocate again in a couple of years, when they change jobs yet again[9]. This traditional form of economic development makes even less sense when you consider the accelerating trend towards working in distributed teams, instead of an employer's physical office.

What if there was a different way to do economic development? What if we give incentives to humans, not corporations?

---

[9] This barrier to relocate is significant. Relocating costs money. As of Sept 2020, approximately 30% of Americans do not have $400 spare to pay for unexpected emergencies. This means they cannot afford to pay to relocate for a job, even if they wanted to move. For more on this, see "US Federal Reserve Survey Economic Well-Being of US Households 2020."

Specifically, humans working in distributed teams, who could relocate and bring their existing job with them?

In the US, in June 2018 I helped the State of Vermont pass a law doing exactly this[10]. The aim of this program was to see if we could have 125 humans relocate to Vermont—anywhere in Vermont—over the next four years. When the program started taking applications in January 2019, there were over 3,000 applications in the first month. Applicants were verified, approved, relocated to Vermont, established new residences and reimbursed within the next four *months*—not four years. Each brought their existing job with them, and as new residents, each immediately started contributing new tax revenue to the state.

The rapid success of this project is even more impressive when you remember that, like many rural jurisdictions, Vermont had suffered years of net migration out of Vermont, with a "brain drain" of people leaving to find jobs elsewhere.

While most of the media coverage on Vermont's "Remote Worker" law has focused on the payments to humans, it is worth noting that relocation reimbursement was only one part of this three-part program. The program also had a matching-grant incentive to create small neighborhood coworking spaces with high-speed internet connections. These professional work environments helped tackle social isolation by fostering human connections; the newly relocated humans worked alongside long term residents, sharing valuable job skills and helping others in the community find employment online. These neighborhood spaces also helped increase foot traffic in the quiet main street areas, which in turn helped other nearby businesses.

Finally, the program fostered practical, personal, contact between applicants and local residents during the application and relocation process. The local residents helped applicants with housing decisions, school choices, finding doctors, package deliveries, and the million-and-one other logistical barriers of relocating. Relocating is stressful in many ways, so this practical real-world help was invaluable. Collaborating like this was strategically important for a few reasons. It helped new arrivals have more realistic expectations of day-to-day life in the new

---

[10] Vermont Senate Bill S.94

location, which reduced the "bounce rate" of people leaving when the reality of life in the new location didn't match their hopes. It helped address concerns of disruption by local residents and it brought both groups together emotionally. New arrivals frequently described being welcomed into the community with more social connections than where they had moved from. These connections played a crucial role in improving the "stickiness factor," with new arrivals more likely to stay instead of bouncing out, and local residents more vested in wanting the new arrivals to stay. This direct, personal, contact also helped share the logistical workload on the humans running this Economic Development initiative.

These three parts of the program combined to help humans feel genuinely welcomed, decide to risk relocating, become a welcomed member of their new local community, and contribute with others to revive the local economy.

Since then, similar programs have been created elsewhere in the US: Utah; Hawaii; Tulsa, Oklahoma; Savannah, Georgia; Topeka, Kansas; and Muscle Shoals, Alabama. Outside the US, countries like Estonia, Portugal, Barbados, the Cayman Islands, and Iceland are also doing versions of this[11]. Each of these programs has slightly different implementation details, but at their core they each provide incentives for humans not corporations. Specifically, humans who can bring their existing job with them when they relocate. Each of these programs has been wildly successful, and I expect we'll see even more of these, especially because of COVID-19[12].

This new approach to economic development—which I call *Distributed Economic Development*—is successful for multiple reasons.

Distributed Economic Development will gradually revive declining rural towns and sleepy commuter towns into more vibrant communities in their own right, while avoiding the rapid

---

[11] While not a national program, some towns in Italy have started providing similar incentives. For more info, see: Santo Stefano di Sessanio, L'Aquia; Gangi, Sicily; and Ollolai, Sardinia.

[12] To track ongoing and new emerging programs, see: oduinn.com/book/locations-for-remotes.

gentrification and displacement problems caused by rapid boom-and-bust cycles of office-based companies. Increased use of local neighborhood coworking spaces, conferences, events, and meetups create longer term stable communities of professional peers that are essential for networking, career growth, and ongoing emotional support.

These humans can build longer-term stable lives in a location, while working for various different distributed employers over the course of their career. This helps them contribute to the local community financially through payroll and sales taxes, as well as by creating new jobs for others[13].

When residents work in distributed organizations, the jurisdiction gains a more stable, diversified revenue stream—human taxpayers continue living in their community, even as they change employers multiple times over their career. This financial diversity helps keep tax revenues more stable and predictable, which is essential for long-term planning and hiring for services like schools, parks, public safety services, public transit, cultural events, and social venues—services that make people want to live there in the first place.

At the same time, this transition to distributed teams will help improve diversity in the overall workforce. Humans who are qualified and seek work are no longer prevented from working simply by the need to reliably and consistently commute between their home and a physical office. For many, simply knowing the size and complexity of the recurring commute or the need to relocate was a barrier to even applying for the job in the first place.

When more people work from home, or work in distributed teams from a neighborhood coworking space, the environmental impact of commuting is reduced. Immediately and significantly—not incrementally sometime in the distant future.

In 2017, carbon dioxide (CO_2) emissions from transportation were 37% of the total carbon footprint of the US[14]. This was the single

---

[13] *The New Geography of Jobs*, by Enrico Moretti, notes that each high-tech job creates five new additional service jobs.

[14] US Energy Information Administration State Carbon Dioxide Emissions 2017 Data, published 2020.

largest source of emissions nationally. For comparison, the emissions from all US electricity generation power plants combined was 33% and all US industrial manufacturing combined was only 19%.

Inventing and mass-producing affordable-for-everyone electric cars, improving public transit, and other measures are all good things to do for the environment. No question about it. However, these all take significant time and money to invent and then to reliably build at scale. Even if mass-produced, affordable, reliable, zero-emissions vehicles existed today, the transition would take time. The average age of cars on the road today is 11.6 years in the US[15] and 10.5 years in the EU[16]. This means it would take at least another decade for these to become the average cars on the road—unless there were significant government policy changes to accelerate this transition.

We don't have that much time.

As more organizations become distributed, we can reduce the number of commuters—and for those who still commute to an office, reduce how often and how far they commute. We can do this *now*. This will help reduce our carbon footprint and help tackle climate change immediately. These reductions are already quietly happening. Energy usage for the entire US *decreased* by 1.8% from 2003 to 2012, largely because of more people working from home[17]. In 2017, people working from home in the US reduced the carbon footprint of their commute by three million tons of greenhouse gases. To get a sense of scale, other ways to achieve that same reduction would require removing 617,000 cars from the road for an entire year—or planting 91 million trees now and accumulating 10 years of carbon reduction from them[18].

---

[15] Average age of light vehicles in the US from 2003 to 2016 (in years).

[16] European Automobile Manufacturers Association "The Automobile Industry Pocket Guide," 2017-2018.

[17] "Changes in Time Use and Their Effect on Energy Consumption in the United States" by Sekar, Williams and Chen.

[18] "5 Stats About Telecommuting's Environmental Impact" by *FlexJobs* and *GlobalWorkplaceAnalytics*.

The case study with government agencies in the State of California[19] show the scale of immediate savings that are possible. Their new "telework policy" encourages existing staff to *not* commute, reduces weekly emissions—and automatically displays these savings on a public dashboard for all to see. The policy and dashboard are still being rolled out across other agencies in California, but as of January 2021, California is now tracking reductions of 408 metric tons *per week* from 11 agencies. The same emissions reduction as cancelling 355 roundtrip SFO-NYC-SFO flights. Each week.

It is worth noting that these environmental improvements are *already happening,* using existing, consumer-grade technologies—simply by encouraging more humans to use the most popular employee benefit, which improves employee retention and *reduces* costs for employers.

Crisply organizing how we work together, even while physically apart, will accelerate this trend, helping distributed teams cross the chasm to becoming the norm, further reducing our global carbon footprint and helping tackle climate change immediately. The environmental benefits from this change cannot be overstated.

While improving how you work with others on a daily basis is itself a competitive advantage for your organization, never lose sight of these larger social, economic and environmental goals. Instead of feeling daunted by the magnitude of it all, just quietly start taking baby steps. Start today. And keep taking relentless baby steps. Every. Single. Day.

Distributed teams are a competitive advantage for your organization, and may help your organization survive the economic fallout of COVID-19. Maybe, just maybe, working together while physically apart will also literally help save our planet.

"Revolution doesn't happen when society adopts new technology. It happens when society adopts new behaviors."

Clay Shirky

---

[19] For more details, see "Environmental Impact."

Acknowledgments

Corrections and Errors

I've tried my best to catch all the errors before publication, yet it still feels inevitable that some will slip through. I apologize in advance for any errors you find. They are all my responsibility.

If you do find errors in this book, please let me know by emailing me at feedback@oduinn.com. Anything that helps make this book better would be very welcome. I'll fix them for the next edition and of course credit you. Since v1.0.0 shipped, I'm thankful for the helpful corrections from: Aki Sasaki, Ben Linders, Brandon Bouier, Chris AtLee, Ian Soboroff, Paul Fitzpatrick and Sheeri Cabral.

Acknowledgements

When I started writing this book, I had no idea how much work was involved. Even after other authors tried to warn me, I still didn't understand the scale of the work involved. I could not, and did not, do this alone.

This book summarizes more than 28 years of discovering what did —and did not—work. All of my learnings came from trial-and-error while working with real human coworkers in real organizations. I am deeply grateful for the patience and tolerance of everyone who suffered through my many experiments while they did their real job. All of the following people played a role in helping this book become a reality—and I am forever indebted to them. While listing people by name risks my forgetting someone from over the years, I have to try—and I apologize now if I forget anyone who helped me along the way.

This book summarizes work in many companies, big and small. A significant turning point was at Mozilla, where I was actively encouraged to talk openly about this work—inside and outside the organization. I owe deep thanks to Mitchell Baker, Brendan Eich, Jim Cook, John Lilly, Mike "schrep" Schroepfer, Debbie Cohen as well as Mike Shaver, Johnathan Nightingale, Johnny Stenback, and Bob Moss. Still close to my heart is the extended Release Engineering family, who were incredibly tolerant of my many different experiments and soon started adding experiments of their own: Aki Sasaki, Armen Zambrano Gasparnian, Ben Hearsum, Chris AtLee, Chris "coop" Cooper, Hal Wine, Joey Armstrong, John Hopkins, Jordan Lund, Justin Wood, Kim Moir, Lawrence Mandel, Massimo Gervasini, Mihai Tabara, Mike Shal, Nick Thomas, Peter Moore, Rail Aliev, and Simone Bruno.

In addition to encouraging my experiments and seeding ideas, the humane leadership of Chris "coop" Cooper, Deb Richardson, Laura Thomson, Mike "morgamic" Morgan, Mike "schrep" Schroepfer and Mikey Dickerson is outstanding to witness in action.

Thanks for candid interviews and encouragement from Andrew Montalenti, Alex Moundalexis, Art Shectman, Angela Welchel, Brad Greenlee, Brenda Stone, Emmanuel "Manu" Tesone, Finn Green, Greg Grossmeier, Greg Horvath, Jody Grunden, John Goulah, John Lewis, Dr Kim Nilsson, Kim Rachmeler, Lisa Gelobter, Marco Zehe, Matt Dunne, Michael MacVicar, Michael Patten, Mike Brittain, Mike Gifford, Mike Loukides, Omer Trajman, Rachel Taylor, Rajesh Anandan, Commander Scott Larson (US Navy), and Sibley Bacon.

During the four (!) years of writing the original book and now this updated edition, I received ongoing practical encouragement along the way from Alan Gates, Ana Cambria, Andrew Sturmfels, Arthur Richards, Arthur R. Ware (Senior), Brian Warner, David Heinemeier Hansson, Deborah Farrell, Doug Belshaw, Eric McNulty, Gene Kim, Jeff Hackert, Jeff Maher, Jez Humble, Josh Elser, Kate Lister, Marjorie Ryerson, Michael Ivy, Molly Pyle, Rose Davidson, Rowena Hennigan and Paul Fitzpatrick.

Alan, Jude, Cary, Scott and the entire crew at Borderlands Books in San Francisco helped with a quiet space for interviews, for focused typing, and for good coffee while stuck on yet another tricky block of text. Not to mention their endless insider industry wisdom, camaraderie, encouragement, and deep persistent love of the written word.

For advice, moral support, lively debates, and countless examples of real-life leadership-by-example, I have to thank Bjorn Freeman-Benson, Bob Ellis, Brandon Bouier, Carol Sexton, Damhnait Harvey, Donald Moxham, Elspeth Henderson, Evan Marwell, Henry Poole, Jeff Higgins, Jen Pahlka, John Lilly, Martin Doherty, Maurice Maxwell, Michael Ryan, Mitch Kapor, Pascal Finette, Sara

Sutton, Stephane Kasriel, Steve Harris, Stuart Drown, and Ted Carpenter.

Linda George has been a wonderfully patient, organized, and friendly editor, bringing calm and detailed reason throughout this entire book project. Catherine LaPointe Vollmer took on the challenge of creating artwork for my unusual "friendly business book about humans" project with grace, humor, and great skill. As the artwork came to completion, it gave me goosebumps. I want to explicitly note that this book *about* distributed teams was created *by* a distributed team—Linda, Catherine, and I live in different time zones.

Finally, this book literally would not have happened without the help, support, and encouragement on a million and one different topics from Antonina Ní Dhuinn, Elizabeth Johnson, Gráinne Killeen, Patricia Higgins, Proinnsías O'Duinn, and Joan Merrigan. I especially thank Jennifer Bury for encouraging me to start writing this book—and then putting up with years of my typing at every possible (and impossible) moment.

Thank you.

John.

Appendices

Terminology

Takeaways

- The terms "distributed teams," "virtual teams," "virtual employee," "remote work," "remote employee," "work from home," "work from anywhere," "telework" and "telecommute" describe very different work location arrangements. These terms are not interchangeable.

- The terms "employee," "sub-contractor," "full-time contractor," "part-time contractor," "temp" and "gig worker" describe legal employment arrangements and are unrelated to your physical proximity to coworkers.

- Using these terms incorrectly can (mis)communicate important human, social context in ways that create a damaging and unhealthy work culture.

Words matter. The terms you use reveal more about your unspoken assumptions and biases than you might realize.

Using terms incorrectly can (mis)communicate important human context in ways that damage trust and unintentionally erode cultural norms. Coworkers can be led to believe that they, and their work, will not be valued—simply because of their physical location. Or that they should not value your work because of your physical location.

If you describe co-located humans as coworkers and describe humans in other locations as something else, you can bias yourself into thinking co-located humans are somehow better. This will, in turn, cause you to bias towards assigning new projects, bonuses and promotions to your co-located coworkers. You might not notice yourself doing this—or you might construct narratives after-the-fact to justify your bias. However, the humans in other locations will notice your bias. They will accurately conclude that their work, and their career path, will be stunted if they remain at that physical location while in your organization. You can measure the impact of your bias by looking at your staff retention data—and noticing how many "remote" employees in exit interviews would *not* recommend your organization to other "remote" candidates.

Being intentionally precise and consistent about the words you use in your normal discussions helps foster a healthy culture for your distributed team.

> *"You keep using that word. I do not think it means what you think it means."*
>
> Mandel Patinkin as "Inigo Montoya" in the movie "The Princess Bride"

Location vs. Employment Status

In recent years, I've had multiple people tell me that they don't plan to hire "remote people," because they don't want to hire gig workers. They are always surprised when I point out that these are very different topics.

I've worked in multiple physical offices where the humans working side-by-side at adjacent desks were a mix of full-time employees, full-time contractors, sub-contractors (employed by other employers) and project-specific part-time contractors. There was no way to know someone's employment status by looking at the individual human, or their assigned seating. The only way to know someone's employment status was to look at their carefully color-coded ID badge.

I've also worked in teams where full-time employees of the same employer worked together for years—even when the humans were in different physical locations, multiple time-zones apart.

Your physical proximity to your coworkers is orthogonal to your employment status.

Distributed Team

The phrase "distributed team" clearly and correctly describes that all humans on the team coordinate their work together, even though they are physically apart from each other. This is not a collection of individuals who each do solo focused work from different locations.

If you are within immediate arms-reach of *every* person on your team, then you are physically co-located. Otherwise, you are part of a distributed team.

Because everyone on the physically distributed team is "remote" from someone, the term "distributed team" makes it clear that everyone on the team shares responsibility to communicate clearly and coordinate their work with coworkers—regardless of whether any individual human is working from a building with the company logo on the door, from their home, a coworking space, a hotel or a parked car!

Example usage: *"I work on a distributed team." "My team is distributed."*

Remote Work(er)

This term usually describes one human being physically separate from other coworkers.

I usually hear this term from someone who believes they are *not* remote—only the other person is remote. Technically, this is physically impossible and tells me a lot about the mindset of the human speaking[1]. Typically, this happens when one human is sitting in an office with a company logo on the door, describing a coworker who is not in the same physical office. Using terminology like this tells me that the person in the office considers

---

[1] To emphasis this point, I invented the term "remoties" to describe the individuals in distributed teams. If any one person on a team is not physically adjacent to *all* others on the team, then *everyone* is remote from *someone*. In this scenario, they are all "remoties". This informal, made-up word "remoties" sounds close enough to "remote" that people notice the difference, stop to think and often discover their own internal bias.

themself to be a first-class citizen in the center-of-their-universe, doing the important work, while they consider the "remote worker" to be a second-class citizen physically located somewhere else, doing less important work. This bias will influence project assignments, bonuses and future promotions.

Another risk with this term is the hidden assumption that the "remote worker" carries all the responsibility for communicating with the rest of the team—a mindset that is incorrect and operationally harmful to the team.

To be explicit, if any member of the team is not able to reach out and tap the shoulder of each and every other human on the team, then everyone is remote from someone—and all share responsibility to make sure communications are clear across the entire distributed team.

This term can also be used when most of a team are co-located and one person is physically in a different location. For more on this, see "The Canary in the Coal Mine."

Example usage: *"I work remotely in a dead-end job." "We have a remote person on our team, but I don't know much about them."*

Virtual Work(er)

A variation of the "remote" term above, the use of "virtual" implies that the human is somehow not as valued as a real human and is therefore somehow more disposable. This term reveals that the human speaking has a first-class / second-class mindset— thinking of themselves as a real, more-important human, while the other human is somehow a virtual(not-real), less-important human.

Because of this mindset, these "virtual humans" are usually only assigned more mundane tasks, which obviously limit their career progression, promotion prospects and of course, retention.

No matter how politely someone says this, it feels to me like virtual humans are treated as second class employees in terms of interesting new projects, career progression and even just basic human empathy—while humans "in the office" are somehow "real (non-virtual) humans" who should be cared for more intentionally.

Example usage: *"We have a virtual employee on our team who takes care of the boring stuff like…"*

Telework(er)

This term, and the related term "telecommute," originated in the 1970s[2] when people working outside the office had to use a telephone landline to "phone in" their work. Computer connection speeds were so slow and technology so expensive that video calls and transferring large files were usually impractical. Communications between coworkers were limited to audio-only phone calls / conference calls, emails with small attachments and slow character-based terminal connections. Because of the physical size of computers and the need for a physical landline telephone, this was usually only done from a fixed home location with plenty of advance time needed for complicated setup and configuration.

Because of the limited communications between coworkers, this was usually reserved for focused, short duration, solo work, or for more routine, mundane work—not prolonged collaborative team work. Coordinating complicated work with others usually required returning to their desk in the office. Because of these technical restrictions, "teleworkers" usually only worked on more routine solo tasks, which obviously limited their career progression and promotion prospects. This impacted retention of teleworkers and discouraged employees from enrolling in a "telework" policy, even if offered.

The declining use of landline telephones and desktop computers, combined with the increased availability of cheap, high-speed internet and laptops, make this term feel increasingly obsolete.

Example usage: *"Our company has had a telework policy for decades, but almost no-one uses it." "If there's a bad storm, I telecommute when roads are closed."*

---

[2] The earliest mention I've found of these terms was by Jack Nilles in his 1976 book "The Telecommunications-Transportation Tradeoff", which is based on his research papers from 1974.

Work From Home

Similar to "telework," the term "working from home" made sense when describing someone working from their fixed residential location outside of a physical office. Like "telework," the use of a desktop computer and a physical landline telephone connection limited work to a predictable fixed location—typically their home. Internet connectivity has improved, however, so video calls, emails with large attachments and prolonged collaborative team work are feasible.

Now that portable laptops, smartphones, high-speed internet and Wi-Fi are the norm, this term feels increasingly obsolete. Of course, some people do actually work online from their actual home. Confusingly, I've heard the phrase "Working from Home" used to describe someone working from a coworking space or a hotel conference venue—or when describing coworkers who travel the majority of the time. I've also heard the terms "road warrior" and "on the road" used to describe coworkers flying in planes or working from airport lounges.

The terms "Work From Anywhere," "Digital Nomad" and "Gray Nomad" are gaining popularity, and at least feel more accurate if there is a need to describe someone's non-permanent physical work location.

Focusing on describing the physical location of coworkers, instead of how teamwork is coordinated, concerns me. Describing the physical location incorrectly bothers me, so I avoid the term "work from home" unless it is somehow relevant that the human is literally working in their place of residence.

Example usage: *"I can work from home sometimes." "Some people on our team can work from home." "I usually work from home, but this week I'm working at a conference center hotel." "There are too many interrupts in the office, so I work from home when I need to do focused work."*

Becoming A Nomad

Takeaways

- Just because you can be a nomad does not mean that you should. Think through the consequences before you decide.

- Prepare in advance, then rehearse.

- Have a fallback plan for internet connections, money and anything else that would block you from safely working while nomadic. Test them regularly.

The phrase "digital nomad" has become popular in recent years, and usually invokes images of hip cool people working on their laptops from various exotic locations around the world.

This is not the only scenario. There is also "semi-nomadic," where you move to a fixed location, work from there for a few months, then move to the next fixed location for another few months. Corporate "expats", military personnel and diplomats are paid to move to a specific location to work for a fixed number of years before relocating to a new location for another fixed number of years. Semi-retired "gray nomads" work part-time online while touring to visit family and friends. Finally, there are the fully nomadic: always on the move, living out of RVs, camper vans and sailboats. Some do this solo. Some do this with their relationship partner. Some travel with their children.

Each of these lifestyles is very different, so it's important to be clear with yourself about your goals, hopes and intentions before you start.

Are You Sure?

Just because nomadic work is possible does not mean that it is a good fit for you personally or professionally. If you're thinking about working from a new, temporary location, I recommend you first quietly and carefully consider a few important questions before plunging into a nomadic life:

- Are you comfortable working on a small, portable workstation for an extended period of time?

- Are you able to quickly diagnose and fix most common issues with your equipment and software?

- Are you able to focus on work in different physical locations?

- Are you able to focus on work amid travel distractions and a disrupted daily schedule?

- Can you adapt quickly to new time zones and working hours?

- Are you comfortable working odd hours or rearranging life in your new local timezone to fit the needs of coworkers in their usual timezones?

- Is your personal life and your personality compatible with spending long periods of time in new locations, without family or close friends nearby?

If you've answered yes to all of these questions, then the nomadic life might be a good fit for you. If you've answered yes to most, but not all of them, a semi-nomadic life might be a better fit. If you don't know, experiment by working while on an extended vacation to figure out what best fits your personality.

Prepare Your Work

Talk to your coworkers and any key clients about your upcoming nomadic work proposal. Explicitly ask for any concerns they might have about your plans—no matter how trivial—and figure out ways to address those concerns. Test and re-test your proposed solutions until everyone is satisfied before you commit to start to travel.

Do you have work tasks that will fall at an unpleasant time for you in your new time zone? If so, can they be handed off or can you trade tasks with a coworker?

Make a note of what time each of your usual work meetings and calls take place—and calculate what that will be your new local time zone. Do not disrupt others by rescheduling these meetings to fit your travel schedule. Instead, for the first few weeks, plan the structure of your day around these existing events, so others are not disrupted, and you are the only person who needs to adjust to your new time zone.

Make sure all recurring calendar invites specify the timezone, so when you start traveling, they will adjust correctly to your new local timezone. For more on this, see "Own Your Calendar."

Carefully check for legal rules prohibiting specific work in specific locations. Some examples include software developers hired by U.S. companies working on encryption software while outside of the U.S., medical professionals accessing patient medical records while outside their medical association jurisdiction, and government employees doing official work while outside of their jurisdiction. There can even be legal restrictions within different regions of the same country, so read the legal small print carefully. If there is any doubt, check with an industry-specific employment lawyer.

Prepare Your Equipment

Make sure your cell phone works with the network technology available in the new location. Most newer smart phones are quad-band and should work anywhere globally, but avoid surprises—check before you go.

If your physical device will work in the new location, then review call charge rates and connection speeds available for your cell phone plan. Some cell phone companies automatically include international calling and data plans, but if yours does not, consider adding an international data plan. If international data plans are too expensive, get a local pay-as-you-go SIM card that you can use in your smart phone, and swap in your original SIM every few days to check for messages. The idea here is to create ways to maintain familiar recurring contact with friends and family, even if they don't remember each new local number you have in each country you visit.

Check the connection speeds on the data plan. When traveling, I use GPS maps on my phone a lot—especially when I don't know the location or the language. This reduces my stress when I'm lost[1]. Using your cell phone as a Wi-Fi hotspot is also a good backup plan in case of Wi-Fi or internet connectivity problems. The Wi-Fi hotspot feature can have different bandwidth limits, so check this as well.

Verify internet connectivity where you will be living, as well as in nearby coworking spaces. Check online reviews carefully[2]. Find other backup locations in case your first preference turns out to be closed or not-as-advertised when you arrive. Even if all is working well, you should occasionally work from your backup work location as a test. As part of this test, notice how long it takes you to get from sitting at your usual work location to being ready to work at your backup location. This will help you be confident that you can quickly handle surprise power or internet outages before an upcoming important work call.

Check for, and bring electrical plugs and voltage adapters that convert between your home and travel locations. Pack a spare in case you lose or break one. Pack a power strip to reduce the need to pack multiple plug adaptors.

Computer backups are less important if all of your work is on cloud-hosted SaaS products and there is literally no unique data on your computer. However, if you have local files, documents or photos, you need backups. If you bring a physical backup disk, carry it separately to prevent the loss of your computer *and* your backups in the same river crossing or mugging. Or avoid this risk by using cloud-hosted remote backup services—and remember to allow time for these backups to complete before you disconnect from the internet and get back on the road.

---

[1] From a street safety point of view, going into a store or doorway to look at directions on your phone is less conspicuous than standing on a street corner looking at a large paper map.

[2] Most reviews mention download speeds only. For video calls and other work uses, you need fast download and fast upload and fast ping times. If in doubt, ask to see their speedtest.net results.

Prepare Yourself

Do all of your regular medical and dental checkups before you start traveling. Check your health insurance for travel coverage. Bring paper copies of proof of insurance, medical prescriptions, medical records, and your doctor's contact info. If you need vaccines for some locations, get those in advance, and bring paperwork proof for when you arrive. Scan images of this paperwork and have the files available in a secure online location in case the paper copies are lost. As a last resort, leave a copy of all of your paperwork with someone you trust.

Visa rules are very tricky and specific, so read the small print carefully. Some countries issue on-the-spot visas when you arrive at the border—others will only let you arrive on the exact date specified on the visa that was issued by their embassy in your home country. Some countries are flexible, if you have a proven trip departing within 90 days. Some welcome you when "tourist" or "doing business meetings," but are less welcoming when you arrive to work there for a while. Some countries will explicitly pay you to move there to work. Again, read and know the exact rules in advance. Find a safe location to hide a photocopy of your passport, along with a spare credit card and some cash. Make sure your passport will not expire for at least six months after the end of your planned travel.

Tell your bank and credit card companies about your travel plans, so they do not think your travel activities are fraudulent and freeze your accounts. Each credit card company has different international fraud prevention systems, so I recommend bringing multiple credit cards, one from each major issuer. When you arrive, use your bank card to withdraw some local currency in small denominations for day-to-day use.

Pack some fun stuff to help you rebalance your non-work life with daily routines. If you jog, do yoga, or swim, bring familiar exercise equipment. Some people upload copies of their favorite movies. Or a favorite pillow. Or a journal. Think about what matters to you and pack for that. For more on this, see "Create New Daily Habits."

Schedule recurring video calls with family and close friends for purely social reasons. Meet in person before you start travel to debug any setup issues—especially if some family members are not comfortable with technology! This pattern of recurring contact will help keep you in eye-to-eye close contact with family and friends while you are traveling. Sometimes these calls might feel like intrusions from another past life into your current adventure; other times they will feel like essential emotional support—if you've just been mugged, missed a critical flight, eaten something that disagrees with you or just need a familiar, friendly person to talk with. They'll also enjoy vicariously being part of your nomadic life, as well as reliving shared stories in later years.

Rehearse

Before you travel, you need to be confident that you have all the equipment you will need. Seasoned road warriors have a "go bag" of carefully chosen tools, evolved over time. However, when you first start to travel like this, I find it best to rehearse.

Pack your bag with all of the equipment you plan to bring with you. Then try doing your normal work from a different part of your house or a nearby location, using only the equipment you packed in your bag.

Notice what did not work. Unpack, fix your packing list, repack your bag and then retry this experiment. It's best to try this and sort out initial problems while you are still near home and can easily go back for that missing cable if needed. Repeat this experiment until you can work routinely from another location near your home for a few days in a row using only what you packed in your equipment bag.

Once this experiment works consistently, upgrade your experiment. Stay somewhere else for a slightly longer period, such as a week, and see if you can still do your normal work using only what you packed in your equipment bag.

Repeat and learn each time.

The idea is to take bigger and bigger baby steps, each experiment building confidence on top of the previous experiment, rehearsing until you are confident you can successfully make the transition to the nomadic lifestyle. Learn before you travel. You want to avoid the scenario of arriving into a country, only to discover that you forgot an essential and hard-to-find cable, disrupting your work plans.

When You First Arrive

Don't expect to be working productively as soon as you arrive in a new country. Instead, reserve the first few days as "vacation"days —not "working" days. Use these first few days to figure out your new environment before you attempt to focus on work. You'll need time to focus on the physical setup of your new home, as well as to figure out the practicalities of grocery shops, internet providers, public transit and coworking spaces. Depending on the distance travelled, you may also have jetlag. Prioritize taking care of all of that before you attempt to focus on your professional work.

If you attempt to focus on work, while also setting up your new life in the new location, and also still recovering from jetlag, you'll be distracted and unproductive in both. This can give coworkers a bad first impression of your ability to work professionally while traveling. Avoid setting yourself up for failure.

Verify your internet connectivity and your fallback plans. At your new place of residence, verify that the connection is good enough to use for your usual professional work[3]. Then, switch to using your cell phone as a hotspot and verify that the cell phone signal and hotspot connection is good enough to use as a backup internet connection[4]. For each of these configurations, make social video calls with friends or family, testing connection speeds, camera lighting and background noise. Repeat these experiments until you are confident you can make professional calls in either configurations. Finally, go to your nearby coworking space and

---

[3] The website "speedtest.net" is an easy way to quickly measure the upload, download and ping response metrics.

[4] Some cell phone plans treat "normal" data usage differently to "hotspot" usage— with different speeds and different fees. Your existing "home country" cell phone plan may include international roaming plans and support hotspot usage—but typically with different speeds in different countries. Read small print carefully before you travel, and test carefully each time you arrive in a new location.

repeat these same two experiments, first on their primary Wi-Fi and then using your cell phone as a hotspot.

Set up a consistent sleep (and work!) schedule as quickly as possible. Make sure that your calendar and group chat programs show your updated working hours, so people know when they can contact you or book meetings on your calendar. For more on this, see "Own Your Calendar."

Now, you are ready for your first day working from your new location.

Create New Daily Habits

Quickly establish a structure for your day, with a consistent sleep and work schedule. This is an important enough topic that I encourage re-reading "Feed Your Soul."

Think about how you typically start and end of your workday when at home. Whether you jog, swim, do yoga, read a book or watch movies, explicitly schedule that on your calendar. Intentionally schedule recurring social video calls to friends and family during the week. The important point is to intentionally continue familiar habits, as closely as possible. This helps life feel comfortable and familiar—even when daily life in a confusing unfamiliar culture in the new location starts to feel overwhelming[5]. Whatever your habits, it is important to clearly denote your workday schedule and maintain a familiar daily pattern while traveling.

It is important to balance life and professional work in your new location. Intentionally plan trips to nearby coworking space events, expat clubs, meetups, or volunteering opportunities. Try a few to see what feels interesting to you. The idea is to find ways to interact with other humans and grow social connections. You can always adjust your plans later, but I've found intentional scheduling of events especially important when first arriving in a new unfamiliar location.

---

[5] The movie "Lost in Translation" does a good job of capturing this hard-to-describe feeling.

Once you have acclimatized to the initial work and life cadence in a new location, it's time start exploring life in your new location. Enjoy! After all, that's why you are a nomad.

When Things Go Wrong

The reality is that not all things will go according to your plan. Things will go wrong. Even when you are still at home, not yet "on the road," things can go wrong. A little advance planning helps reduce disruption whenever something does go wrong.

Working on your laptop at a sidewalk café sounds great. However, when you're focused on your work, it is easy to not notice incoming risks. Laptops are stolen in broad daylight from cafés while people are typing on them. Reduce this risk by sitting at a table indoors, far from the door—ideally in a corner, with your back to a wall, so you can see people approaching you. This also reduces the risk that people can see what you are working on.

On public transit, smartphones can be snatched out of people's hands even while they are being used. Reduce this risk by not standing near the doors (snatch-and-grab as the doors are closing is a frequent tactic).

If you are driving a car, avoid parking the car, putting all of your valuables in the trunk, and then walking away. This is a clear invitation for nearby watchful thieves. Instead put all of your valuables in the trunk before you start driving, so that when you arrive and park, there is no need to open the trunk in front of any watchful eyes.

These are all good security tips in most major cities. The risks increase in locations where your "normal" laptop and phone are relatively more exotic (and hence have more resale value on the black market).

Consider travel insurance. If your policy covers stolen equipment, know what serial numbers, police reports, and other paperwork will be needed!

In most cases, the data on your laptop or phone is far more valuable than the actual laptop or phone hardware. Use a password manager[6] to protect login information for all of your accounts and any client data you might have. If your device is stolen, login to your password manager and disable access from that stolen device. Use a password manager with two factor authentication as this will help prevent people from breaking into your accounts before you notice the theft.

Make sure you regularly commit code into a hosted source code repository, and store critical work files in Google Drive, Dropbox or other cloud-hosted services, so that no important information is lost forever with the stolen hardware.

Find nearby, trusted, repair shops where you can quickly repair or replace a device in case you drop, or spill liquids on it.

If you store all of your documents, emails, code and other work on secure cloud-hosted systems, the theft of any laptop or phone is still expensive and annoying—but not career threatening. Instead of losing unique, valuable work that would need to be re-created, you replace the hardware, update the password manager, restore the files from their cloud-hosted locations and quickly get back to work.

A habit I developed was to repeatedly ask myself "What could possibly go wrong?"—and create a list of these scenarios. For each scenario, I then figured out contingency plans. Make time to plan this in advance: it is much harder to think through these scenarios when you are stressed because something went wrong, and sometimes it's too late at that point. Over my years of traveling and working from various locations around the globe, I've had many things go wrong—and each time I was very grateful to have pre-planned contingency plans ready.

---

[6] For recommendations on specific tools to use, see: oduinn.com/book/tools-for-remotes.

Script for Making a Job Offer

Before

Making a formal offer to a candidate is not something you should delegate.

If your company requires a formal written offer to be sent by your HR department, make sure it is first sent to you, so that you can personally review it for errors. I've occasionally caught typos in salary, start date or title, so I now always do this. Ask them to not send it until after you make a verbal offer. Make the video call yourself. If HR insists on being present on the video call, that's fine —but you get to do the talking.

To make sure I'm organized, I schedule a block of preparation time on my calendar immediately before the offer meeting.

Don't call the candidate out of the blue; schedule a time to discuss next steps. As with all other calls during the interview process, this call should be on video. Everyone should be comfortable working this way.

During

At the start of the call—before discussing anything else—I reconfirm that the candidate has 30 minutes free, is in a place where they can talk freely, and is able to take notes. If needed, I wait while they get a pen and paper.

Start by mentioning that your coworkers liked meeting him or her during the interviews. Briefly describe some of the enthusiastic responses from interview debriefs. Be honest about strengths, gaps, and weaknesses found by the interviewers. This is not about flattery; this gives the candidate a realistic summary of interviewer feedback[1].

---

[1] I'm surprised how infrequently this is done. I've only had three people discuss this with me—and it's important for me to feel that I am joining a group of people who gave me serious evaluation and consideration, and want me to work there (compared to a group that was split about me-as-second-choice, and their first choice turned down the job offer).

Segue to the job offer: "As you probably guessed, I'd like to make you a formal job offer now. This will sound a little more formal than usual as I go through this checklist of items, but it is important that I don't miss anything. I'll stop at specific points to ask for questions, but there's a lot to cover and it is important to get this right. Please take notes as we go, and ask questions at each stopping point. Anything to ask before we start? Ready?"

The following sequence is important.

I intentionally discuss money at the end because many people fixate on a certain base salary and listen *only* for that in the offer. If you start with base salary and it is not a number they are excited about, they will not even hear the rest of the offer details. Ironically, this might prevent them from hearing information about other compensation that might be worth far more, financially, than their base salary.

- Start with work details: formal title, who they would be reporting to, location (or full-time remote!) and the project they would work on when they start.

- Stop and ask for questions.

- Review benefits such as medical insurance, retirement contributions, vacation allowance, and training budgets.

- Stop and ask for questions.

- Discuss total compensation, in this specific sequence: Start with quarterly or annual bonus and how that math is calculated. Give examples of percentages for the last several quarters. Describe stock options, if appropriate, including vesting schedule and today's approximate strike price. Include a disclaimer; this might change by the time they start. Discuss how spot, individual, or ad hoc bonuses are determined. Describe the signing bonus, if appropriate. Then, list the base salary.

- End with "…which brings us to a total annual compensation of …," and state the total amount.

- Stop and ask for questions.

- Take a deep breath, and then ask, "So, having covered all that, now I have to ask. Do you formally accept this offer?" Cross your fingers.

If the candidate says "no," remember that they went this far through the interview process, so they must have been interested in the job at some point. At what point did they lose interest? It is totally reasonable to gently ask for details.

Maybe they're concerned about something that you can easily fix, like the start date, the nature of their first project, or a small increase in base salary needed for a home mortgage. It might be the vacation policy. Or title or responsibility. Or the base salary, bonus, or stock options. Maybe they decided to stay at their current company, because they were promoted or started a cool new project.

Perhaps they don't-believe-bonus-is-real (bitten by bait-and-switch bonus numbers in a previous job). Solve this by having them talk with accounting or other employees about historical bonus numbers.

If they are concerned about the vacation policy, one possibility would be to increase their base salary and agree that they can take unpaid time off at a time of convenience for everyone[2].

If the candidate has no intention of accepting an offer, they will usually tell you during the interview process—as soon as they decide they are no longer interested. At the latest, they would say something at the start of this formal offer call, as soon as you said, "I want to make you a formal offer, but before I do—do you have any questions?" Importantly, they would tell you *before* you start describing the details of the offer. If the candidate waits until after you have fully described the terms of your offer, perhaps they are intentionally holding something back. Maybe they wanted to see if your offer was better than another (undisclosed) offer they had in hand. Maybe they were hoping to use your offer as leverage in their current job, where they'd decided to stay. Maybe they pretended to be interested in a job simply to learn about your upcoming projects—a form of industrial espionage—before

---

[2] Many companies now have a "no vacation" policy, allowing employees to take as much (or as little) vacation as they need, knowing many people don't take enough vacation. Expiring vacation days trigger some people to actually take vacation. Also, when someone leaves a company, accrued vacation must be paid, which is tracked as a liability in the company finances. A "no vacation policy" eliminates this financial liability.

accepting a job with your largest competitor. Regardless, hearing a candidate say "no" at this point is a red flag. If you can, gently find out why. This information will help improve your hiring process with the next candidate.

If the candidate says "maybe," carefully try to find out why. Is it because they want to make sure that the written offer letter matches the verbal offer? Is there an unasked question that needs to be answered? Are they listening to your offer only to use it as a bargaining chip for an increased offer elsewhere? While this hasn't happened to me often, it does happen.

If the candidate says "yes," be grateful. Say "thank you"—and mean it! As the hiring manager, you should be at least as excited as the new hire! Let that eagerness show. You have several reasons to be grateful. All of the focused attention you spent interviewing candidates for this role was worth it and is now over. Your understaffed team will finally have the additional help they need —this is always an exciting boost to everyone's morale.

If the job can be done on a range of different types of computers, such as Mac, Windows, or Linux, ask the new hire if they have a preference. Ask if they have an email address preference[3]. Find out what t-shirt size and fit they prefer for later swag gifts.

Start calendar haggling about start dates. Be aware that it's easy to pressure a new hire into starting as soon as possible, and sometimes new hires feel they need to start immediately to make a good impression. Instead, as the hiring manager, I encourage the new hire to do a graceful transition from their soon-to-be-former employer—as I would like them to treat me when they decide to change jobs in the future. I also encourage taking time off to decompress and reset between jobs, explicitly noting that I want them to start on Day One with a fresh brain—eager to dive into a lot of new work, not tired, stressed out and looking forward to a vacation.

---

[3] Many companies standardize on the format of email addresses, which is fine, but it is easy to set up additional email aliases. Some people I've worked with have strong personal attachments to the specific format of their email address. Asking about their preferred email address is a nice, easy to implement, personal touch.

Only once did I not follow my own script here. I urgently needed one specific new hire to start as soon as possible. A strategic project was unstaffed and already overdue when it was reassigned to my team. As part of the job offer, I explained my usual approach about start dates. Then I apologized that I was not going to follow my usual approach. I explained the urgency of the project and asked him to start immediately after leaving his current employer. I still wanted him to give his current employer enough notice for a graceful transition, but asked him to start with us the day after he left his current employer. I promised that he would be able to take a multi-week vacation within a few months—as soon as the project was completed—even though he would not have accumulated enough official vacation time by then. He reluctantly agreed.

During the project, I reminded him in one-on-ones of my promise. A few months later, when that project was out of crisis mode, I made sure he took that long vacation—even though he now had mixed feelings about it because of his sense of ownership on the other high-priority projects still on our team's plate.

Over time, I learned that his work-hard-until-burnout-and-then-quit mindset caused him to keep changing jobs, becoming more resentful of his employers each time. As his direct manager, I kept actively encouraging him to take significant vacations to recover between high-pressure projects. At one point I needed to give him an ultimatum: he had 48 hours to pick a location and date for his next vacation, or else I would pick for him. The next day, when I presented my choices for vacation destinations, he relented.

As a point of pride, I note that at time of writing he remains an outstanding engineer, continues to do outstanding work, is no longer burning out, has stayed in this job longer than any other, and for the first time in his career, he has used up his company vacation allowance—repeatedly!

After

Send offer paperwork the very same day, by courier. Email the tracking information to the candidate as soon as you send the paperwork, so they can track it themselves.

If you use an online signing service for contracts, the service will automatically send an email to the candidate. You should still email them personally, letting them know to look for the paperwork that was sent electronically. I adopted this habit after one eager candidate delayed signing for several days. I thought the candidate was backing out of their acceptance, but they hadn't received the paperwork. The candidate thought we were slow to make a written offer, and was waiting to give notice at their current employer.

When I eventually phoned the candidate, we figured out that the automated emails for their electronic job offer were hidden in their spam folder. Both sides were frustrated by this delay. After that lesson, I always email personally and separately.

How NOT to Work

The Simple Sabotage Field Manual

In 1944, during World War II, the US Government put a lot of thought into how to disrupt the effectiveness of companies working inside enemy territories. The Office of Strategic Services (later renamed to the Central Intelligence Agency) wrote a small book called the Simple Sabotage Field Manual[1], for distribution to Allied sympathizers willing to help disrupt and sabotage companies working in Axis countries.

As you might expect, most of this wartime field manual covers physical sabotage, explosives, and so on. However, the last few pages describe how to disrupt and delay work in an office environment, without being identified as a saboteur. I was surprised to find how many of these same tactics I've encountered in modern organizations with broken team cultures.

Why mention this here?

Firstly, I hope that reading about these counterproductive behaviors help demonstrate what *not* to do[2].

Secondly, as someone writing a book intending to help people work *more* effectively, regardless of their physical location, I found it interesting to find a book on how to work *less* effectively.

---

[1] "Simple Sabotage Field Manual" by US Central Intelligence Agency.

[2] Note: When this field manual was written in early 1940s, the word "conference" meant a larger, formal, company meeting—not today's usage of the word. For simplicity of reading, substitute "meeting" whenever you see the word "conference."

UNCLASSIFIED

SIMPLE SABOTAGE
FIELD MANUAL

Strategic Services
(Provisional)

(11) *General Interference with Organizations and Production*

(a) Organizations and Conferences

(1) Insist on doing everything through "channels." Never permit short-cuts to be taken in order to expedite decisions.

(2) Make "speeches." Talk as frequently as possible and at great length. Illustrate your "points" by long anecdotes and accounts of personal experiences. Never hesitate to make a few appropriate "patriotic" comments.

(3) When possible, refer all matters to committees, for "further study and consideration." Attempt to make the committees as large as possible — never less than five.

(4) Bring up irrelevant issues as frequently as possible.

(5) Haggle over precise wordings of communications, minutes, resolutions.

(6) Refer back to matters decided upon at the last meeting and attempt to re-open the question of the advisability of that decision.

(7) Advocate "caution." Be "reasonable" and urge your fellow-conferees to be "reasonable" and avoid haste which might result in embarrassments or difficulties later on.

(8) Be worried about the propriety of any decision — raise the question of whether such action as is contemplated lies within the jurisdiction of the group or whether it might conflict with the policy of some higher echelon.

(b) Managers and Supervisors

(1) Demand written orders.

(2) "Misunderstand" orders. Ask endless questions or engage in long correspondence about such orders. Quibble over them when you can.

(3) Do everything possible to delay the delivery of orders. Even though parts of an order may be ready beforehand, don't deliver it until it is completely ready.

(4) Don't order new working materials until your current stocks have been virtually exhausted, so that the slightest delay in filling your order will mean a shutdown.

(5) Order high-quality materials which are hard to get. If you don't get them argue about it. Warn that inferior materials will mean inferior work.

(6) In making work assignments, always sign out the unimportant jobs first. See that the important jobs are assigned to inefficient workers of poor machines.

(7) Insist on perfect work in relatively unimportant products; send back for refinishing those which have the least flaw. Approve other defective parts whose flaws are not visible to the naked eye.

(8) Make mistakes in routing so that parts and materials will be sent to the wrong place in the plant.

(9) When training new workers, give incomplete or misleading instructions.

(10) To lower morale and with it, production, be pleasant to inefficient workers; give them undeserved promotions. Discriminate against efficient workers; complain unjustly about their work.

(11) Hold conferences when there is more critical work to be done.

(12) Multiply paper work in plausible ways. Start duplicate files.

(13) Multiply the procedures and clearances involved in issuing instructions, pay checks, and so on. See that three people have to approve everything where one would do..

(14) Apply all regulations to the last letter.

(c) Office Workers

(1) Make mistakes in quantities of material when you are copying orders. Confuse similar names. Use wrong addresses.

(2) Prolong correspondence with government bureaus.

(3) Misfile essential documents.

(4) In making carbon copies, make one too few, so that an extra copying job will have to be done.

(5) Tell important callers the boss is busy or talking on another telephone.

(6) Hold up mail until the next collection.

(7) Spread disturbing rumors that sound like inside dope.

(d) Employees

(1) *Work slowly*. Think out ways to increase the number of movements necessary on your job: use a light hammer instead of a heavy one, try to make a small wrench do when a big one is necessary, use little force where considerable force is needed, and so on.

(2) Contrive as many interruptions to your work as you can: when changing the material on which you are working, as you would on a lathe or punch, take needless time to do it. If you are cutting, shaping or doing other measured work, measure dimensions twice as often as you need to. When you go to the lavatory, spend a longer time there than is necessary. Forget tools so that you will have to go back after them.

30

(3) Even if you understand the language, pretend not to understand instructions in a foreign tongue.

(4) Pretend that instructions are hard to understand, and ask to have them repeated more than once. Or pretend that you are particularly anxious to do your work, and pester the foreman with unnecessary questions.

(5) Do your work poorly and blame it on bad tools, machinery, or equipment. Complain that these things are preventing you from doing your job right.

(6) Never pass on your skill and experience to a new or less skillful worker.

(7) Snarl up administration in every possible way. Fill out forms illegibly so that they will have to be done over; make mistakes or omit requested information in forms.

(8) If possible, join or help organize a group for presenting employee problems to the management. See that the procedures adopted are as inconvenient as possible for the management, involving the presence of a large number of employees at each presentation, entailing more than one meeting for each grievance, bringing up problems which are largely imaginary, and so on.

(9) Misroute materials.

(10) Mix good parts with unusable scrap and rejected parts.

(12) *General Devices for Lowering Morale and Creating Confusion*

(a) Give lengthy and incomprehensible explanations when questioned.

(b) Report imaginary spies or danger to the Gestapo or police.

(c) Act stupid.

(d) Be as irritable and quarrelsome as possible without getting yourself into trouble.

(e) Misunderstand all sorts of regulations concerning such matters as rationing, transportation, traffic regulations.

(f) Complain against ersatz materials.

(g) In public treat axis nationals or quislings coldly.

(h) Stop all conversation when axis nationals or quislings enter a cafe.

(i) Cry and sob hysterically at every occasion, especially when confronted by government clerks.

(j) Boycott all movies, entertainments, concerts, newspapers which are in any way connected with the quisling authorities.

(k) Do not cooperate in salvage schemes.

Further Reading

Books

Here is a list of books that I've found helpful over the years. I've personally bought and given away multiple copies of each of these books to people I encounter who would find them helpful, and I still routinely sit down to re-re-read specific sections.

- *An Illustrated Book of Bad Arguments* by Ali Almossawi

- *Becoming A Technical Leader: An Organic Problem-Solving Approach* by Gerald Weinberg

- *Better Allies: Everyday Actions to Create Inclusive, Engaging Workplaces* by Karen Catlin

- *Complications: A Surgeon's Notes on an Imperfect Science* by Atul Gawande (A collection of true short stories about high-stakes decision making with only partial information)

- *Crucial Conversations: Tools for Talking When Stakes are High, 2nd Edition* by Kerry Patterson, & Joseph Grenny

- *Death March* by Edward Yourdon

- *Elements of E-Mail Style* by David Angell & Brent Heslop

- *Free Agent Nation: The Future of Working for Yourself* by Daniel Pink

- *Getting Things Done: The Art of Stress-Free Productivity* by Dave Allen

- *Hire Fast and Build Things: How to recruit and manage a top-notch team of distributed engineers* by Stephane Kasriel & Jacob Morgan

- *Hiring Engineers* by Marianne Bellotti

- *It worked for me: In Life and Leadership* by Colin Powell

- *Joel on software: And on Diverse and Occasionally Related Matters That Will Prove of Interest to Software Developers, Designers, and Managers, and to Those Who, Whether by Good Fortune or Ill Luck, Work with Them in Some Capacity* by Joel Spolsky

- *Managing Humans: Biting and Humorous Tales of a Software Engineering Manager* by Michael Lopp

- *Peopleware: Productive Projects and Teams* by Tom DeMarco & Tim Lister

- *Remote: Office Not Required* by Jason Fried & David Heinemeier Hansson

- *The Checklist Manifesto: How to Get Things Right* by Atul Gawande

- *The Culture Map: Decoding How People Think, Lead, and Get Things Done Across Cultures* by Erin Meyer

- The *CultureShock!* series (various authors)

- *The Death and Life of Great American Cities* by Jane Jacobs

- *The Five Dysfunctions of a Team: a Leadership Fable* by Patrick Lencioni

- *The Future of Work: How the New Order of Business Will Shape Your Organization, Your Management Style and Your Life* by Thomas Malone (Describes the shift from "command-and-control" management to "coordinate-and-cultivate," and the new skills that will be required to succeed)

- *The Mythical Man-Month* by Frederick Brooks

- *The Ultimate Guide to Remote Work* by Wade Foster, Danny Schreiber, et al.

- *The Virgin Way: If It's Not Fun, It's Not Worth Doing* by Richard Branson

- *The Year Without Pants: WordPress.com and the Future of Work* by Scott Berkun

- *Time management for System Administrators: Stop Working Late and Start Working Smart* by Thomas Limoncelli (Practical time management advice, even for people who are not system administrators)

- *Virtual Teams Across Cultures: Create Successful Teams Around The World* by Theresa Sigillito Hollema

- *What Color is your Parachute?* by Richard Bolles

Websites

Here is a list of websites and blogs that are continuously refreshed with new information. I've found these useful.

- "Jobs for Remoties": oduinn.com/book/jobs-for-remoties
- "Tools for Remoties": oduinn.com/book/tools-for-remoties
- "Locations for Remoties": oduinn.com/book/locations-for-remoties
- The GitLab team handbook: about.gitlab.com/handbook
- "Why We (Still) Believe in Working Remotely": blog.stackexchange.com/2013/02/why-we-still-believe-in-working-remotely
- Joel Spolsky's "Guide to Standing Out & Attracting Top Talent": careers.stackoverflow.com/resources/joels-guide
- Global Workplace Analytics: globalworkplaceanalytics.com
- Ada Initiative, Ally Skills Workshop Initiative: frameshiftconsulting.com/ally-skills-workshop
- Upwork: upwork.com
- Flexjobs: flexjobs.com
- We Work Remotely: weworkremotely.com
- 1 Million for Work Flexibility: workflexibility.org
- All Things Remote Work: remote.co
- Freelancers Union: freelancersunion.org
- TRaD Works (**T**elecommuting, **R**emote **a**nd **D**istributed) Forum: trad.works
- Toptal freelance talent network: toptal.com

About the Author

John O'Duinn has written code and led teams in organizations ranging from four-person startups to nonprofits to multinationals —including the US Government as part of the Obama White House, for the US Digital Service.

In addition to technology, John loves growing a culture where diverse groups of humans work well together in a distributed global workplace. He has worked in distributed companies of one form or another for 28 years and led distributed teams for 14 years. Over the last seven years, he has consulted at government agencies and large organizations in transition; mentored fast-growing distributed companies; run workshops and presented at universities, startup incubators, and conferences. He helped write the State of Vermont's "Remote Worker" law—a very different approach to Economic Development which has been so wildly successful that he now helps write policies for multiple other jurisdictions world-wide. He has lived and worked in 13 cities across four continents.

John received his B.Sc. and M.Sc. in Computer Science from Dublin City University, co-wrote a chapter of The Architecture of Open Source Applications, Volume 2, and was a founding committee member of IEEE RelEng. He has a Shodan black belt in Aikido, loves travel, and is on track to fill his passport again.

Made in the USA
Las Vegas, NV
18 August 2022

53445029R00213